Illinois Studies in Communications

Illinois Studies in Communications

Series Editors

Sandra Braman, James W. Carey, Clifford G. Christians, Lawrence Grossberg, Thomas H. Guback, James W. Hay, John C. Nerone, Paula A. Treichler, Ellen A. Wartella, and D. Charles Whitney.

Books in the Series

Fifties Television: The Industry and Its Critics
William F. Boddy

Hollywood and Broadcasting: From Radio to Cable
Michele Hilmes

The American Radio Industry and Its Latin American Activities, 1990-1939
James Schwoch

60 Minutes *and the News: A Mythology for Middle America*
Richard Campbell

60 Minutes and the News

and the News

Richard Campbell | **A Mythology for Middle America**

Foreword by
James W. Carey

University of Illinois Press
Urbana and Chicago

© 1991 by the Board of Trustees of the University of Illinois
Manufactured in the United States of America
C 5 4 3 2 1

In a different version, portions of this book appeared earlier in
Richard Campbell, "Securing the Middle Ground: Reporting For-
mulas in *60 Minutes*," *Critical Studies in Mass Communication* 4
(December 1987): 325-50, and Richard Campbell and Jimmie L.
Reeves, "Covering the Homeless: The Joyce Brown Story," *Critical
Studies in Mass Communication* 6 (March 1989): 21-42. *Critical
Studies in Mass Communication* is a publication of the Speech
Communication Association.

In a different version, portions of this book also appeared earlier
in Richard Campbell, "News as Drama: Mystery and Adventure
in the *60 Minutes*," *Television Quarterly* 23, no. 3 (1988): 51-64.
Television Quarterly is a publication of the National Academy of
Television Arts & Sciences.

This book is printed on acid-free paper.

Library of Congress Cataloging-in-Publication Data

Campbell, Richard, 1949-
    60 minutes and the news : a mythology for Middle America / Richard
Campbell.
        p.   cm. — (Illinois studies in communications)
    ISBN 0-252-01777-3 (alk. paper)
    1. 60 minutes (Television program) 2. Television broadcasting of
news—United States. I. Title. II. Title: Sixty minutes and the
news. III. Series.
PN4888.T4C36   1991
791.45′72—dc20   90-45335
                                       CIP

For Mom and Dad,
Christopher and Caitlin,
and especially Dianna

Contents

Foreword   *James W. Carey*   xi

Acknowledgments   xiii

Introduction   xv

1 From Iconoclast to Institution, from News
     to Common Sense   1

2 News as Narrative, Reporter as Character   25

3 News and Mystery: Heartless Villains, Heartland Virtues   43

4 News and Therapy: Moral Meanings and Tough Questions   68

5 News and Adventure: The Quest for Authenticity   93

6 News and Arbitration: Managing the Social Margins   113

7 News and the Myth of Individualism   137

8 Like Clockwork: The Search for Center   158

Appendixes   184

Notes   247

Index   273

Foreword

Any reflection on television in the network era reveals, among other things, a paradox at the very center of its history. If we consider the evolution of entertainment programming—drama, situation comedy, action, and adventure—the record reveals a steady improvement from the early 1950s at least through the late 1970s. During that period television discovered itself, discovered how to make programs, and showed steady progress in the arts of conception, execution, writing, directing, and acting. Despite the mythology of a golden age in the 1950s, television drama and comedy matured around 1970, and the networks brought forth a steady stream of distinguished programs, programs we continue to catalog and study, programs that might be eventually welcomed into a transformed household of art.

However, the history of television news, from John Cameron Swayze to Dan Rather, undermines our simple confidence in the progressive laws of evolution. Television news certainly has evolved technologically. Lightweight portable cameras, satellite transmission, and videotape, among other things, transformed the parameters of time, space, and organization of the news. Television news has also matured commercially: from a loss leader to a profit center. But the journalistic highlights in the history of television news are closer to the beginning than the end of the network era. *See It Now, Person to Person,* and other creations of Edward R. Murrow, the yearly roundups when distinguished correspondents gathered to review the state of the world, the searing documentaries on McCarthy, farm workers, and poverty are things we must reach back some distance to retrieve. The documentary tradition of television, along with good talk and discussion, has migrated out of the networks and affiliated stations and into cable and public broadcasting. What remains, however visually arresting, is rarely more than tabloid journalism and a headline service.

An ambiguous exception to all this is *60 Minutes.* Created more than twenty years ago, the program broke new ground in television by, in effect, breaking the tradition of the documentary, applying the model of the magazine (rather than the newspaper or feature film) to television news, and, in the spirit of that time, merging the techniques of and blurring the line between fact and fiction, the short story and journalism. The ambiguity of this achievement is attested to by the controversy surrounding the program from the outset. But, controversial or not, *60 Minutes* is the one journalistic development in the network era that stands out as a creative moment against a background of technological advancement and journalistic decline.

I first heard Richard Campbell speak about the CBS news program *60 Minutes* at a convention in 1985. I felt then, and even more so now, that Campbell had watched *60 Minutes* more attentively and interpreted it both more critically and generously than any other writer on the subject.

The book that follows is the product of that attentiveness and critical understanding. It shows a "close reading" of a hundred episodes of *60 Minutes*—on tape, in script—over a twenty-two-year period and presents that reading in effortless prose, mercifully free of inflated jargon or obscure language. Campbell is a critical observer of the program, however. He is neither part of the apparatus of its production, sales, and justification nor of the apparatus of critical iconoclasm that enjoys nothing more than making a mess.

Campbell instead reads the program as a citizen and countryman. He knows how it works because he knows something of how his culture works. He is sensitive to the narrative structure and fictional techniques of *60 Minutes* because he has a nuanced understanding of the stories his compatriots like to tell one another about one another. He is acutely aware of how the journalists who star on *60 Minutes* insinuate themselves into the stories, for he knows something of the "characters" and "roles" American journalists long to play. And, finally, his close watching and reading of *60 Minutes* yields a firmer grasp of those mythologies, those values, that perplex and engage Americans and therefore thread their way through our news stories as much as our fictions. Richard Campbell herein provides an exacting analysis of American culture through the instructively ambiguous achievement of one of the few recent highlights of television journalism.

—James W. Carey

Acknowledgments

This book represents an off-again, on-again project that has spanned nearly ten years. There are many people to whom I owe thanks. At *60 Minutes* I am grateful to Don Hewitt, Mike Wallace, Roy Brunett, and Beverly Morgan who gave me their insights, time, and help. I am indebted also to CBS News Archivist Samuel Suratt and CBS News for the right to display pictures from *60 Minutes* taken from video images and to print the written transcripts of four *60 Minutes* segments in the appendixes of this book. All copyright and right of copyright in these images and transcripts and in the broadcasts are owned by CBS Inc. These images and transcripts may not be copied or reproduced or used in any way (other than for purposes of reference, discussion, and review) without the written permission of CBS Inc.

In addition, a number of other individuals and institutions have contributed to this project along the way. I would like to thank the staff at the Motion Picture, Broadcasting and Recorded Sound Division of the Library of Congress in Washington. I am grateful to Liz and Jim Kehoe for taking me in and treating me well during my research trips to Washington. Thanks to Marlene Hoffmann, Stephanie Sauer, and Brian Mikula, who typed and transcribed various parts of this project. I am also indebted to the Danforth Foundation, Northwestern University, and the University of Michigan, which supported some of the research for this book at different stages. I am grateful to my former teachers and colleagues at the University of Wisconsin–Milwaukee, where I got the idea for this book, at Mount Mary College in Milwaukee, where I began the preliminary writing, and at the University of Michigan, where I finished the project. I am also indebted to all my students who contributed insights and tolerated various stages of my thinking on *60 Minutes* in virtually every course I have taught at Mount Mary, UW–Milwaukee, and Michigan.

I am grateful to reviewers, friends, and colleagues who have read parts or all of the manuscript and who helped me with suggestions and resources along the way: Robert C. Allen, Dianna Szczur Campbell, Don Kubit, Dan Leab, Jack Lule, Tom Mascaro, Michael Schudson, John Stevens, and Mary Ann Watson. I am especially grateful to Leah R. Vande Berg, who guided the early stages of the project; to James Carey, who wrote the Foreword and gave me the best single piece of advice: "Tell me what you know about *60 Minutes*"; to my friend and mentor David Eason, who taught me the value of storytelling and helped me find my own voice as a writer; and to my colleague and friend Jimmie Reeves, who had coffee with me whenever I needed to talk and who contributed a number of important ideas to the final draft.

I am also grateful to the University of Illinois Press, especially Richard Wentworth, Lawrence Malley, Karen Hewitt, and Mary Giles, my manuscript editor, for supporting this project through three different rewrites of the manuscript.

Finally, I would like to thank my family: my grandmothers, Rose Yankovich, who is nearly ninety, and Edith Campbell, who died in 1977 but whom I still think about often; my parents, Molly and Dick Campbell, who are a continuous source of support and encouragement; my son Christopher, now eleven, who was two years old when I began this project; and my daughter Caitlin, now seven, who was born three years into the project. Their presence and laughter kept the whole thing and everyday life in perspective. Most of all, I would like to thank my wife of twenty years, Dianna, who encouraged me a long time ago to become a college teacher. Her energy, humor, honesty, love, tolerance, criticism, and support are the common ground where I can always return.

Introduction

In the early 1980s, I once tried to explain to my Croatian grand-mother—also in her early eighties—why I had abandoned a perfectly fine job as a high school English teacher to enter a doctoral program in radio, television, and film at Northwestern University. From her vantage point in Dayton, Ohio, there were only two possible reasons. First, she thought that her grandson might be after Walter Cronkite's anchor position at CBS. But when Dan Rather got that job, she had to revise her thinking. Next, she speculated that her grandson, armed with a doctorate in radio-TV-film, would certainly be qualified to fix her television set which had been recently complicated by cable.

My grandmother has always been a touchstone in my life—a good antidote to whenever I get to feeling particularly elite and academic. When I do get back to Ohio, I take my grandmother to church and may occasionally watch television with her (I also make a few adjustments to her set so she knows my education was not wasted). Over the years, her favorite shows have included *Lawrence Welk,* studio wrestling, *Dallas,* and *60 Minutes.* Her viewing habits, however, defy the typical elitist, academic characterization of television watchers as "couch potatoes." When she feels particularly good, my grandmother argues with television. She paces the floor. She yells at the characters. An FDR Democrat, she talks politics with television. I've seen her almost curse Ronald Reagan, Mike Wallace, or a *60 Minutes* villain.

Like my grandmother, *60 Minutes* has been another touchstone in my life. I have been watching it for fifteen years—carefully for the past ten. On occasion, I also have yelled at the reporters or at the program's sinister villains. More often, however, I yelled because I just wanted this project to be over—I was tired of watching *60 Minutes.*

But I always come back, drawn by the program's stories. For me, *60 Minutes,* more than any other show on television, explains the opening line of Joan Didion's *White Album:* "We tell ourselves stories in order to live."

This book interprets the stories of *60 Minutes,* the CBS news magazine that began in 1968 and has become one of the most watched and economically successful programs in television history. It is unlike most books about television news because it is not written by an insider. Like my grandmother, I am a viewer—both a fan and a critic. Unlike my grandmother, I have worked briefly as a print reporter and as a broadcast news writer. But rather than write about *60 Minutes* from the inside, which has been done by Don Hewitt, the program's creator and long-time executive producer, and Mike Wallace, the program's lead correspondent, I look in from the outside and see what we are all permitted to see Sunday after Sunday.

This project also is not a definitive history of *60 Minutes.* I will discuss history, but that perspective may be gleaned better from other books about *60 Minutes* including Hewitt's *Minute by Minute,* Wallace and Gary Paul Gates's *Close Encounters: Mike Wallace's Own Story,* and Axel Madsen's *60 Minutes: The Power and the Politics of America's Most Popular TV News Show.* In addition, the Museum of Broadcasting in New York did a *60 Minutes* retrospective in the mid-1980s which generated a small booklet and audio transcript.

This is also not entirely an academic book. I try to write from my grandmother's couch as well as from the ivory tower. Although I realize that students and researchers studying television and news constitute my primary audience, I write here—although not always successfully—for editors, producers, and reporters. And I try to write for other viewers and fans—like my father, a retired salesman and avid reader, who beats me regularly at Scrabble. A bright man who taught me how to ride a bike, fillet a fish, and correct a slice, he tactfully commented after reading two pages of a "structural analysis" paper that I once wrote about television news, "This is nice." So, in part, this book is for him.

In order to speak to these distinct audiences, I do not locate my interpretation of *60 Minutes* among the intellectual strategies (with apologies to journalists and my father) of data collection and statistical methods, or content analyses of reportorial bias, or psychoanalysis, or postmodernism, or the ideological lexicon of power and domination—although the way I think about news has been influenced by some of these perspectives. Rather, coming from the broad populist perspective of American cultural studies, I regard the news of *60 Minutes* as culture—as dramatic storytelling, as compelling contemporary mythology. I view *60 Minutes* in much the same way as a cultural anthropologist—as a rich storehouse of stories and meanings, and as a key development in journalism's history. At least one *60 Minutes* reporter has also noticed a connection between anthropology and the program. Harry Reasoner in his autobiography writes: "In anthropology you are as interested in cooking pots and games as in thrones and religions; so is *60 Minutes.* So we erratically touch on art and trivia and pool hustlers and old ladies who own Rolls-Royces as well as on rip-offs and shahs and chancellors. This is, given the world we live in, as it should be."[1]

I also regard journalism not merely as a job or a profession, but as a vibrant and ritualized cultural system akin to religion, academia, science, and art, in that, through its stories, it tries to make sense of a fragile and often contradictory world. And other than teaching (I have to defend my own vocational prejudices here), journalism may be the most important profession and cultural system, given that most of us learn much of what we know about our communities and our world through the drama and ritual of news. In their own ways, then, a variety of cultural systems, including the mass media of journalism, are up to the same thing. And James Carey asks those of us who make sense of mass media to "grasp hold" of news and culture with words such as *myth, ritual,* and *story* in order "to see in a miraculously discontinuous world persistent practices by which that world is sedimented and held together."[2]

Journalists, academics, and other readers may fault my approach, for I am not concerned here specifically with the "intentions" or production influences of *60 Minutes.* Although I have interviewed the creator of the program and its leading reporter, my focus is not on the particular individuals who make *60 Minutes* each Sunday. I believe that the meanings of *60 Minutes's* segments are social as well as individual, always richer and larger than the sum of their parts. The program's complexity—and contradictions—cannot be fully explained by Don Hewitt's personal vision or Mike Wallace's tenacity or Morley Safer's wit or Harry Reasoner's midwestern charm.

Nor can *60 Minutes* be fully explained by the gifted field producers who have fashioned its stories over the years: Joel Bernstein, Greg Cooke, Grace Diekhaus, Marion Goldin, Norman Gorin, Jim Jackson, Barry Lando, Paul Loewenwarter, William McClure, Harry Moses, Drew Phillips, Philip Scheffler, Jean Solomon, Suzanne St.

Pierre, John Tiffin, David Turecamo, Al Wasserman, Joseph Wershba, and Palmer Williams, to name just a few. And while on-screen reporters and backstage producers ably create *60 Minutes,* the program's cultural meanings are always something more than the best work and intentions of producers, reporters, and editors. Once the program gets into my grandmother's living room—and twenty million other living rooms—the meanings of *60 Minutes* become as diffuse and diverse as the electromagnetic spectrum itself.

But I am also not chiefly concerned here with measuring the "impact" or "effects" of *60 Minutes* on this diffuse and diverse audience, which would require a different perspective and method. My focus is not on the individual "messages" of particular *60 Minutes* narratives, but rather how those public narratives—taken as a pattern, as a larger whole—come to signify meanings and how those recurring meanings wind through our culture.

Nor am I interested here in re-working and highlighting the concerns that have been raised about *60 Minutes* by magazine and newspaper critics.[3] I have not investigated questions of bias or libel (although Don Hewitt speaks with a certain pride about never having lost a libel case).[4] Nor do I examine charges of unfair editing techniques.[5] Nor have I looked closely at the powerful backstage role of the field producer in comparison to the more limited role of on-screen reporters.[6] Mike Wallace in *Close Encounters* has addressed some of these issues and charges, including the program's flair for "show biz," "ambush interviews," and "tendentious editing."[7]

Finally, I have not looked closely at the relatively minor role women have played in the program over the years—both as on-camera reporters and as interview subjects.[8] Once again, I have tried to limit my focus to the program's creation and maintenance of Middle-American myths, which I acknowledge here are largely male mythologies. (John Fiske goes so far as to suggest that television news stories circulate their particular meanings in the guise and form of "masculine soap opera.")[9]

Embedded in much TV criticism—both academic and popular— is an implicit and elitist definition of the medium as some monolithic, menacing, technological, postmodern commodity that threatens the so-called purity of modern print culture. I would like to be more generous here and instead acknowledge that television, like the book publishing industry, is also a widely disparate and contradictory collection of stories and commodities—a collection of often popular and profitable contemporary myths.

Given the recent movements in cultural studies away from the "texts" of programs and toward the audience, some scholars may regard the spotlight here on the stories and myths of *60 Minutes* as a step backward. Yet in our academic criticism of the privileged stance of the interpreter and in the rush to reconstruct and embrace elusive audiences, I am concerned about the academy ignoring what is actually *on* television—for the development instead of totalizing theories *about* television and its viewers. Television constructs and circulates public discourses that are different from private meanings. We need also to attend to these larger *public* narratives and myths that map and guide our individual viewing.

I am, nevertheless, indebted to recent developments in cultural studies focusing on the relationship between programs and viewers.[10] Although my analysis is essentially textual, I do not mean to discredit the variety of viewer responses to *60 Minutes.* I do believe, however, that the analysis of text and the analysis of audience may constitute separate research problems. Whereas John Fiske argues that "meanings occur only in the encounter between texts and subjects,"[11] I contend that the producers of texts, the producers of *60 Minutes,* construct formulaic ways to read the texts—public maps for meaning—and I am concerned here with interpreting those maps. I believe with Horace Newcomb and Paul Hirsch that television "research and critical analysis . . . must somehow define and describe the inventory" that makes "multiple meanings" possible.[12]

What I do is see—as a viewer, a fan, and a critic. Since the early 1980s, I have carefully watched and taken notes on more than a hundred episodes of *60 Minutes* containing more than three hundred individual segments from programs airing between 1968 and 1990. In order to view the older programs, I made three extended trips to the Library of Congress in Washington, where almost all episodes of *60 Minutes* are copyrighted and available for viewing.[13] Through the University of Michigan graduate library, I made extensive use of the CBS written transcripts from the program. I also relied on *60 Minutes Verbatim*—a book in which CBS News published the written transcripts of 114 *60 Minutes* segments from the 1979-80 television season.[14]

What I have come to see over time is an important cultural artifact, one of the most influential programs in television history. Each week—like clockwork—*60 Minutes* attempts to organize a complex world for millions of us and, therefore, bears a special, often unacknowledged, responsibility for its particular perceptions and the kind of television sense it makes of our compelling and contrary world. For better or worse, *60 Minutes* is one of television's quintessential efforts in depicting everyday life. As journalist Tom Wicker acknowledges, "Television has become a condition of being. It may on occasion be inconvenient, intrusive, even harmful, but . . . we depend on television for perception as we depend on air for breath. And that's the way it is."[15]

In his powerful speech before the 1988 Democratic Convention, Jesse Jackson said, "I am here to make sense," a taken-for-granted role and responsibility that *60 Minutes* also takes on weekly. What I hope to do here is to make sense of the ways *60 Minutes* makes sense. As the dominant piece of furniture-technology in most of our homes, television and its programs have stitched themselves into the fabric of our individual and social identities. Ultimately, my task is to unstitch the stories of *60 Minutes,* turn them inside out in order to see them in new ways—the ways they comment on our public values and national character.

Although my choice of *60 Minutes* as the site to confront television appears microscopic, I hope to use this special program telescopically—to reveal larger vistas of American television and news, as cultural forms, connecting individuals to places in a larger world.

Such a microscopic approach—the focus on a single television news series—perhaps appears to constitute a limitation of this study, what the anthropologist Clifford Geertz might call an "extended acquaintance with extremely small matters," and as a result, "intrinsically incomplete."[16] But the study of culture, like culture itself, is never complete, always ongoing, and what I can hope to do is understand some key moments in a key contemporary text. To use Geertz's phrase, I am "rescuing the said" of *60 Minutes* discourse so I might reconstruct how the program makes sense by telling stories.[17]

Doing cultural analysis affords a researcher the benefit of drawing on a variety of perspectives and disciplines in the search for sense. As the following chapters attest, I am especially grateful to developments and work in sociology, anthropology, linguistic and literary theory, and both British and American cultural studies. Carey has addressed the limitations and strengths of such cultural analysis: "It does not seek to explain human behavior, but to understand it. It does not seek to reduce human action to underlying causes or structures but to interpret its significance. It does not attempt to predict human behavior, but to diagnose human meanings. It is, more positively, an attempt to bypass the rather discrete empiricism of behavioral studies and the esoteric apparatus of formal theories and to descend deeper into the empirical world."[18] Cultural studies then, for Carey and Geertz, is "not an experimental science in search of law but an interpretive one in search of meaning."[19]

Distinguished from cultural studies, the social science practices that guide much American media research are not unlike the dominant conventions that direct professional journalism. Both suspect interpretation, subjectivity, values, imagination, culture, and symbol, at best, as red flags—as problems to be avoided, dismissed, or worked around—and, at worst, as dangerous contaminators of reports that aim to explain carefully "what's really going on here in the world."

Generally, however, journalists and social scientists claim different terrain—the former, the practical world of common sense; the later, the esoteric world of expert knowledge. But these worlds often collide. A reporter must, on occasion, turn the expertise of academia into the common sense of news reports. And the academy is often unhappy with the results. Among peers, academics like to discredit certain kinds of descriptive research by labeling it "journalistic," while reporters (like Andy Rooney of *60 Minutes*) make a great living attacking the "gobbledygook" of academics.

But I argue that the boundaries between the academy and journalism overlap in important ways. After all, both modern science and contemporary reporting developed as nineteenth-century products of utilitarian rationality and realism which rejected imagination, romanticism, and the subjective. Both focus on a world "out there." Both search for external clues to that world (in the form of data, quotes, measured effects, and visual "actualities"). Both attend to information, fact, and message rather than to ritual, symbol, and meaning. Both value detachment from ideology in their work (a posture which locates scientists and reporters in superior positions above the fray), and are, in turn, valued by society for their apparent success at remaining detached. Both employ the omniscient third-person point of view in their writing in order to fortify their detachment and enhance their superiority.

Yet this latter value, in particular, is a purely narrative construction. However unwilling we are to admit that this is partly what we do, academia and journalism are in the business of telling stories. Instead, conventional journalism invokes the metaphors of science—fact-gathering, objectivity, information— rather than the metaphors of literature—characters, conflict, drama. And in her comparison of news and science, Gaye Tuchman reminds those of us who are academics that "the professionally objectified form of writing scientific articles tells a story. It contains its own inherent logic . . . and associated narrative form, and so structures what can and will be reported as science. It bounds what can be said and will be said."[20] Both journalists and scientists, like all professionals, create symbolic borders through the narratives we each write—narratives which often mask their own conventional contrivances.

Opposing the postures of routine journalism and conventional communication studies, my task in analyzing *60 Minutes,* then, becomes the construction of a "reading" of the program and its "sequence of symbols—speech, writing, gesture—that contain interpretation." My job here, more like that of a literary critic, is to "interpret the interpretations."[21] Within this context, I reject any notion that news—or my study—is objective, neutral, and value-free; making news reports and studies about those reports are always interpretive, value-laden acts. We all have our stories to tell—in our own ways.

Why is such a search for meaning in *60 Minutes* important? Because most of us learn, in fragmentary fashion, about the rest the world through mass media—and through news stories. News plays a crucial role in the construction, maintenance, and repair of that shared knowledge. To find common ground—to unmask for a moment our shared commonsense beliefs—is an important undertaking. It is "a quest for meaning" that attempts to make sense of "those forms and practices, those durable features, that withstand the vicissitudes of modern life."[22] But Carey says that merely to name those "durable features" is not enough—that the study must then connect the forms and practices of *60 Minutes* to its specific cultural heritage and to those individual threads that help secure us, however fragilely, in a collective world where we *must* tell stories in order to live. I try to make these connections.

The stories of *60 Minutes* speak to common themes, to ties that bind. Each Sunday it carries on backyard, over-the-fence conversations with its community of viewers. Like my grandmother, we talk back to the show. Or we write letters to the program (sometimes a hundred thousand per year), either to praise it, condemn it, or demand that Mike Wallace or Morley Safer look into some scam.

In more academic terms, the program is one key repository for our contemporary mythologies. Such an argument may affront many journalists who regard myths as primitive, amorphous, and subjective while revering news as sophisticated, methodical, and neutral. However, thinking of news as mythology helps reveal how the individuals and institutions of journalism organize experience and create meaning.

In a compelling interview series first broadcast on PBS in 1988, the late mythologist Joseph Campbell complained to Bill Moyers about the dearth of modern myths. He thought that our failing in contemporary technological societies is our inability to acknowledge the importance of myth to the sustenance of culture. While I agree with Campbell on the second point, I think we need only to look at *60 Minutes* to discover a cultural menagerie of modern American myths alive and healthy. In the chapters that follow, I hope to uncover some of those myths, place them on display, and critique this powerful contemporary storyteller.

Chapter 1 locates the development of the program amid competing definitions of news and common sense. It measures *60 Minutes* against the news metaphor that has dominated the practice and discussion of journalism in this century—reporting as science. In sharp contrast, a challenger to the preeminent model, the dramatic story, serves as the metaphor that has guided the creation and development of *60 Minutes*. Chapter 2 extends the discussion of common sense to its most pervasive cultural container, the narrative form. I identify here those particular narrative conventions that distinguish *60 Minutes*.

Moving from the discussion of news conventions, chapters 3-6 offer close analysis of four formulas that organize *60 Minutes*. In these four chapters, following John Cawelti's definition of formula, "a combination or synthesis of a number of specific cultural conventions with a more universal story form,"[23] I explore how a variety of conventions or characteristics contribute to each particular narrative type. For instance, chapter 3 details the most pervasive *60 Minutes* formula, news as mystery and the reporter as detective; chapter 4 examines news as therapy and the reporter as analyst; chapter 5 highlights news as adventure and the reporter as tourist; and chapter 6 features news as arbitration and the reporter as referee.

The final two chapters, representing a search for meaning, mark a departure from the description and interpretation of narrative formulas. In chapter 7, I argue that *60 Minutes* ultimately creates and celebrates a mythological tribute to American individualism. In chapter 8, I take up a discussion of the grace and sin of America's most watched television news program. Examining first its potential and limitations for initiating social change, I move to an exploration of the variety of cultural binds and contradictions the program "solves" for us week to week. Finally, I offer my own contradictory, liberal-populist attitudes toward a program that I simultaneously want to commend and condemn.

I argue in the end that *60 Minutes* is contemporary storytelling, enriching and simplifying, transforming and distorting experience. *60 Minutes* locates us in its world—a world we share—gives us characters to identify with and take exception to, and bridges the jagged gap between the private and the public domains. The stories and discourse of *60 Minutes* carry a mythology for middle America—what David Thorburn might call "consensus narrative."[24] It is a mythology in search of middle ground and common sense. In other words, it is this powerful mythology that, like church, draws both an immigrant Croatian grandmother and her Northwestern Ph.D. grandson back to this same place Sunday after Sunday.

From Iconoclast to Institution, from News to Common Sense

1

> News reading, and writing, is a ritual act and moreover a dramatic one. What is arrayed before the reader is not pure information but a portrayal of the contending forces in the world.
>
> —James Carey

> [T]here is a need in humans for myth, for symbols, to construe and order a confusing and hostile environment—just as there is a need for food, water, shelter, and sex—and the absolute truths of science do not provide this myth.
>
> —Walker Percy

> Journalists act as the custodians of realism and common sense. . . .
>
> —Mary Mander

It is no accident that *60 Minutes* was born in the late 1960s. In a time when even middle-class consensus and common sense were shaken, this often iconoclastic news magazine emerged, along with *Laugh-In* and *The Smothers Brothers Comedy Hour,* as a topical prime-time *variety* show. These programs represented television's irreverent challenge to traditional institutions whose leaders—network executives among them—generally seemed baffled by what the decade had wrought. Each of these shows made its own sense of the Vietnam War, racial unrest, political assassinations, campus protests, the drug culture, free love, and feminist and African-American challenges to elite white male authority.

CBS aired that first *60 Minutes* on September 24, 1968—some nineteen months after *The Smothers Brothers* premiered on CBS and eight months after *Laugh-In* started on NBC. *Laugh-In,* which rated as the most-watched program in America from 1968 through 1970, died on network prime time in 1973. *The Smothers Brothers*

1

Comedy Hour, which aired on all three networks during its contro-versial run, passed away on NBC in 1975. *60 Minutes,* however, kept ticking—one of only a handful of shows, including *The Ed Sullivan Show, Meet the Press, Gunsmoke,* and *The Tonight Show,* to endure on television for twenty years or more.

60 Minutes initially struggled to find viewers, alternating with the *CBS News Hour* in a Tuesday night time slot, often on opposite ABC's *Marcus Welby, M.D.,* America's most popular program during the early 1970s. Over the next few years, *60 Minutes* moved to 6:00 P.M. (EST) Sunday, to 8:00 P.M. Friday, then back and forth between 6:00 or 9:30 Sunday evening. In December 1975, CBS scheduled the news magazine into its now familiar Sunday prime-time slot at 7:00 P.M. (EST), where it has remained.

During the 1976-77 season, *60 Minutes*—at number eighteen—first snuck onto the list of top twenty most-watched shows. The next season, amid a plethora of sitcoms, cop shows, and prime-time soaps, it cracked the top ten. It has been there ever since.[1] At its ratings peak during 1979 and 1980, *60 Minutes* ranked as America's most widely viewed program, ahead of *Three's Company, That's Incred-ible, Alice, M*A*S*H, Dallas, Flo, The Jeffersons, The Dukes of Hazzard,* and *One Day at a Time,* which rounded out the top ten that season. Over the next six television seasons, it ranked among the top four programs in each of those years, climbing to number one again during the 1982-83 season.[2]

The story of *60 Minutes* is also any self-respecting capitalist's vision of the American Dream. From rags to riches, from its early low-rated, marginal status as feisty iconoclast to its full-blown devel-opment as a powerful CBS institutional fixture, *60 Minutes* has made close to $1 billion for the network.[3] By 1980, "a commercial minute on *60 Minutes* sold for a record $230,000."[4] By 1985, the program's six and one half minutes of national advertising time were worth $350,000 per minute.[5] By 1990, like other top-rated shows including *Roseanne* and *Cosby, 60 Minutes* commanded nearly $400,000 per minute for its now seven minutes of national advertising slots.[6] Because CBS owns *60 Minutes* and does not have to pay fees to an independent production company, the program can generally make back its production costs for any given program after selling only one or two minutes of commercial time. Its inventor, guiding light, and executive producer Don Hewitt rightly calls it, "the biggest money-maker in the history of broadcasting."[7] And any single *60 Minutes* program reaches a bigger audience than any other single news form in the history of American journalism.[8]

That first *60 Minutes* broadcast back in 1968 featured the kind of news variety that would become the staple of *60 Minutes*. Leading with a story on the Nixon-Humphrey presidential campaign, *60 Minutes* showed exclusive footage from the hotel rooms of both candidates from the nights they were nominated. Next came "Cops," a segment on the tensions between Middle America and police departments. Mike Wallace's opening question to Attorney General Ramsey Clark captured the iconoclasm that was Wallace's trademark during those early years: "I think Dick Gregory has said that today's cop is yesterday's nigger. Do you understand that?"[9] A short satirical "Viewpoint" essay by Art Buchwald followed on how journalists gauge public opinion by reading each other's columns. The closing segment highlighted excerpts from Saul Bass's *Why Man Creates,* a clever animated history of human creativity originally made for Kaiser Aluminum.[10]

Taking his cue from the cultural variety offered in *Life* and *Time* magazines, Don Hewitt's television magazine sought to counter the often tedious one-hour, single-subject news documentaries that generally drew small audiences in comparison with other prime-time fare. He argued, "Instead of dealing with issues we [will] tell stories," and went on to create a "multi-subject" format with an emphasis on "personal" journalism. "If we package reality as well as Hollywood packages fiction," Hewitt maintained, "I'll bet we could double the rating."[11]

The contemporary prototype of the tough news editor with keen entrepreneurial instincts, Hewitt has indeed doubled the rating. And along with the dictates of the managerial types currently running the networks, Hewitt's success with the magazine format has played a part in the demise of the traditional, single-subject news documentary which generally drew low ratings and even lower profits. *CBS Reports,* NBC's *White Paper,* and ABC's *Close-Up* are all gone. Hewitt says of all three programs: "[They] seemed to me to be the voice of the corporation, and I didn't believe people were any more interested in hearing from a corporation than they were in watching a document."[12]

In place of the documentaries are other news magazine clones—

3

ABC's long-running *20/20* and *Prime Time Live*—and the breezy syndicated tabloid shows *A Current Affair, Inside Edition,* and *Hard Copy,* among others. Hewitt regards them all as part of his contribution to television news: "The main legacy of the show is that it has changed the face of television. In our wake came *PM Magazine, That's Incredible!, 20/20,* God knows how many NBC magazines . . . *Inside Edition, A Current Affair, USA Today [on TV].* They just keep coming out of the woodwork for a very simple reason. They look for the profit or loss thing and say, 'That's the way to make money.' "[13] Fortified by national commercial spots reaching nearly twenty million U.S. homes each week, a typical episode still finds *60 Minutes* following the formula: multiple subjects and personal narratives.

For example, at the outset of their February 4, 1990, program, the character-reporters introduce themselves after previewing the evening's three stories: Mike Wallace, who started with the program in 1968; Morley Safer who joined in 1970; Harry Reasoner, who began with Wallace in 1968 but left for ABC from 1970 through 1978; Ed Bradley, who came aboard in 1981 to replace Dan Rather (1975 through 1981), who left to take Walter Cronkite's job; and Meredith Vieira and Steve Kroft, who both came over in 1989 from CBS's thirtysomething version of a news magazine—the defunct *West 57th.* Vieira and Kroft were added when Diane Sawyer (1984 through 1989) left to work for ABC's *Prime Time Live.* At the end of the introductions, low-seniority reporter Kroft also mentions that Andy Rooney will follow that evening's three featured stories with his weekly essay.[14]

After Jeep Cherokee, Wausau insurance, and AT&T advertisements, Ed Bradley on this particular night, in front of the traditional *60 Minutes* "magazine cover," begins the first segment. In this moving narrative titled "One American Family" (produced by Grace Diekhaus), Bradley introduces a Hollywood "model family" coping with AIDS. The mother, Elizabeth Glaser, was infected with the HIV virus during a routine blood transfusion in 1981 while giving birth to a daughter. When the daughter died of AIDS in 1987, the family discovered that both the mother and a surviving younger son now also carry the virus. The husband, Paul Michael Glaser, television-actor-turned-director, has not been infected. The story features concerned politicians, movie stars, and movie star-turned-politician

4

Ronald Reagan, shown doing a public service spot for Elizabeth Glaser's Pediatric AIDS Foundation.

This powerful news drama attempts to make sense of the conflict between public taboos and private anguish, between hope and despair. Like many *60 Minutes* stories, amid the horror of human experience the program offers comfort at the end. As the Glasers, arm-in-arm and backs to viewers, walk down their suburban street, Elizabeth Glaser's voice-over covers the scene, names the conflict, and tries to resolve it: "You walk outside and you appreciate your life—even though it's horrible—because you have it. And you learn to love what you have now."

Cut to the ticking *60 Minutes* stopwatch.

Following advertising for a VISA-sponsored Paul McCartney tour, Subaru, US Sprint, and two CBS promotions for upcoming shows, Mike Wallace introduces the next segment, "The McMartin Pre-School" (produced by Lowell Bergman). This story, Wallace says, is about "the longest, the most expensive criminal trial in U.S. history." It updates a segment that *60 Minutes* did three years earlier on two California preschool employees, Peggy and Ray Buckey, mother and son, charged with child abuse. After the six-year case, both were acquitted "on 52 counts of sodomy, rape, oral copulation, and conspiracy," although Ray Buckey was to be retried on thirteen other deadlocked counts.

It is again a story about private humiliation and public outrage. With Wallace's skillful commonsense voice-overs stitching the narrative together, interviews of the acquitted pair are pitted against parents and child advocates who don't think justice has been served. Continuing the boxing metaphor, the segment ends with Ray Buckey vowing dramatically to fight the thirteen remaining counts: "There's no end to what they've done to me. I can't just put this behind me. . . . I'll fight them because I have no other way to go. I'm not going to roll over for something that I never did."

Cut again to ticking stopwatch.

Next, advertising features Enterprise Rent-A-Car, Maytag, a promo for *Murder, She Wrote* which follows *60 Minutes*, an affiliate promo for a wind-chill index chart, American Airlines vacation packages, and another local promo for a syndicated series. Steve Kroft introduces the third segment, "The Selling of Retin-A" (produced by Suzanne St. Pierre), a story about the cozy and questionable rela-

5

tionship between drug companies and medical research. Focusing on the drug Retin-A, an FDA-approved acne cream, this report addresses larger problems regarding the "commercialization of science."

Touted as a wrinkle-removing miracle drug by academic researchers, the drug still has not been approved for that purpose by the FDA. Concerned about its long-range effects, some researchers also weren't convinced that the drug worked as a wrinkle remover. Yet a national press conference called by medical school researchers regarding its potential to repair aging skin tripled the sales of Retin-A for Ortho Pharmaceutical Corporation and its parent company Johnson and Johnson—companies which gave large grants to these researchers and helped them set up press conferences as a way of distributing "scientific information."

The episode distinctively features *60 Minutes* "suspects"—researchers from the University of Michigan and Boston University—who refuse to talk directly to *60 Minutes*. As with many of the program's "villains," they seem suspicious in their refusals. The segment ends as Kroft, a mediator between the expertise of science and the common sense of viewers, tells of a congressional investigation into the drug company and a lawsuit filed by another university which claims it owns the patent on Retin-A.

Cut to stopwatch.

Like clockwork, Gallo wine, Lincoln's Town Car, Kellogg's Nut and Honey cereal, and New York Life Insurance advertisements follow. Ed Bradley introduces Andy Rooney's commonsense essay on magazine advertisers who fail to disclose the actual prices of products. Rooney needles Chanel No. 5, Marlboro cigarettes, Madza trucks, and, ironically, Chrysler—including the Jeep Cherokee, a sponsor featured at the beginning of the program. *60 Minutes* may be the only show in network prime time that can make fun of its own advertisers.

60 Minutes is also the only show in prime time that prints excerpts of letters from its audiences—many of them critical of the program. In celebrating diversity through this segment, although the letters are few and heavily edited, *60 Minutes* openly engages in an ongoing dialog with selected viewers. Nearly 80,000 letters—110,000 in 1981—are received by the program each year.[15]

On this particular night, following commercials for Advil, GM

6

parts, Nicorette nicotine gum, and three promos for CBS shows, Mike Wallace updates a story from June 1989 and then reads from the three chosen letters. The final excerpt offers a hostile critique of *60 Minutes*: "As far as I'm concerned, you can retitle your program SIXTY SECONDS because that's about all I can stand of your liberal garbage. . . ." After he finishes reading this letter, Wallace neatly defuses the barb with a smile. Positioned beside the ubiquitous stopwatch, he closes the show: "I'm Mike Wallace. We'll be back next week with another edition of *60 Minutes*."

Fade to black.

The credits role over audio and video from the first story shown that evening. An announcer provides information on where to write for a $4 transcript of the program: *60 Minutes* Transcripts, 267 Broadway, New York, NY 10007. The information appears visually again over the stopwatch.

Fade again to black.

This 1990 program dramatically recalls Mike Wallace's conclusion from that very first 1968 episode: "And there you have our first *60 Minutes* broadcast. Looking back, it had quite a range, as the problems and interests of our lives have quite a range. Our perception of reality roams, in a given day, from the light to the heavy, from warmth to menace, and if this broadcast does what we hope it will do, it will report reality."[16]

60 Minutes then, taken as a whole, offers a kind of rising and falling action among its three major narratives, capped each week by Andy Rooney's essays and letters from viewers. This structure also loosely follows the original plan for the program's reporters, which according to Morley Safer meant, "Every program should have one sweetheart and one son of a bitch . . . Safer is witty. Wallace is crotchety."[17] Within this comfortable structure, viewers too are situated in a middle ground between nice and tough reporters, between light and heavy pieces, between warmth and menace, between the factual trappings of news and the fictional feel of drama.

The Contested Nature of News

Before its emergence from marginal iconoclast to popular institution, *60 Minutes* was a product of, and a participant in, a late-1960s' battle over what constituted news. This fight was waged primarily on two fronts. From above, Vice President Spiro Agnew, in his famous "heartland speech" (delivered from Des Moines) in November 1969, attacked East and West Coast newscasters and editors in the "privileged" journalism hierarchy.[18] This was an attack on journalism's alleged liberal agenda, its failure to remain "objective," and its increasing opposition to government positions on the Vietnam War.[19]

From within journalism itself, however, along a second front there was a conflict between old guard editors and managers (many of whom Agnew was attacking) who believed in objective news and, from below, young turk reporters who questioned traditional conventions. For the young radicals, according to the sociologist Michael Schudson, " 'Straight news' was not only drab and constricting—it was itself a form of participation, a complicity with official sources [like Agnew] whose most alarming feature was that it so self-righteously claimed to be above partisan or political consideration."[20] So the old guard was caught in the middle, under siege from two directions: from the establishment right and from its own discontented left. It was a battle over changing and competing definitions of common sense.

In the late 1960s the perception of the growing government manipulation of news institutions (despite Agnew's self-serving concerns) helped spur on the discontented "adversary culture" within journalism. This reporter counterculture sparked a renewed interest in what Schudson calls "two submerged traditions" in reporting: "a literary tradition and a muckraking tradition"—both of which *60 Minutes* has drawn heavily upon.[21]

Whereas most editors—in the sixties and today—cordon off news from entertainment and document from drama (distinctions that are often arbitrary and also self-serving), Don Hewitt intriguingly and honestly offers *60 Minutes*' connection to a storytelling tradition as a key to the program's popularity: "You're there because somebody is telling you a story."[22] The sustained power of *60 Minutes* partially rests then on this celebration of a literary tradition. In order to make sense of the world, for example, *60 Minutes* adapts familiar story forms long associated with American fiction genres such as the classical detective mystery. As I will explain in chapter 3, this literary formula, in fact, also has strong ties to the earlier muckraking tradition. Within these formulas and traditions the reporters of *60*

Minutes perform—not as neutral, antiseptic journalists—but as dramatic and often heroic characters. Their mission is to make common sense of an enigmatic world through the narrative.

The sixties forced institutional reexamination, and journalism as well got caught up in self-study. In the battle over what constituted news in the late 1960s, then, two competing models vied. Schudson labels these the "informational" and "story" models which developed initially throughout the late-nineteenth century.[23] At issue seven decades later were not only the scientific versus dramatic models of reporting, but also which model best constituted common sense.

Defining News as Common Sense

Common sense is, indeed, familiar terrain to Don Hewitt. In discussing the popularity of *60 Minutes*, Hewitt partly attributes its achievements to his own common or "sixth sense": "I do everything at my fingertips. I'm probably the least intellectual person in this shop. Everybody around here is smarter than I am, much smarter. But I've got the best fingertips. I've got the best sixth sense."[24] Journalism textbooks have long praised common sense as "indispensable for the reporter" and celebrated reporters who are "inquisitive, perceptive and healthfully skeptical"[25]—qualities implicit in Hewitt's understanding of his own sixth sense.

But what is common sense? On the luminous side, it represents the kind of shared knowledge that allows us to live together in a contemporary yet contradictory democracy. It is found daily in our newspapers, on our televisions, in our conversations. It is in the iconoclasm, humor, and uncommon wisdom of an I. F. Stone, or the clarity and comfortable acumen of Ellen Goodman's best essays. On *60 Minutes*, it is the program's ability to penetrate pretense and artifice, to lay bare the heart of indifferent institutions tangled in veins of red tape.

Yet common sense has a shadowy side. It is elusive, amorphous, and often contradictory, characteristics that belie its own intuitive definition as practical, anti-intellectual, and transparent. For example, there is an urban common sense that views small-town life as narrow, naive, and oppressive; and there is a pastoral conventional wisdom that perceives the city as embattled, hurried, and heartless. The borders of common sense then are precious but contested and often contrary spaces. And although common sense is identified as a solid, Middle-American virtue, slippery footing marks its definitional terrain.[26]

I argue that the consensual, taken-for-granted knowledge served by the news also shares the elusive terrain of contemporary common sense.[27] The term connotes "conventional wisdom"; it does have a "natural," "that's the way things are" quality about it. The cultural anthropologist Clifford Geertz discusses its aura as "matter-of-fact," "down-to-earth," "colloquial wisdom."[28] Because of its transparency, any "ordinary" person should instinctively recognize conventional wisdom; it is "what anyone with common sense" already knows. Despite its transparency, however, like myth, painting, religion, television, and news, common sense is also a "cultural system." Geertz notes, "It can be questioned, disputed, affirmed, developed, formalized, contemplated, even taught, and it can vary dramatically from one people to the next."[29]

In exposing common sense as a cultural system, Geertz has defined five possible features: (1) naturalness ("of courseness"); (2) practicalness ("materially useful"); (3) thinness ("simpleness or "literalness"); (4) immethodicalness ("unapologetically ad hoc"); and (5) accessibleness ("open to all . . . solid citizens," "anti-expert," "anti-intellectual").[30]

Most news story structures—whether the inverted pyramid model of a front-page New York *Times* story or a fourteen-minute *60 Minutes* detective drama—fit major parts of Geertz's definition. First, news stories appear *natural* and transparent in that they do not call attention to their own construction; they do not ask the reader or viewer to demand, "Now why did the reporter choose that word or pick these quotes or why did they show that image or edit at that point?" As Ted Glasser and James Ettema have pointed out, the naturalness of the news story and "the *naturalness* of common sense . . . posits an unproblematic view of the world."[31] This commonsense feature recalls former CBS news anchor Walter Cronkite's famous evening sign-off: "And that's the way it is. . . ."

In the day-to-day uncritical consumption of news, then, reports seem natural rather than manufactured. Reporters at *60 Minutes* or the New York *Times* seldom explicitly share with readers and viewers their ideological stances, their corporate roles, or the selection process by which assignments are made and story angles chosen. News stories present a vision that although "reality" may be complicated, it is ultimately controllable by professional reporters who can recognize the real and transform it into transparent and sense-making news stories.

Second, news stories are *practical* because they serve the day-to-day—or Sunday-to-Sunday—deadline pressures of journalism. The news report as common sense responds to "particular needs" then serves those needs "directly and practically."[32] For example, it is simpler to re-present a new experience or issue in terms of the detective formula or the inverted pyramid news model than it is to create an entirely new form to accommodate and retell that experience or issue. As Glasser and Ettema contend, "Among journalists . . . news is not a theoretical construct but a practical accomplishment. . . ."[33]

Third, commonsense news stories are *thin* because they advocate a literal or descriptive posture. The thinness of commonsense news suggests that "facts" are transparent and generally unambiguous.[34] Such descriptive facts and details only tell us "what is going on here" without plunging explicitly into analytical reflection or the multitude of contradictions that saturate "the real." News stories are marked off and categorized apart from opinion pieces and political columns. After all, as the conventional wisdom of journalism dictates, readers and viewers in a democratic society will make up their own minds concerning the practical information provided in the transparent stories of America's evening newscasts and front pages.

Fourth, common sense is *immethodical,* as Glasser and Ettema note, because it "expresses itself not in formalized methods or codified laws but in a culture's store of proverbs and other opportunities for conventional wisdom."[35] In journalism, for example, such catch phrases as "sticking to the facts" or "telling both sides of a story" function as "proverbs" which often justify particular reports without exposing the construction of those reports to self-examination. The first proverb assumes facts are natural; the second assumes experience is two-dimensional. In addition, news reports are immethodical because they seldom make analytical connections among the stories that appear together on a front page or in a *60 Minutes* broadcast. Nor are clear connections made between a week's worth of front pages or a month's worth of *60 Minutes'* programs.[36]

Fifth, common sense is *accessible,* Geertz contends, in that its comprehension seemingly requires "no esoteric knowledge, no special technique or peculiar giftedness, and little or no specialized training. . . ."[37] *60 Minutes* stories then—as cultural forms of conventional wisdom—appear accessible because they often take expert knowledge offered by a variety of sources on multiple subjects and shape that knowledge within the familiar confines of news narratives. The explanations of experts may be reduced to four or five sound bites (or quotes in print) embedded within practical news formulas.

Reporters often draw upon common sense to resist the rhetoric of politicians, public employees, and business leaders, making them say "what it is they really mean." Mike Wallace, for example, often resists the jargon and privilege of politicians or business people on behalf of viewers, demanding instead clarification and common sense. He might ask, "Do you really expect the American people to buy that?" He says that this interview strategy is meant to "test the morality" and "get the heart started" of an interview subject.[38]

Common sense, however, also repels self-scrutiny. Status-quo values or political arrangements are often taken for granted in news stories as "the way things are." By its very immethodicalness, its very opposition to analytic coherency, common sense contains no abstract strategies for critiquing elite or competing points of view and therefore certifies class or political divisions as natural and given. Common sense, then, inadvertently maintains these divisions by its inability to assess the ways in which class and political hierarchies are *not* natural and given. Therefore, when Democratic and Republican leaders on *60 Minutes* espouse ties to Middle-American virtues, what is also going on, according to John Fiske, is the ability of those in power "to naturalize their social interests into 'ordinary' common sense" coded in taken-for-granted news narratives.[39] Political elites, then, use the rhetoric of common sense to move up and down the social hierarchy to forge a bond with the middle.

A key distinction of common sense, then, is its dexterity in withstanding definition and close examination. By clinging to codes of detached professionalism, journalists further insulate themselves from scrutiny by claiming that only they are adequately qualified—through the common sense of practical, street-wise experience—to critique their profession.[40] However, because commonsense journalism focuses on objects, sources, and data out in the world, it rarely turns its lens back on the profession itself. In the history of *60 Minutes*, for example, only one program ("Looking at *60 Minutes*") in September 1981 specifically addressed a few of its own more controversial practices, including chasing unwilling sources down the street and concealing reporters' identities. Common sense, then, lacking the mechanisms for diligent and sustained self-analysis, is a perfect form of knowledge and object of celebration for journalism, a profession which does not know how to examine systematically its own devices and structures.

As with any shifting cultural process, commonsense knowledge is forever contradictory, incomplete, and fickle. As Stuart Hall and his colleagues warn, common sense is fragmentary and inconsistent "precisely because what is 'common' about it is that it is not subject to tests of internal coherence and logical consistency."[41] Coherence and consistency allegedly belong to another realm of knowledge — the domain of the expert.

Experts and the Well-informed Reporter

The sociologist and former reporter Robert Park, who made one of the earliest connections between news and common sense, distinguished common sense from analytic knowledge — or "knowledge about" — which is "formal, rational, and systematic."[42] Instead, Park defined common sense as synthetic knowledge — or "acquaintance with" — "the sort of knowledge one inevitably acquires in the course of one's personal and firsthand encounters" with daily experience.[43]

From a journalist's viewpoint, knowledge about resides in contemporary culture in the realm of experts or "primary definers," to use Hall's term: those institutional leaders who dominate news stories as privileged sources and establish the initial definitions or "primary interpretations" of news topics.[44] Often at the edges of conventional wisdom, specialized knowledge about is typically possessed by highly trained practitioners across a variety of professions (medicine, law, politics, education) and is inscribed in their expert vernacular. These primary definers who dominate routine news are also often central character-subjects in *60 Minutes* stories.

The division of labor in modern, technological societies has led to a "growing gap" between those with expertise and those without it, and the increasing dependency of laypersons on expert sources.[45] Depending on our own fields of expertise, a privileged few of us may function from time to time as news sources and experts. More commonly, however, sitting at home watching *60 Minutes* or reading the daily paper, we are also laypersons—practitioners of common sense. In this mode we are more often synthetic rather than analytic readers and watchers of news.

The widening gap between common sense and expert types of knowledge has created the need in contemporary society for a skilled arbiter. Terming this arbiter the *well-informed,* Alfred Schutz and Thomas Luckmann contend that this person is distinguished from the layperson by an unwillingness to "unreflectively" accept the point of view or "judgment of the expert." On the other hand, unlike the expert, the well-informed generalist lacks expertise in any particular specialized field.[46] However, with privileged access to experts and their special realms of knowledge, the well-informed command a critical, mediating symbolic station in modern cultures—a station located on the vistas between "expertness and the lack of it," between primary definitions and conventional wisdom.

60 Minutes's reporters are perhaps the exemplars of what Schutz has called "the well-informed citizen."[47] Acting as agents for the mass audience, *60 Minutes*'s reporters fashion news stories addressed to common sense. And a primary mission of the well-informed reporter is to take specialized knowledge and transform it into common sense. The journalistic convention of the quote in print or the sound bite on *60 Minutes* often locates knowledge about within the context of acquaintance with. Once within this ad-hoc milieu of conventional wisdom, reporters may defend their stories as natural, as the-ways-things-are, thereby rendering them transparent and no longer subject to critical inquiry that questions reporter assumptions and conventions.

Despite apparent transparency, however, the commonsense narratives of *60 Minutes* do invite criticism, most publicly from well-informed types who serve newspapers as television critics. The neutrality edict of "informational" journalism—which these critics generally value—appears at odds with the rich storytelling and dramatic intrigue often generated in any given *60 Minutes* segment. Both reportorial impulses, however, represent opposite sides of the coin of common sense. According to many orthodox editors, television critics, and much of the public, journalism should appear neutral, report descriptive information, and be a window on the

14

world. The prevailing argument goes: keep drama separate from documents, entertainment separate from information. These professionally manufactured oppositions are the stuff of common sense; they naturalize their own borders in a way that may prevent us from seeing that they are not mutually exclusive and are arranged by historical (rather than natural) forces.

The routine distinction, for example, between hard and soft news has to do with widely accepted masculine perceptions of how reality divides and works. Not only is the hard-soft news designation a commonsense way for journalists to sort gentler features from rugged news, but these categories also elevate particular reports—the timely, descriptive account or the tough, investigative piece—to a higher status. Soft features (often written by women in journalism's history) traditionally have been relegated to a lower position in the news hierarchy, inside a newspaper or as the final story of a *60 Minutes* program. In the conventional wisdom of newspaper critics of television, soft features are aligned with pandering popularity, while hard news marks the important information needed in a democracy.

From the very beginning *60 Minutes*'s strategy was to play on the distinction between hard and soft news metaphors—metaphors that have become part of the taken-for-granted, orthodox conventions of daily reporting. CBS News biographer Gary Paul Gates also certifies the hard–soft, fact–fiction categories as natural and given: "With *60 Minutes* [Don Hewitt] conclusively demonstrated that slick entertainment and journalistic quality could be combined. . . . The program's best and most memorable pieces were its hard-hitting, investigative reports on political corruption and other front-page subjects. But what gave the show an extra dimension—and accounted for much of its appeal—was its back-of-the-book features on popular personalities."[48]

When Mike Wallace reflects on the growing popularity of the program, he too locates this power in the hard-versus-soft distinction: "At that time [early 1970s], it was only Morley [Safer] and me who were up front on the broadcast, and he was doing more essays, profiles, things of that nature. I was doing the harder stuff. And then [Dan] Rather came [in 1975], and he began to do some of the hard stuff, too. Those were the years, in effect, that made the reputation of *60 Minutes*."[49]

While the reporters on *60 Minutes* track down a criminal, expose a con game, confront a bureaucrat, or laud a movie star, the overall structure of the program does juxtapose harder-edged, investigative segments with lighter feature pieces. However, like all language, these conventional distinctions between hard and soft, fact and fiction, are also often arbitrary and immethodical. These dualisms have become so entrenched as taken-for-granted, commonsense oppositions that they frequently conceal the territory where they spill into one another.

The Information Model: News as Science

The hard news label in journalism, in part, grew from the convention of regarding news as "just the facts, please." And despite journalism's ties to literary traditions, since the late nineteenth century institutional journalism has aligned itself more closely with science, information, and objectivity. When Adolph Ochs bought and reinvented the New York *Times* in the late 1890s, one strategy he employed sought to counteract the large-circulation New York papers of William Randolph Hearst and Joseph Pulitzer with an elitist "informational" paper that carved out a smaller audience among wealthy businesspeople, political leaders, and intellectuals.[50] In opposing his paper to the more dramatic, narrative journalism of the Pulitzer and Hearst papers, Ochs positioned the *Times* as the "paper of record" filled with the texts of treaties, court reports, congressional hearings, and federal documents—an alternative to the "common," middle-class storytelling that went on in the large-circulation papers. Ochs's strategy was not unlike television marketing schemes today which target smaller, upscale yuppie viewers who control a larger percentage of consumer dollars than their representative numbers among the population.

The icon status of the *Times* as the preeminent institution for democratic, pristine information, as distinct from tainted tabloid stories, obscures the economic strategy that appeals to elitist interests within the market. With Hearst and Pulitzer papers capturing the bulk of working- and middle-class readers, Ochs and the *Times* forged an alliance between facts and high social status. In other words, in the hierarchical class scheme the so-called objective, informational model for reporting was regarded as inherently superior to storytelling for making sense of experience. The *Times* eschewed overt storytelling and marketed itself around the notion that information and story were mutually exclusive categories. The rise then of an objective ideal was connected as much to elitism and corporate strategy as to any moral sense of journalistic neutrality.[51] In fact, at its root this tendency in objective journalism is anti- not pro-democratic in spirit.

In the history of journalism, the trappings of science have been a pervasive and recurring strategy for establishing and maintaining journalism's legitimacy as a powerful institution.[52] One journalism textbook, for example, makes explicit reference to the metaphor: "The journalist and the scientist perform different roles for society, but there are similarities in the goals, subject matter, techniques, and attitudes of the two professions. One of the central arguments . . . is that journalists can improve traditional reporting skills by drawing on techniques of gathering information developed in the sciences . . ."[53]

This model achieved its status and dominance, not by being "scientific," which is outside the boundaries of the utilitarian, anti-intellectual imperatives of routine journalism. Rather, reporters implicitly reached a consensus that the strategy of neutral conventions was a practical, economical, commonsense blueprint for organizing events and issues within severe time and space constraints. As Schudson notes, the science metaphor represented a crucial tactic in transforming conventional journalism into its preeminent position: "Reporters in the 1890s saw themselves, in part, as scientists uncovering the economic and political facts of industrial life more boldly, more clearly, and more 'realistically' than anyone had done before."[54]

Conventional journalism continues to mask the objective–subjective conflict by submerging the identities of reporters under a wave of so-called scientific practices. In the "objective" report the self of the reporter disappears as attention shifts to the (re)presentation of facts—"what's really going on here." Gaye Tuchman locates this convention in the "web of facticity," which includes the separation of hard news from opinion, the use of quotation marks, sound bites, and neutral word choices, the presentation of "both sides" of an issue, and the use of the detached third-person point of view, among others.[55] Because it is practical and efficient, "facticity" helps establish journalism as an apparently neutral, legitimate institution with the power to frame occurrences, identify reality, sell news, and make common sense of widely disparate experiences for audiences. In conventional, factual news reports, however, readers and viewers are seldom privy to the relationships of reporters to their sources, to their communities, to their corporate employer, or to the commodity nature of news reports. Over time, validated by the consensus of conventional wisdom, these personal and economic elements are buried in naturalized, institutionalized practices.

In tracing the metaphors that have been used to talk and think about journalism, Jack Lule argues that the science metaphor limits meaning: "The ruling metaphor of news as science has allowed news to be experienced in a particular, limited way. It encourages talk of bias, truth, fact, source, objectivity; it discourages other kinds of talk, such as theme, scene, language, meaning, genre, convention. Oddly, it is not that news as science says too much; it says too little. . . . News as science discourages contemplation of the *meaning* of the method, style, structure, convention and language that flows through the unreflexive heart of the news."[56] Lule, a former writer for the Philadelphia *Inquirer,* calls for opening discussion on journalism to incorporate its dramatic dimensions. Thus far, such discourse has generally been closed or used to discredit news reports.

The news-as-science metaphor shuts down certain meanings by limiting discussion of "real" news to its datalike or descriptive dimensions rather than its emotive or analytical possibilities. Margaret Morse frames the argument this way: "In critical discourse, only the journalistic, objective model of news is legitimized, while news in a subjective mode is generally considered nothing but an aberration or degradation of news values, deplored as 'show biz,' 'glitz,' and 'glitter' atypical of the news profession. However, news in a subjective mode can have a far more powerful impact on what we perceive as 'real' than the old news based on print."[57] Although marginalized by tradition and convention, the news-as-story metaphor potentially could extend rather than limit the commonsense language used to define news. Indeed, in a world where everyday life is increasingly represented in the journalistic and social science metaphors of arcane statistics and opinion polls, the search for new, popular, and richer metaphors becomes even more imperative.

Unlike the expert domains of medicine, economics, law, or science, "informational" journalism does not usually require or demand years of specialized training beyond learning basic data-gathering and formula-writing techniques. "Reporters," David Eason points out, "have no special method for determining the truth of a situation nor a special language for reporting their findings. They make sense of events by telling stories about them."[58] In other words, reporters work in the *acquaintance-with* world of the narrative—which is a different place than the *knowledge-about* world inhabited professionally by those of us who belong to cults of expertise.

Whereas the common sense of informational journalism conceals its storytelling impulses, there is a model of well-informed journalism which foregrounds the drama of news over objective conventions. Occasionally calling those conventions into question, this model also represents a competing view of common sense. Designated "literary journalism"—sometimes dubbed "new journalism"—this mode of reporting achieved prominence in the 1960s. It presented an iconoclastic alternative to the facticity-neutrality ideal of corporate journalism and dramatically set the stage for *60 Minutes*.

The Dramatic Model: News as Story

60 Minutes materialized at a time in the late 1960s when there was less and less consensus about what constituted appropriate commonsense responses to social dilemmas. Faced with so many anomalies by the end of the decade, institutions were not totally trusted in their ability to oversee and direct the social order. As a result, status-quo organizations in our culture lost much of the favor, homage, and credibility they had commanded.[59] Not only fringe protest movements, but also Middle Americans as well began to suspect the privileges and power of traditional authority. This breakdown of faith in institutions, in part, paved the way for programs such as *60 Minutes* to tell their dramatic stories, which usually championed the individual oppressed by menacing institutional authority.

In the early part of the 1960s, Tom Wicker contends that neutral or "objective journalism" (which "reported mostly the contents of official documents, or statements delivered by official spokesmen") was entrenched as the dominant model, a model which analyzed experience and "statements only in the most obvious terms." According to Wicker, the "press had so wrapped itself in the paper chains of 'objective journalism' that it had little ability to report anything beyond the bare and undeniable" facts.[60] Thus, as the decade confronted a myriad of problems, the detached conventions of routine journalism offered few or unsatisfactory avenues for exploring partial or distorted institutional responses to social upheaval.

As a result, by the end of the 1960s "objectivity became a term of abuse." Schudson argues that "critics claimed that urban planning created slums, that schools made people stupid, that medicine caused disease, that psychiatry invented mental illness, and that the courts promoted injustice. . . . And objectivity in journalism, regarded as an antidote to bias, came to be looked upon as the most insidious bias of all. For 'objective' reporting reproduced a vision of social reality which refused to examine the basic structures of power and privilege."[61] From the shifting commonsense perspective of some critics, then, both expertise and professionalism across a variety of fields became suspect.

A number of reporters responded to journalism's inadequacies by stretching the framework of conventional journalism and adapting practices from a variety of alternative models in order to strengthen the conventional model. So, for example, in the "advocacy journalism" of the late 1960s, some reporters privileged their own values and viewpoints in their writing, claiming that mere routine recording of institutional sources would fail to confront larger moral contexts.[62] On the other hand, another model, "precision journalism," attempted to push journalism in the direction of social science by contracting the objective framework rather than expanding it. Precision journalists argued that only by applying rigorous methods using surveys, sampling, and questionnaires could a reliable and valid portrait of social change be reported.[63]

While some reporters led reporting toward science, however, others pushed journalism toward art. The literary model of the 1960s adapted presumably fictional storytelling techniques to nonfictional material. A leading proponent and practitioner of literary journalism, Tom Wolfe, saw the "new form" as merging the *content* of the journalist with the *form* of the novelist in order "to create in one form both the kind of objective reality of journalism" and "the subjective reality" of the novel.[64] Wolfe also argued that the literary model offered what the dominant model did not: "It was more intense, more detailed, and certainly more time-consuming than anything that newspapers or magazine reporters . . . were accustomed to. . . . [We] had to gather all the material the conventional journalist was after—and then keep going. It seemed all-important to *be there* when dramatic scenes took place, to get the dialogue, the gestures, the facial expressions, the details of the environment. The idea was to give the full objective description, plus something that readers had always gone to novels and short stories for: namely, the subjective or emotional life of the characters."[65]

Although Wolfe recalls a print mode here, his description could apply as well to *60 Minutes*. Writers such as Wolfe, Joan Didion, Norman Mailer, Hunter Thompson, Gay Talese, and Truman Capote—like Don Hewitt, at times contemptuous of conventional print journalism—turned to this literary model in the 1960s in an attempt to fill in gaps they perceived in the routine reporting of history.[66] Their often self-reflexive and iconoclastic treatment of social problems infused their writing with a perspective that allowed them to confront—both personally and professionally—assumptions about social realities which institutional journalism either took for granted or was incapable of probing.[67]

So the new journalists often moved from newspapers to such magazines as *Mother Jones, New West, Esquire, Rolling Stone,* even *The New York Times Book Review,* and finally to full-length books. Literary journalism reached beyond a factual report of Ken Kesey's drug experiments to probe the nuances of the 1960s' drug and hippie culture (Wolfe's *The Electric Kool-Aid Acid Test*); beyond a thousand-word story of the 1967 March on the Pentagon to an intense 320-page "history as novel—novel as history" document of that event's location in the social atmosphere of the 1960s (Mailer's *The Armies of the Night*). And on *60 Minutes*, beyond the conventional two-minute network news package to the dramatic fourteen-minute television magazine-style report.

Hewitt, indeed, values his program as "personal journalism" that attempts to present "reality" in narrative form.[68] A part of that personalization involves rethinking the metaphors for reporters; instead of neutral conduits or mirrors, Hewitt would endow his news narratives with dramatic characters. He refers to *60 Minutes'* reporters as "a repertoire company of reporters . . . and what they do mostly is take you along on the story with them."[69]

Another literary journalist, Mark Kramer, again like Hewitt, partially defines personal journalism by distinguishing between the corporate or "institutional voice" of most conventional reporting and

21

"a reliable voice on the scene" found in literary journalism.[70] The former is represented in print by the detached third-person point of view and in broadcast by disembodied voice-over narration; the latter is represented in print through first-person accounts that admit the self of the reporter and in broadcasting through the dominating screen presence of the *60 Minutes* reporter.

One early convention of television news—borrowed from print journalism to further the appearance of neutrality—edited reporters and their questions from the final report, leaving only the "testimony" of the interview subjects described in voice-overs by off-screen reporters.[71] Even today the conventional two-to-three-minute television package, the centerpiece of the network evening news, may often feature reporters only in voice-over narration. In contrast, *60 Minutes*'s reporters, like Mailer in *Armies of the Night,* transcend convention and become central characters. In *60 Minutes,* for example, the reporter may appear in as many as forty or fifty shots in a 120-shot, fourteen-minute segment.

With unconventional journalism providing new metaphors—character, story, drama—for the ways in which we speak about journalism, critics and scholars began to distinguish among different kinds of literary journalism. For example, David Eason divides it into two camps: "ethnographic realism" and "cultural phenomenology."[72] He differentiates the approaches by the way reporter-writers respond to contradictions between image and reality, between observing and living, and between stories and experience. Those writers practicing "ethnographic realism" (Wolfe, Talese, Capote, and Gail Sheehy, among others) confronted "cultural fragmentation" and the disintegration of common ground "by giving accounts of 'what it is that's going on here' that suggest 'This is reality.' The realism of the text constitutes the subculture [hippies, Hell's Angels, prostitutes, for example] as an object of display, and the reporter and reader, whose values are assumed and not explored, are cojoined in the act of observing."[73] These writers believed that although it was difficult task, complexity and ambiguity could be sorted out and that a moral order underpinning reality could be reclaimed. These reporters exchanged one commonsense journalistic metaphor moored in neutrality for another anchored in storytelling.

In contrast, literary journalists of "cultural phenomenology" (Didion, Mailer, Thompson, Michael Herr, and John Gregory Dunne, among others) critiqued common sense. They described, as Eason contends, "what it feels like to live in a world in which there is no consensus about a frame of reference to explain 'what it all means.' " Instead of claiming that their work represented "reality," these writers and journalists focused rather "on the experiential contradictions that call consensual versions of reality into question."[74]

On one hand, "ethnographers," or realists, tried to expand and ultimately repair the dominant, institutional model which held that social reality could be described by reporters who in the 1960s merely had to work harder at observing and unraveling the tangle of facts and experiences available to them. The "phenomenologists," or modernists, on the other hand, sought to demystify the conventional model, expose the weaknesses in the symbolic border between objectivity and subjectivity, and describe a world in which the referent and the experience are bound together in complex ways. This latter group of reporters challenged conventional wisdom and implied that meaning "is not something that exists out there independent of human consciousness, but something that is created and recreated in acts of interpretation and expression."[75]

For these reporters, the world was not logical or commonsensical. At times they doubted the ability of their own narratives to make sense of things. Joan Didion, for example, offered this comment on a 1960s' set of experiences as diverse as Robert Kennedy's funeral, the Mai Lai massacre, and a woman "who put her five-year old daughter out to die on the center divider" of a California freeway: "Certain of these images did not fit into any narrative I knew."[76]

Some critics contend that the enigmas of the decade demanded a new journalistic form that could deal better with social contradiction. Although both forms grappled with the lack of consensus in society, ethnographic realism—far more than the phenomenological model—assumed that it was still possible not only to narrate social reality but also to organize and order, explain and contain it through commonsense storytelling. However, after the tide of Vietnam, Watergate, and intense social upheaval ebbed, the wave of more iconoclastic inquiry and personal reporting that characterized both kinds of literary journalism also subsided.

A form of the "new" journalism, a television brand of "ethnographic realism," spilled over from the 1960s in the practices and stories of *60 Minutes,* however. This program in its twenty-plus-year history has evolved dramatically from its iconoclastic position at the margins of news in the late 1960s and early 1970s. Ironically, over time *60 Minutes* has managed to *institutionalize* its own story model as a viable and prosperous challenger to the enduring—and still dominant—pseudo-science news model. The feisty iconoclasts have become popular icons.

The narrative formulas employed by this profitable and popular news enterprise carry forward a commitment to making sense of the world. The stories of *60 Minutes* share with us a public vision of common sense—"our storehouse of narrative structures."[77] In cataloguing the inventory of features that conventional wisdom and news reports have in common, Glasser and Ettema conclude, "For the journalist . . . not the least part of common sense is the wise choice of a narrative form—'the story.' "[78] And despite reporters who would and must cling to fact and information metaphors as foundations for commonsense news, all reporters in the end are essentially storytellers who offer—not precise transparencies—but narrative interpretations of experience.

News as Narrative, Reporter as Character

> We live entirely, especially if we are writers, by the imposition of a narrative line upon disparate images. . . .
>
> —Joan Didion

> There's a very simple formula if you're in Hollywood, opera, publishing, broadcasting, newspapering. It's four very simple words: tell me a story. . . . A good broadcaster commands attention when he says, "Come here, I want to tell you something. . . . I want to tell you a story."
>
> —Don Hewitt

For a long time now, critics have tried to account for the allure of *60 Minutes* and for the meaning of a "popular" news program. Was it the CBS decision in 1975 to use *60 Minutes* to counter Sunday evening children's programming on other networks? Was it the arrival in 1975 of Dan Rather, fresh from the White House beat and the press's symbolic triumphs during Watergate? Was it because, as Mike Wallace argues in his book *Close Encounters,* we discovered the program on Sundays "instead of visiting relatives or going for a late afternoon drive" during the Arab oil embargo.[1] Or is it the program's sense of drama?

Most critics, journalists, readers, and viewers—operating from a commonsense premise—separate news and entertainment, document and drama, science and art—distinctions that sometimes become so rigid that they fail to illuminate shared ground. As Walker Percy has reminded us: "Although science and art are generally taken to be not merely different but even polar opposites—the one logical, left-brained, unemotional, Apollonian, analytical, discursive, abstract; the other intuitive, playful, concrete, Dionysian, emotional—the fact is that both are practiced at a level of abstraction, both entail transactions with symbols and statements about the world, both are subject to confirmation or disconfirmation."[2] In fact, on that very first program in 1968, Harry Reasoner in his closing comments intriguingly aligned *60 Minutes* not with the science traditions of journalism but with impulses in art. "All art is the rearrangement of previous perceptions," Reasoner offered, "and we don't claim this [the first *60 Minutes* broadcast] is anything more than that, or even that journalism is an art, for that matter. But we do think this is sort of a new approach."[3] In 1968, *60 Minutes*, however, did not spring full-blown from a dry bed as a "new approach." Rather, it developed from the informational and narrative wellsprings of earlier CBS television documentary work, particularly *See It Now* and *CBS Reports*. Both *See It Now* and *CBS Reports* practiced a kind of television journalism lodged somewhere between neutral and narrative traditions. Both programs also provided the direct training ground for many *60 Minutes* producers.[4] *See It Now* in particular introduced the investigative model of journalistic practice to television news.[5]

Co-produced by Fred Friendly and Edward R. Murrow, *See It Now* ran on CBS from 1951-58.[6] Don Hewitt directed the premiere episode on November 18, 1951, which marked the first time live shots from both the East and West coasts aired simultaneously. Hewitt continued to serve as director through the tenure of the show. Palmer Williams, for many years managing editor and second in command on *60 Minutes*, also worked as an associate producer on *See It Now*.[7] Beginning as a weekly half-hour program, *See It Now* by its fifth year had expanded to one or one-and-one-half hours. Generally regarded as "the first and definitive" news documentary on American television, *See It Now* sought "to report in depth — to tell and show the American audience what was happening in the world using film as a narrative tool."[8]

CBS Reports was produced in the beginning by Friendly and featured Murrow as its chief reporter; it filled a gap between *See It Now* and *60 Minutes*.[9] Premiering in October 1959, fifteen months after *See It Now* was canceled, *CBS Reports* initially ran twelve times a year, then went to a biweekly format in 1960-61 and became a weekly series during the 1961-62 television season. Between 1962 and 1965, it aired on a less regular basis (ten to twelve times per year). Both Hewitt and Williams served at different times as executive producers. When *60 Minutes* came along in 1968, the two programs briefly alternated in a Tuesday evening time slot. Since the late 1960s, while *60 Minutes* more fully developed the narrative tradition in television journalism, *CBS Reports* stuck closer to conventional practices and was produced sporadically through the 1980s before it was finally scrapped.[10]

Although *CBS Reports* in general carried on the traditions of *See It Now,* as the 1960s wore on the literary model of reporting was playing a more significant role in the program. When it began, Friendly hinted at the importance of narrative tradition to *CBS Reports:* "Though based on truth, the programs still have to have stories of their own, with the basic outline of beginning, middle and end."[11] Friendly did not like the label of "documentary" for the program and described the early shows as "stories" which called for strong plot lines. Both *See It Now* and *CBS Reports* developed narrative techniques that *60 Minutes* would later exploit as it pushed the television news documentary more in the direction of news drama.[12]

Narrative News Conventions

To account for television's early exploration of conventions and inventions that challenged traditional "objective" journalism, Thomas Kuhn's arguments offer insight on how alternative professional practices take hold. Kuhn suggests that certain scientific models gain their status because "they are more successful" than others in solving problems practitioners regard as central to their profession.[13] The dominant, "objective," commonsense model of journalism, when not confronted by the turbulent social change that characterized the 1960s (when literary journalism confronted objectivity), had been able to handle the "few problems" that "reality" might impose upon journalism. Maintenance of the neutral model required practitioners to believe that the images created in news stories faithfully presented "the reality" the story sought to represent. Maintenance also required practitioners to believe that they could detach themselves from the experiences they covered. They finally believed that differences between the story and the experience were essentially seamless; they believed that they had not altered the reality that had been transformed into reports.

In his analysis of television news, Stuart Hall focuses on the taken-for-granted "language" of television and on the complex yet transparent relationship between experience and narrative structure: "The raw historical event cannot, *in that form,* be transmitted by . . . a television newscast. . . . To put it paradoxically, the event must become a 'story' before it can become a *communicative event.*"[14] In other words, *60 Minutes* and news must make sense of personal and social phenomena by telling stories. The narrative process provides the program with a common ground for understanding ourselves and multiple realities.

Daily local and network news programs represent this conventional middle ground in television journalism. These programs may appear to audiences as factual, neutral, and transparent documents which merely mirror reality; however, a tightly ritualized process underpins this apparent transparency. As John Fiske notes, "news is as conventional as any form of television; its conventions are so powerful and so uninspected because the tyranny of the deadline requires the speed and efficiency that only conventions make possible. The types of stories, the forms that they will take, and the program structure into which they will be inserted are all determined long before any of the events of the day occur."[15]

The conventional strategies embedded in the television news process include presenting experience in terms of two conflicting points of view (i.e., "telling both sides of a story"), eliminating overt value judgments, citing expert testimony through sound bites, and reporting the news through detached, invisible voice-over narration. Through such practical conventions journalists—mediators between the referent and the experience—lay claim to professional virtues such as credibility, fairness, and neutrality.

In addition, another source of reportorial power emanates from audiences who "pretend that the reporter is not present in the story." Mary Mander argues that "This invisibility of the professional, while required by the conditions of his practice, is created or called forth by the public. It is the public, moreover, which creates the power wielded by the reporter. In this respect, the modern journalist resembles the shaman who pretends his acts are magical because pretense is demanded of him by the society in which he lives. Like the shaman, the reporter is a kind of official who is vested with authority by the public, and it is incumbent upon society to believe in him."[16]

This belief is predicated on our desire to make common sense of reality and our faith in reporters to help us with that task. Mander further suggests that the reporter and audience share a "tacit contract" which "grants the reporter the right to know what he is talking about"; that is, because the reporter narrates stories by "tacit convention," virtually "no attention is paid to his human limitations."[17] Therefore, the public endows the reporter with a kind of "all-knowing perspective"—the perspective of the well informed.

Obscured in the process and pretext of this tacit "canon of objectivity" are the narrative structures inherent in news which feature a beginning, pose a set of conflicts, and provide resolution or closure. As an often-quoted 1963 staff memo from former NBC news president Reuven Frank outlined, these narrative strategies are an integral aspect of television reports: "Every news story should, without sacrifice of probity or responsibility, display the attributes of fiction, of drama. It should have structure and conflict, problem and denouement, rising and falling action, a beginning, a middle, and an end. These are not only the essentials of drama; they are the essentials of narrative."[18]

What makes Frank's memo unusual, of course, is that narrative style is generally viewed as antithetical to the process of making neutral reports. A "news story" appears to represent a value-free vision of the world while at the same time it constructs that vision through a narrative process, generally regarded as an imaginative, personal mode for organizing experience. While we often speak of the informational aspect of the news, the *story* of news is usually exnominated, concealed by commonsense conventions established by journalists over time.

News Conventions of *60 Minutes*

Part of the particular style of *60 Minutes* foregrounds narrative structure over more traditional journalistic tendencies.[19] *60 Minutes* has redirected the structure of television news programs away from the appearance of facticity—describing and listing information in neutral reports—and toward the narrative intrigues of character, setting, plot, and conflict. The program's style of "personal" reporting or literary journalism did indeed apply the narrative techniques of realistic fiction to journalism. The power and popularity of *60 Minutes* reside in the emotion and drama of the program—and in the performances and adventures of reporter-characters—

rather than in adherence to the older print standards and science metaphors.

Although *60 Minutes* may break from certain traditional journalistic conventions, it relies heavily on its own set of conventions, as does all news facing time and space constraints. From week to week, viewers know these reporters through the roles they play as characters and through five conventions or maps which shape the narrative terrain of the program: (1) representation of reporters as characters; (2) construction of multiple stories; (3) mediation of dramatic tension; (4) control over the frame; and (5) direction of the discourse. With the aid of these cues, the *60 Minutes* narratives try to position audience members in a sociocultural common ground from which they are invited to share the reporter's stance.

Representation of Reporter-Characters.

Mainstream journalism minimizes the role of reporters and their relationships to news reports. In print, we often know a reporter only by byline; in daily broadcast news, a reporter typically appears in only one or two shots in any given network package. In *60 Minutes*, however, the reporter may be represented in as many as sixty shots in a 120-shot segment.[20] Take, for example, "Brown vs. Koch" (1/24/88), a personal drama that features the story of an allegedly mentally ill, homeless woman, Joyce Brown, and her legal battle with Mayor Ed Koch and the city of New York. While these title characters appear in approximately thirty shots in this 121-shot segment, reporter Morley Safer appears in thirty-six shots.[21]

In *60 Minutes* reporters emerge not merely as recorders of information but as participant-performers who are intimately involved with their subjects. Through such presentations—reporters performing as detectives, referees, therapists, and tourists—the program offers role models on how to attend to the world. In combination with their powerful dual role as narrators, the reporters are the only characters on *60 Minutes* permitted to address viewers directly. (This privileged reporter shot is customary of most television news; in fact, when an interview subject gazes at the camera for too long, convention is violated and the shot is usually considered ruined.) Given such dominant narrative standing, *60 Minutes* reporters outline what questions to ask, how to distinguish good from evil, how to interpret and resolve contradiction, and how to make common sense of experience.

Reporters then in *60 Minutes* often take on heroic dimensions. Morley Safer, for example, is searched by British guards before driving his car into the streets of Belfast as part of a story on war-torn Northern Ireland ("Life and Death in an Irish Town," 5/17/81). Ed Bradley strolls hand in hand across a New York street with Lena Horne as part of a story in which both appear as heroic models of African-Americans who have overcome a white-dominated world ("Lena Horne," 12/27/81). Before moving to the *CBS Evening News* anchor job in 1981, Dan Rather, dressed in native costume, trudges through the hills of Afghanistan with anti-Soviet guerillas ("Inside Afghanistan," 4/6/80). Harry Reasoner plays cards and challenges the Las Vegas gambling industry ("Black Jack," 5/17/81). Wallace accompanies investigators on a raid of a counterfeit jeans operation in Hong Kong ("Fake," 12/27/81) and parleys face-to-face with the Ayatollah Khomeini in Iran early in the hostage crisis ("The Ayatollah," 11/18/79). Diane Sawyer during her tenure on the show walks the halls of 10 Downing Street with the prime minister of Great Britain ("Mrs. Thatcher," 2/17/85).

In fact, when Sawyer joined the program in 1984, Hewitt, in order to toughen her on-screen persona, assigned her to "some dirty face stories" to places such as Iran where she appeared "in no makeup and wearing a babushka."[22] Burton Benjamin, former executive producer of the *CBS Evening News,* has argued that part of the reason for the program's success derives from the reporters, who unlike reporters on regular evening newscasts, become "participants in their stories, . . . players in the drama."[23]

Construction of Multiple Stories

60 Minutes also differs from traditional television newscasts and documentaries in its use of multiple story lines within a single narrative, a device more commonly associated with serial dramas such as day-time soaps or prime-time programs such as *Dallas* or *L.A. Law.*[24]

60 Minutes's multistory configuration is constituted, first, through the construction of smaller, single-story units suited to the personae of individual reporters. The title and the "byline" of the producer are set within a full-screen, glossy magazine frame complete with "page borders." Meanwhile, in the foreground, the reporter-narrator directly engages the viewer and verbally begins the dramatic prologue. Through these contemporary storytelling strategies, the opening narration supports the magazinelike frame and presents the report—often explicitly—as drama.

Mike Wallace, for example, begins "The Scarlet 'A' " (8/25/85), a story about child abuse, this way: "In Nathaniel Hawthorne's *The Scarlet Letter,* Hester Prynne is forced to display the big red 'A' for committing the sin of adultery. Today the Scarlet 'A' stands not for adultery but for abuser, child abuser. . . ." *60 Minutes* frames a Diane Sawyer interview with Gloria Vanderbilt as a fairy tale: " 'Once upon a Time . . .' is the opening line of fairy tales, and it's also the memoir of a woman who has lived a fairy-tale life, including the childhood terrors that go with fairy tales" ("Once upon a Time . . . ," 8/25/85). In a final example, Harry Reasoner begins "Tales of the Texas Rangers" (12/29/85), "In the American attitude, the Texas Rangers come pretty close to Mom and apple pie as being beyond criticism. After all, they are the stuff of legend." Mike Wallace suggests regarding the program's drama and appeal, "our pieces are constructed almost like morality plays."[25]

Within the three reports which comprise the bulk of the program, other plot lines unfold as *60 Minutes* reporters elicit tales from interview subjects. For example, in "Saddam's Body Guard" (1/20/91), Safer induces a former Iraqi soldier to tell stories of beheadings, acid baths, and assassination plots within Saddam Hussein's military hierarchy. Reasoner in "Wheeler Dealer" (10/27/85) gets a "confessed swindler" and former New York City lawyer to tell this story about coaching witnesses in malpractice suits to fake injuries on the witness stand: "We would have canes in our office, wheelchairs. I mean, the stuff you see in— in the old movie *Fortune Cookie,* you know, the guy sitting with bandages and canes. We would set people up with walkers, and then they would come in for the jury appeal of that. It was done all the time." At this level, then, reporters present mini-stories within the larger narrative.

Asked in his pre-*60 Minutes* days if "there is a real dramatic structure in a good interview" with "a beginning, middle and end, and a point of climax," Wallace responded: "Absolutely. You can only hope that you'll have the wit, flair and ability to respond to the flow, in order to make the interview more and more interesting as it builds. . . . But there should definitely be a story 'line' in the interviewer's mind as the interview begins."[26]

"The Sting Man" (4/12/81) illustrates the technique. In an interview with Melvin Weinberg, a convicted swindler who helped the FBI set up congressmen in the ABSCAM scandal, Wallace asks his interview subject to tell stories about Weinberg's days as a con man. Weinberg provides a rousing tale about the time he was thrown out a window and conned by an Arizona Indian tribe. These stories add a rich dimension to the larger narrative conflict in which Wallace asks Weinberg to "characterize congressmen for us." In the interview, Weinberg conjures up characters, labels congressmen as "crooks" and "perverts," and establishes a class conflict between himself and the lawmakers.

Finally, other forces situate *60 Minutes* within the broader narrative spectrum of television. Significantly, the program finds a middle ground between the live dramatic ritual narratives of fall football and the detective fiction of *Murder, She Wrote.* In her analysis of television and narrative, Sarah Ruth Kozloff offers a third element to the definition of television narrative beyond story—"what happens to whom"— and discourse—"how the story is told." She adds the concept of schedule—"how are the story and discourse affected by the narrative's placement within the larger discourse of the station's schedule."[27] *60 Minutes* does not reside arbitrarily between sports and detective tales; rather, the centering of the program here constructs a world in which television news participates in the narrative flow that bridges sports mythologies and crime fiction.

In accounting for the program's sustained large viewership, Mike Wallace argues that "there's a sense of renewal each year, and we inherit that sense of renewal on Sunday afternoons. . . . We've turned a fresh page. It's a new season of NFL [National Football League], and it's a new season of *60 Minutes*."[28] It makes sense, then, to read *60 Minutes* as part of the narrative rhythm of television rather than merely as an anomaly, a news document somehow oddly misplaced between sports and mystery. Given that the detective formula is the dominant story form in *60 Minutes* segments (chapter 3), the program appropriately serves as a bridge to *Murder, She Wrote,* which *60 Minutes* promoted for many years in anonymous voice-over narration during closing credits. *60 Minutes* continues rather than disrupts the narrative continuity—the familiar confines of setting, problem, plot, character, drama, and resolution vital to the texture of American television.

Of course, a final and vital part of television's narrative rhythm features the commercials that cement the programs together. While CBS promotions within *60 Minutes* provide plot summaries for *Murder, She Wrote,* commercials embedded between segments tell their own stories that often affirm the common sense of heartland virtues—individualism, freedom, populism, tradition, nationalism, and unspoiled nature—promoted in many of the *60 Minutes* segments. Whereas advertisements are criticized for disrupting the continuity of a particular program, just as often those commercials may promote a continuous narrative flow. For example, General Motors may sell us the "heartbeat of America" or tell us that "the great American road belongs to Buick" between segments, and a *60 Minutes* story may travel that heartland road to champion an embattled Iowa farmer fighting insensitive bureaucracies. Again, American Airlines may promise "blue skies, white sand, no troubles, life is grand" in its travel packages, and a *60 Minutes* adventure story may follow to whisk us away as we accompany reporters to exotic lands (chapter 5).

Mediation of Dramatic Tension

In *60 Minutes*, confrontations generally pit individual against institution, nature against culture, tradition against change, honesty against deception, humanity against technology, in order to build dramatic conflict. Generally, however, the reporter-narrator mediates the conflict by (1) siding with one of the oppositional pairs (e.g., supporting the individual in battle against menacing bureaucracies) and/or (2) by interposing a "third term" (such as *community* or *family*) in the narrative that locates viewers *between* an individual victim and a villainous institution.[29] This new term or concept resolves the narrative problem by empowering the individuals pitted against institutions, by shifting focus from the central conflict, or by offering synthesis.

In their study of myth at work in the news reports of the British recapturing the Iranian embassy in London in 1980, Graham Knight and Tony Dean illustrate how third-term mediation works to resolve tensions between narrative oppositions constructed in British news stories.[30] The British Special Air Service Regiment (S.A.S.) that car-

34

ried out the assault was described by the print media as calm, patient, and humorous at the same time it was described as ruthless, swift, and deadly. News accounts 'resolved' these conceptual tensions by introducing the term *discipline* as mediator.[31] This term resolves the contradiction of a social force that appears to be both law-abiding and lawless.

The same study illustrates the use of the concept *efficiency* to provide a mediating function between violence and heroism: "No matter how ruthless, chilling, murderous, deadly, or unsavory the actions of the S.A.S., they are ultimately efficient. . . . So long as their heroic quality is also established in other ways, and so long as force is used with economy and efficiency, their mythical goodness remains intact, indeed is strengthened."[32] Knight and Dean argue that the news accounts foregrounding mediating third terms—*discipline* and *efficiency*—resolved tensions between "excitement and order," war and peace, life and death, which were established as fundamental conflicts in the process of transforming this particular experience into a news narrative.

In *60 Minutes*, a number of celebrity interview segments illustrate the point. Generally, these interview subjects are introduced as famous, wealthy, or successful (or any combination), but they are evaluated partially in terms of how many Middle-American virtues they demonstrate or affirm in spite of their fame, wealth, or success. For example, in "Shirley" (4/8/84) Mike Wallace approves and thereby locates Shirley MacLaine within the space of centrist virtues when he tells us: "She has none of the usual trappings of a movie star, no entourage. . . . In fact, she lives downright modestly for someone who commands huge salaries." *Modesty* then becomes a third term that resolves tension between rich and poor, success and failure. In "More Than a Touch of Class" (4/7/74), Wallace interviews Glenda Jackson, also identified as successful and famous, who tells Wallace that she does not "believe in privilege of any kind." In his narration, Wallace draws attention to her "growing up as a shop girl" in a modest section of London and her refusal to move to a "glamorous," elite Hollywood setting. As narrator, Wallace arbitrates abstract conflicts between the acclaimed and the commonplace by describing Jackson as ordinary and intelligent—in other words, full of common sense—in spite of privilege. Here implicitly, *common sense* is the third term positioned between contrary cultural tensions.

Controling the Frame

60 Minutes lays out its images, centers, and contains those experiences the program chooses to transform into narratives. What is included in the frame directs our attention, suggests what is important, and inscribes a particular reading based on narrative formulas and conventions. Two narrative strategies give substantial control to the program's reporters.

First, *60 Minutes* employs the reverse-question technique that is a staple of all television news—and fictional filmmaking. Often limited to a one-camera situation during field interviews, reporters have to edit in their questions and reaction shots later because the camera focuses on only one subject during the actual interview. As Peter Funt describes the technique: "With the camera aimed at him, the reporter re-records all of his questions so that they may be spliced together with the answers. Although the networks insist that reverse questions match the original questions as closely as possible, there is no denying that the reporter is allowed to polish his performance, while the interview subject's answers must stand as first delivered."[33]

Barbara Walters, reporter and interviewer for ABC News, also suggests how such a technique favors the reporter: "If you do a recorded interview, one of the advantages for the reporter is that he always comes out on top; he's always right. You've never seen a *60 Minutes* interview, or any taped interview, in which the reporter gets the worst of it."[34] Coupled with this privilege, of course, is the ability of *60 Minutes* and any news organization to edit together the sound bites (or quotes) and reporter reaction in any manner that supports a particular narrative point of view.[35]

Second, in reinforcing the narrative structure, *60 Minutes* consistently offers its reporters more visual or frame space than its subjects. Over the more than twenty-year history of the program, reporters are almost always shot at a greater distance than the characters they interview. Frequently, in the reaction or question shots, interview subjects appear in extreme close-ups—usually with the top of the head cut from the frame. These shots contrast with the medium shots of the reporter, normally shown from mid-waist with space revealed overhead. This greater space granted to the reporters may be read on one level as the print counterpart to detachment and neutrality.

Mike Wallace says, however, that in his case at least, the greater distance the camera allowed him was, in part, because his ruddier, pock-marked complexion created problems with lighting.[36] Burton Benjamin, who regarded the close-up as a "privileged" shot for interview subjects, has said CBS News had a policy not to shoot reporters tighter than interview subjects: "If we did that [frame reporters in close-ups], the reporters would be shown as equal to the figures they're interviewing."[37]

But Don Hewitt says he never heard of this rule. Although Hewitt does agree that reporter and interviewee should not be depicted visually in a similar way, he contends that this has more to do with variety in shot selection. Like varying sentence length in print, camera-to-subject distances should also provide visual variety. When juxtaposed shots of a *60 Minutes* reporter and an interview subject suggest roughly equal camera distance (as in Ed Bradley's January 1988 interview with Lee Hart), Hewitt contends that this is "a mistake."[38] This still does not account, however, for why the interview subject, and not the reporter, is the one most consistently shot in the tighter close-ups.

At another level of meaning, the greater distance afforded a *60 Minutes* reporter can also be read as support for the function of reporters as arbiters of narrative tension. The reporters are endowed with the appearance of more room in the narrative. They have more space within which to operate. They appear in greater control. Victims and villains are shot in tighter close-ups; they are in less control and often cut off from the place around them. The preferred shot for the reporters on *60 Minutes*, however, is the middle or medium shot which symbolically centers the reporters in a common ground region between close-ups and long shots where they mediate narrative tension.

Direction of the Discourse

In addition to the powerful on-screen presence of *60 Minutes*'s reporters as dramatic characters, they function also in dual roles as narrators. Frequently they step out of their character roles in the story to address the viewer directly in both on-screen and voice-over narration. The technique is like that used in fiction when a character steps out of the plot to direct the discourse — the telling of the story. The narrators of Thorton Wilder's *Our Town* or F. Scott Fitzgerald's *The Great Gatsby* perform such dual functions as character-narra-

Two shots from a 1975 story, "What Became of Eldridge Cleaver?" demonstrate the visual space usually granted to the reporter in comparison with the tight close-up framing of many *60 Minutes* interview subjects. (© MCMLXXV–CBS Inc. All rights reserved.)

tors. Nor is this style unlike character-narrators in literary journalism. Norman Mailer, for example, in *Armies of the Night,* switches back and forth between character in the drama and commentator on the drama of the 1967 March on the Pentagon.

In *60 Minutes* as in most television news narratives, the voice of the reporter dominates. As Todd Gitlin observes, "The images depend on the narration, not the other way around."[39] Don Hewitt agrees: "It is your ear more than your eye that keeps you tuned to television. . . . I've always used a sort of analogy: if you were watching the [presidential] inauguration which is essentially the same pictures on all three networks, and you like Peter Jennings but ABC loses its picture, you stay with them and listen to Jennings until the picture comes back. But if you lose the audio, you go somewhere else. You're there because somebody's telling you a story."[40]

In fact, when the written transcripts of *60 Minutes* are read without visual counterparts, they still make sense as narratives; however, the visuals without the narration do not cohere as news reports. Long stretches of each *60 Minutes* narrative feature voice-overs situated on top of the visuals in the post-production process. This gives the reporter a great deal of control over the sense and rhythm of the program.

For example, in "Why Me?" (5/18/75), a segment about seniority rights and affirmative action, Morley Safer performs metaphorically as a referee in the central scenes, placing himself between four white and four black security guards. However, his appearance as a neutral referee is deceptive given how much control he exercises over the narration. In this segment there are 126 discrete shots, and Safer's is the only voice heard until shot forty-seven. While on one hand, the story seems to present a detached reporter-referee who presents the issues, Safer's control of the narration endows him with an authoritative voice, in control of the facts. Viewers are invited, encouraged, through the dominance of Safer's voice and image, to identify with him — the character-narrator at the center of the drama.

Through narration the reporter may also control the construction of particular characters. In "Liberté, Egalité, Fraternité" (4/26/81), Dan Rather on location in Paris narrates a story about French anti-Semitism. A number of French Jews are interviewed, but throughout the story the "other side" remains faceless, nameless, and allusive. In devising the villain for this narrative, Rather conjures up a foreboding image of a neo-Nazi movement solely through narration. He indicts the anonymous villain for claims of genetic superiority. The reporter, however, does not tell us why neo-Nazi or other anti-Semitic groups remain unrepresented in the story. *60 Minutes* transforms their absence into a narrative asset by constructing a mysterious and terrifying force that haunts the story. Rather emerges heroically for naming the menace and stalking it through the streets of Paris.

Through narration and voice-overs, *60 Minutes* attempts to locate a common ground through first-person point of view. These masterful reporter-narrators often include viewers as colleagues; we share in their authority as well-informed citizens. The "we" point of view personalizes reporters and creates a sense of intimacy absent in the detached third-person point of view of most corporate print journalism. The "we" point of view creates one side of a conversation which implicitly includes "us"—the implied viewers—as the other side.

In "Momma" (10/14/84), for example, Morley Safer compares Mary Eugenia Charles, prime minister of the Caribbean island of Dominica, to "certain school teachers we've all had at some times in our lives." And in "Mister Right" (12/14/75), an interview with then presidential candidate Ronald Reagan, Mike Wallace speaks for "all of us," commenting that Americans are "disillusioned over politics" and "dishonesty" in government. He tells Reagan on our behalf: "We're always in trouble . . . no matter who we elect." Here the reporter serves as moral arbiter, naming certain virtues that we Americans demand of our political candidates.

These first-person accounts ultimately mediate the distance between viewer and reporter and include us as characters in the adventure. The audience, then, is constructed as part of the story. Robert C. Allen notes, "Television frequently provides us with on-screen characterized viewers—textual surrogates who 'do' what real viewers cannot: interact with other characters and respond in an ideal fashion to the appeals, demands, and urgings of the addresser."[41] Both power and danger reside in "the regime of the 'fictive We' " which, as Robert Stam notes, "claims to speak for us, and often does, but just as often it deprives us of the right to speak by deluding us into thinking that its discourse is our own."[42]

Thus, the narratives of *60 Minutes*, while following in the traditions of *See It Now* and *CBS Reports,* have over time adopted a particular set of conventions now shared by a wide range of television news programs from ABC's *20/20* to the new wave of tabloid news programs heavily criticized in the conventional press for their provocative, dramatic portrayals and reenactments of news. In addition to the commodity legacy of *60 Minutes*, the program has opened up the definition of news to mean explicitly drama and story.

Yet the program still must endure scrutiny under commonsense definitions of news stories as mere neutral documents. Hewitt says he gets tired of defending the conventions of his program: "I went up to speak to this group and the first question was, 'You guys are really "show biz," aren't you?' And I spent an hour defending myself, getting nowhere. Went off to speak at Yale . . . and the first question was, 'You guys are really "show biz," aren't you?' And I said, 'You bet your ass we are. Next question.' I wasn't going to spend the hour talking about that. What is *Newsweek* when its got the Cabbage Patch Doll on the cover?"[43]

Ironically, a 1989 issue of *Newsweek,* in previewing new network news programs planning to include dramatic reenactments of events, asks, "When reality is rebuilt, is it still reality?"[44] In scrutinizing the conventions of the visual image and the right of broadcasters to produce news, the magazine story, of course, takes the arbitrariness and reconstruction of its own printed words and world for granted. This print critique of television is a commonsense critique which, in assuming its own transparency, fails to account for the contrivances of *Newsweek*'s own symbolic terrain. It presumes that it represents "the real" while television news drama and reenactments border on fiction. We could, of course, ask the reality question of the *Newsweek* article, a conventional front-page news story, or this book. When words are selected to make sentences to form paragraphs, how has some original, pure, unrepresented experience been revealed? The point is that "reality"—as if there were a single, genuine reality—is always rebuilt in the news, whether it is a reenactment of a presidential assassination or the routine coverage of yesterday's press conference. Symbolic convention and interpretation, whether in print or broadcasting, are the only ways we have to both transmit and make sense of experience. As James Carey reminds us, "We first produce the world by symbolic work and then take up residence in the world we leave produced. Alas, there is magic in our self-deceptions."[45]

In order to make symbolic sense, *60 Minutes* adapts familiar story forms long associated with American fiction genres such as the adventure melodrama or the detective mystery. Inside these formulas the reporters of *60 Minutes* act—not as detached, off-screen journalists—but as involved characters. Their avowed mission is to organize an often contradictory world. *60 Minutes* enjoys its wide popularity because it is arguably the most successful, and certainly the most popular, of all news forms and institutions—print and broadcast—in converting that world and slices of its experiences into commonsense stories.

The conventions of *60 Minutes* with its far-reaching impact on television journalism nevertheless derive from and combine a variety of techniques and formulas employed by the objective, interpretive, investigative, and literary traditions in print history. The following chapters describe and interpret four particular *60 Minutes* reporting formulas: news as mystery, news as therapy, news as adventure, and news as arbitration. All have features in common with the older print metaphors for news. However, the unifying attribute of all formulas used by *60 Minutes* is the symbolic reliance on dramatic models which foreground news as narrative and reporters as characters.

News and Mystery: Heartless Villains, Heartland Virtues

3

What is a reporter except a kind of house detective, scavenging through the bureau drawers of men's lives, searching for the minor vice, the half-forgotten lapse that is stored away like a dirty pair of drawers.

—John Gregory Dunne

60 Minutes developed its hallmark as . . . the broadcast that looked into the dark and grimy corners of American culture.

—Mike Wallace

It is this boring into the center of society to find it rotten that constitutes the fundamental drama of the American detective story. It is not a personal but a social mystery that the detective must unravel.

—*Habits of the Heart*

Located somewhere on a continuum between conventional and literary journalism resides the investigative tradition in reporting. *60 Minutes* owes a substantial debt to this muckraking spirit. At the turn of the century, like their counterparts in the 1960s, some reporters shared dissatisfaction with the conventions of journalism. In the middle of moving from production to consumption, from farms to factories, as hundreds of thousands of immigrants poured into American cities, the country that journalists of the early 1900s wrote about grew increasingly enigmatic.

Dissatisfied with conventional journalism, a handful of reporters turned from writing shorter newspaper accounts to magazine articles and books in order to deal with broader issues and trends. They wrote both factual and fictional accounts on topics ranging from big business and government corruption to urban problems faced by immigrants to labor and management conflicts and race relations to the unsavory practices of the meat industry. President Theodore Roosevelt in 1906 dubbed these reporters—who included Ida Tarbell, Lincoln Steffens, Ray Stannard Baker, and Upton Sinclair—"muckrakers."[1] It was a mantle Roosevelt meant as derision, but the reporters wore with pride.

Muckrakers, like *60 Minutes* reporters and most Americans, believed in common sense and the individual. They distrusted established institutions which sought to convolute sense through political corruption or indifferent bureaucracy. Muckrakers undertook to protect ordinary citizens from such corruption and bureaucracy.[2] In his study of this era, C. C. Regier defines muckraking "as the exposing of evils and corruption for the real or ostensible purpose of promoting righteousness and social justice."[3] Lincoln Steffens's *The Shame of the Cities,* Ida Tarbell's *The History of the Standard Oil Company,* and Upton Sinclair's *The Jungle* all promote and develop these themes. Steffens has said of his own journalistic investigations, "When I set out to describe the corrupt systems of certain typical cities, I meant to show simply how the people were deceived and betrayed."[4] The afterword to Sinclair's fictional account of the Chicago meat-packing industry identifies the book's major themes as the "capitalist as a heartless scoundrel and the workingman as an oppressed hero."[5]

In constructing stories which portrayed authority and bureaucracy as villainous and the middle and working classes as heroic, the muckrakers applied a literary, dramatic narrative structure to what they perceived as the realities of their times.[6] This journalistic model was a response to middle-class Americans who had grown "impatient with traditional wisdom" and corrupt leadership in business and government.[7] This investigative model—also a reaffirmation of common sense—provides the organization for a substantial number of *60 Minutes* narratives.

Although the muckrakers of the early 1900s drew upon narrative devices to structure their reports, their chief influence was still the rational model of science; facts still reigned supreme.[8] These reporters continued to use many of the conventions of neutral reporting, yet a number of features separate this mode from the neutral model. Quoting Michael Schudson, "The investigative tradition distinguishes its aggressiveness from objective reporting's passivity."[9] The investigative report also requires more time and space. A typical assignment for a reporter at a daily newspaper might include two or three different stories in a single day; an investigative assignment, however, might require that one or more reporters cover a single topic or issue for an extended time. Such, for example, was the case with Carl Bernstein and Bob Woodward's coverage of Watergate in the 1970s.

The two modes as well are occasionally distinguished from each other by their handling of sources. Whereas conventional reporting generally relies on official government or status-quo spokespersons as prime sources, investigative reporting may be regarded as "the development of sources within the counter-elite or other dissidents of government."[10] This difference, according to some journalism critics, explains in part why the official White House press corps "missed" the significance of the initial events of Watergate, because these reporters, committed to the conventional model, relied too heavily on official announcements.[11] It was two relatively obscure Washington *Post* reporters from outside that corps, using techniques associated with the investigative mode (including interviews with nonofficial sources), who began to penetrate the official government facade.

Along with *60 Minutes*, the major investigative model for contemporary journalism is Woodward and Bernstein's *All the President's Men,* their 1974 account of how they covered Watergate for the *Post.* What is most significant about the book, for this study, is the explicit use of the detective metaphor as a model for reporting — a journalistic model closely shared by broadcasting counterparts at *60 Minutes. All the President's Men* blurred distinctions between journalism as neutral information and journalism as dramatic story. Indeed, the promoters of one paperback edition claimed it as "the most devastating detective story of our time"; they filled the cover material with newspaper testimonials: " 'One of the greatest detective stories ever told' — *Denver Post;* 'A devastating political detective story' — *San Francisco Chronicle;* 'Reads like first class whodunit' — *Cleveland Press.*"[12] The writer-reporters became media stars themselves — characters in the larger American drama. A movie chronicled their exploits. And although Don Hewitt's television brand of detective stories predated *All the President's Men* by six years, he uses that Watergate story as a touchstone for his own program: "*60 Minutes* is the adventures of five reporters, more fascinating to the

American public being themselves than Robert Redford and Dustin Hoffman were playing Woodward and Bernstein."[13]

This use of the detective metaphor is especially interesting because *All the President's Men* has become a major symbol for tough, factual, investigative journalism *and* reads like a fictional mystery story.[14] There is irony in the premise that the reporting profession, which zealously defends itself as a fact-gathering institution, organizes experience on the model of the detective story, largely regarded as a creation of the imagination.

More explicit references to the detective metaphor can be found in textbooks from the Watergate era which showed aspiring reporters how-to-do journalism. For instance, according to one journalism text, "Sherlock Holmes would have made an 'ace' reporter. Relying on no one method, he gathered information by whatever approach was appropriate to the task at hand, and confirmed what he learned by a second method where possible. . . . Journalists today should heed Holmes."[15]

As much as the investigative model—especially as it is employed by Woodward and Bernstein—foregrounds the story aspects of a report, it does not abandon the conventions of the neutral ideal. For example, the detective role model constructed in *All the President's Men* is characterized by reportorial detachment from personal and moral dimensions. The reporters are indeed interested in "what is real here," not what should be or why it happened. As Daniel Schorr points out in a 1974 review of the book, Woodward and Bernstein "display a fascination with recounting how they did it rather than what it all meant. It is an exciting narrative in itself. But, for the perspective on the trauma of the nation, look elsewhere."[16] Thus, like their classical detective counterpart Holmes, who is distinguished in his stories by his detachment from the cases he covers, Woodward and Bernstein disconnect themselves and their reporting from an explicit moral relationship to the events of Watergate.[17]

This neutral pose frees reporters from confronting a variety of concerns that might complicate their quest for clues. Neutrality, both in reporting and detective fiction, presumably allows the appropriate distance from which the reporter and the detective can see the "whole picture" and more easily tell fact from fiction, reality from illusion. Both classical detectives and conventional reporters are generally more interested in "what is" rather than "why it is" or "what ought to be." "What is" generally incorporates the set of rules that constitute the unstated moral imperative of common sense. Ted Glasser and James Ettema argue that contemporary investigative journalists "set aside consideration of the normative 'ought' and concentrate instead on documentation of the empirical 'is' by limiting their investigative stories to violations of widely held values."[18]

In classical detective fiction, the neutral posture allows the detective to penetrate illusions often associated with emotional and moral confusions suffered by victims or perpetrated by criminals. The reporting described and practiced in *All the President's Men* relates to detective fiction's allegiances to plot and action—to the "story." These practices include a strong sense of professionalism characterized by alleged moral detachment, superior reasoning techniques (which allow reporters to ferret out the appropriate clues), and the transformation of events and issues into a game or puzzle.[19] A reportorial stance which mimics patterns of the classical detective formula in news reports not only supports the allegiance to narrative structures but also simultaneously prevents the reporter from discussing (or worrying) about self-reflexive aspects of journalism. These aspects include the relationships of reporters to one another, to their sources, to their stories, and to the institution and conventions of journalism. Discussion and interpretation of these issues remain concealed by convention.

Commercial reporting and detective fiction developed together in the nineteenth century as products of a gradual cultural and philosophical shift which valued science over religion, and realism over romanticism. As products of the "utilitarian culture" of that century, both took shape around the notion of conforming to "what is" or realism.[20] That is, as the gap between science and art—as separate means of arriving at truth or reality—widened, those applauding science had less and less use for creativity and romanticism as an appropriate route for understanding the world. Likewise, the invention of the fictional detective story, as personified by its cerebral, rational detectives such as Arthur Conan Doyle's Sherlock Holmes and Edgar Allan Poe's Auguste Dupin, can also be read as an expression of faith in the ability of science and the "scientific mind" to gather facts and solve problems.[21]

By the end of the nineteenth century, the identities and methods of both reporters and detectives were bound to a view of a world teeming with data that must be discovered, rationalized, organized, and transformed into frames of reference for the public to use in the explanation of immediate experience. Both news reports and detective stories in the nineteenth century, then, can be interpreted, according to Schudson, as vehicles for the new rationality of a utilitarian culture "in which the normative order moved from a set of commandments to do what is right to a set of prudential warnings to adapt realistically to what is."[22]

The Mystery Formula

60 Minutes not only advances this commonsense tradition of faith in reason—in the individual's ability to figure out "what's going on here"—but its dominant story form also merges reporting practices with the literary traditions of the detective mystery. The *60 Minutes* mystery formula features characteristics that, on the surface at least, closely resemble those of the classical detective story. This form reveals a criminal situation and a series of actions to make sense of it through: (1) identifying the crime and distinguishing victims, villains, and bystanders who provide evidence and obstacles; (2) searching for clues of criminal violation; (3) stalking and revealing the transgressors; and (4) explaining or resolving the transgression.[23]

Supplying Crimes and Characters

The reporters introduce themselves and the alleged injustices, which may range from murder or political intrigue to deviation from commonsense values. After they identify major characters, settings, and the crime, the reporters introduce us to other characters who refuse to talk or who try to hinder the search for evidence. But in the end the reporter fits the puzzle together. Like Sherlock Holmes, the *60 Minutes* reporter ends the tale posed in front of the trademark magazine-cover frame, explaining to us—armchair Dr. Watsons—the missing evidence, the fate of the villains, and any apparent contradictions.

The *60 Minutes* reporters carry no weapons, but rely on rational instincts and their ability to expose other characters. Like tidy Columbos, they look like detectives, often wearing trench coats when searching for clues, a detail Don Hewitt notes with pride: "Those scenes of Mike Wallace on a stakeout in a trench coat are great if they produce anything. . . ."[24] And like their fictional counterpart, the *60 Minutes* detective often succeeds where traditional investigative agencies, victims of mediocrity or inferior intelligence, fail. Finally, following the tradition of the classical detective, we know little about the reporters—about their private lives and values, about their relationship to their large parent conglomerate CBS or to the stories they tell.

Unlike classical detectives, the *60 Minutes* reporters are real; they create and enact television performances guided by our expectations that detectives solve problems and reveal truth. The character-reporters of *60 Minutes* resolve fourteen-minute story conflicts and reaffirm that social order is at work in the world. Unlike fictional detectives, these reporters are not lone wolves, but employees in a giant media operation. They are dependent on a team of field producers, researchers, editors, and others in resolving their stories.

The mystery segments of *60 Minutes* often explicitly frame the saga as detective story. For example, in "Warning: May Be Fatal" (12/14/75), a story about "potential lethal pollution" of Virginia chemical plant workers, Dan Rather suggests: "What we have here in no small way is a whodunit." Occasionally, reporters even make direct allusions to the similarities between their sagas and the classical detective fiction of Doyle or Poe. Rather, for instance, begins "Equal Justice?" (8/24/80), a story about a black New Jersey political candidate allegedly framed for kidnapping, this way: "Tonight the strange case of Mims Hackett." And Mike Wallace introduces "The Stolen Cezannes" (10/14/79) similarly: "The case of the stolen Cezannes is not just the tangled tale of . . . three purloined paintings."

Searching for Clues

Reporters in these segments charge off to untangle evidence, stopping first at the place of the violation, where the crime's details and intrigue are recalled. They lead us to arenas where clues reside and where the injustice is resolved. In these scenes, *60 Minutes* visually solves one story conflict between safety and danger by displaying the reporter at the scene of the crime, a place once full of peril but now rendered safe by the passing of time and the reporter's presence. For example, in "John Singer's Coming Back" (3/12/89), Harry Reasoner takes us to "the body," the tombstone of John Singer, a Mormon whose belief in bigamy and defiance of state laws ended in his death. Reasoner retraces the crime and describes the details in this place in Utah, once the site of intrigue and death. Again, "Land Fraud and a Murder" (3/2/75), a story about organized crime activity in Arizona, involves "dubious land sales" and "shady characters." Morley Safer takes us to a dark stairwell in a public parking garage to reconstruct a murder. He points to blood-stained clues and shows us a newspaper photo with the victim lying in the very place that Safer now occupies. The segment also features safe, intimate interviews in which characters reveal clues. As in most *60 Minutes* mystery segments, the reporter, featured in an intimate mid-chest shot on the safe sets of a CBS studio, presents the final summary and explanation.

Challenging Villains

Another mystery element often includes a segment in which the reporter confronts a villain, an unwitting representative of an evil institution, or a bewildered witness or bystander. For example, "From Burgers to Bankruptcy" (12/3/78) tells a story about deception in the food franchising business. Mike Wallace, in a trench coat, confronts an executive from a burger franchising company and tries to spark a response. When the executive no longer will talk, Wallace stakes out his restaurant and in the parking lot challenges an employee—who nervously tells Wallace, "I'll watch what I'm saying"— with information about the executive's past. These dramatic confrontations display the reporter in apparent danger so that the tension later can be balanced against the safety provided by the reporter's revelation of the crime.

Occasionally, *60 Minutes* makes direct references to the narrative news villain. For instance, in "Who Shot Barbra?" (4/10/88), "a bizarre story of hired assassins and love gone sour," Morley Safer tells us early in the narrative "the real villain of the piece will remain a free man." By the end, Safer has presented enough evidence to convince us of the villain's guilt despite his free status. Again "Making of a Murderer" (2/17/85) is a story about a boy who is sexually abused by his adoptive father. The boy later kills the father. During an interview with the social service agency that placed the boy in the home, Safer asks the head of the agency: "Is there a major villain in this tragedy?" She responds, "I think a lot of people share the honor of being the villain." When Safer counters, "And you're one of them?" she answers, "Mm-hmm."

Solving the Crime

The explanation scene is one of the major patterns of action in the detective formula, representing "the goal toward which the story has been moving." That goal is the resolution of the tale's conflict, or as John Cawelti states, "the pleasure of seeing a clear and meaningful order emerge out of what seemed to be random and chaotic events."[25] Detective writer P. D. James comments on the explanatory power of the formula, "No matter how difficult the problem, there is a solution. All of this is rather comforting in an age of pessimism and anxiety."[26]

60 Minutes, too, makes clarity out of chaos in its detective formula. In "Your Money or Your Life" (3/19/78), for example, a world of normalcy is represented by Americans pitted against a world of deviance—foreign "terrorists" who threaten U.S. businesspeople abroad and citizens at home. Dan Rather restores clarity by explaining how we can minimize threats. Rather is located in this segment squarely between the worlds of normalcy and deviance, neither part of the chaos of terror, nor a member of the unsuspecting, victimized public. As detached hero of this narrative, Rather however does empathize with the normal, vulnerable world portrayed in the story. At one point he responds to a statement about terrorism in the United States: "Do you believe that? That scares the hell out of me." Such dramatic vulnerability actually heightens the reporter's credibility as a heroic figure who can identify with us, live with contradictions, and manage to interpret and resolve them.

In this scene Rather briefly resembles the hard-boiled American private detective typified by the works of Dashiell Hammett and Raymond Chandler in the 1920s and 1930s.[27] In this model, which has its television variations in Jim Rockford and Thomas Magnum, detectives are vulnerable, reflective, and far less detached; they are morally and emotionally involved in their investigations. Hard-boiled stories, in fact, have more in common with the literary journalism of cultural phenomenology. These private eyes live in a world where the boundary between reality and illusion is hazy. They are as interested in "what ought to be" as "what is." In hard-boiled fiction, detectives emerge as characters defined and determined by explicit moral codes rather than as mere functions of plot and dramatic tension. The world of clues becomes a means for revealing aspects of a more personal, more complex social order. As a form of ethnographic realism, *60 Minutes*, however, rarely looks to this model. With the program generally affirming the separation between observed and lived experience, *60 Minutes* steers clear of reflective "ought" questions in its search for describing "the real." More personal involvement on the part of the reporter would ultimately violate orthodox journalistic codes regarding the appearance of moral neutrality.

In most *60 Minutes* mysteries there is not a specific denouement featuring "the actual apprehension and confession of the criminal." But this is not a necessary requirement of the formula. According to Cawelti, "the classical story is more concerned with the isolation and specification of guilt than with the punishment of the criminal."[28] Some segments of *60 Minutes*, however, occasionally do offer denouement. "Another Elvis?" (8/12/79), for instance, weaves a tale about characters who pay money to shady record companies in return for recording careers. The disreputable president of a Nashville company (who, we learn, had a previous criminal record in forgery and white slavery), is apprehended and subsequently confesses to the reporter, who has caught the villain in a lie. Mike Wallace reports at the end of the segment that this character has "quit the business" and now "thanks" *60 Minutes* for turning his life in an honest direction. In this segment, the reporter dissolves conflict by placing himself between innocent victims and insensitive villains. Ultimately, he wraps up the case, reinstitutes safety, and champions justice as the villain promises to reform.

The Case of the Intrepid Reporter

In order to offer a more detailed illustration of how the mystery formula operates in *60 Minutes*, I have chosen a model segment that illustrates the general features highlighted above. "The Death of Edward Nevin" (2/17/80, Appendix B) is a story about a man who died as a result of secret army bacteria tests carried out in major U.S. urban centers in the early 1950s. Harry Moses produced the segment and also plays a minor on-screen role; Dan Rather serves as the reporter. This mystery narrative ran fourteen minutes, thirty-nine seconds, and contained 102 separate shots.[29]

Sequence 1 lasts thirty-four seconds and features one shot. Besides the references to "fiction, "tale," "story," and "mystery" in the introductory narration (which displays Rather posed before the traditional *60 Minutes* magazine frame), the reporter-detective conjures up American virtues, including patriotism and freedom: "Occasionally we run across a story that is so unusual it seems it should be fiction. The death of Edward Nevin is such a tale. He was an immigrant whose life could be the story of every Irishman who came to these shores. Edward Nevin was a patriot, a man who worshipped freedom, and yet a man whose death, so his family says, came at the hands of the country he loved. Until recently, the death of Edward Nevin was a mystery. . . ."

Visually, a dramatic conflict between the individual and technology is set up in the magazinelike frame appearing behind Rather, featuring ominous test tubes and the name "E. Nevin." Verbally, an individual-institution tension is posed in the personalization of Edward Nevin (including references to his background and values) and in the depersonalization of the institution (implied in the terms "government experiment" and "death . . . at the hands of the country he loved"). Featured here also are the conflict between life and death, and a clue about the institution as the "villain" responsible for Nevin's death. A more subtle tension is evoked by the visual presence of Rather against the absence of the institutions. The background test tubes also visually support a verbal counterpart—"a secret government experiment"—the concrete embodiment of institutional forces.

Sequence 2 includes fourteen shots and lasts two minutes, eighteen seconds. Here we are introduced to three major characters—the detective, the victim, and a well-meaning Dr. Wheat, an "expert" who does not have the expertise to solve this particular crime and who remains puzzled throughout the narrative. This sequence reconstructs the mystery. Visually, medical garb, shots of Wheat in the hospital, and shots of a medical journal article not only personalize him, but also endow him with credibility as a professional.

Shots at Nevin's grave site fit the classical detective pattern of the story that begins with a body; the detective then has to figure out how it got there and who did it. Rather is firmly established as the reporter-detective in this sequence as he displays detective conventions, donning a trench coat and investigating a cemetery—the site of the body—in order to gather evidence. Old home-movie shots of Nevin personalize the victim as an individual who stands for virtues such as health, vigor, and domesticity. This sequence supports specific characters by granting them both verbal and visual presence—Rather, Wheat, and Nevin as familiar, accessible individuals. At the same time, the absence of government responses and portrayals makes these aspects of the narrative more abstract and unknown, and therefore, more menacing. Rather closes this sequence with a cryptic reference to the mysterious bacteria that claimed Edward Nevin, "the bacteria that appeared from nowhere to kill him. And where it came from was a mystery."

Sequence 3 contains ten shots and lasts one minute, eight seconds. It introduces a new character and reveals more about the villain. This sequence, as does sequence 2, establishes the credibility and professional aura of a second expert. As this sequence opens, a long, high-angle outdoor shot reveals a Dr. Messelson at Harvard University. This shot contrasts with an interview that features Messelson and Rather. We see formulas on a blackboard and stacks of books. The professor of biochemistry tells Rather about the presence of yet another character, Messelson's former assistant, who is too frightened to come forward with evidence. In the final shot featuring the professor, despite his expertise, he admits his ineffectiveness at stopping the government experiments with live but allegedly benign bacteria: "But I didn't know who the right people were to talk to. I don't think." As with Dr. Wheat, long shots amid professional settings (as opposed to living rooms in homes) establish professional legitimacy. As these experts reveal that they lack the solution to the crime, the camera moves in closer, significant because one characteristic of the mystery formula is the presence of so-called expert characters who cannot figure out the crime's intricacies.

Space in the visual frame is gradually taken away from both Wheat and Messelson when they reveal they cannot solve the puzzle. In contrast, Rather as detective hero is portrayed in juxtaposition to Messelson in medium shots and in each shot the reporter-detective is granted more space than the professor. Rather, as the voice of common sense and the well-informed citizen, receives greater visual space in the narrative.

In this two-shot series, Dan Rather receives more "room" in the frame than his interview subject, a Harvard professor of biochemistry.(© MCMLXXX–CBS Inc. All rights reserved.)

This sequence conveys the painstaking detective task of accumulating evidence. Rather notes that *60 Minutes* had to travel three thousand miles to "pick up the trail." That quest provided more information about the crime and about the "villain," the military, specifically "a U.S. Army biological warfare experiment in San Francisco." It is significant that Rather, as opposed to Messelson, reveals this information. Even though Rather may have learned this from the expert doctor, it is the reporter who appears superior, both through his greater visual space and his revelation of crucial pieces of evidence. Messelson says he "told people in government" but did not have the right connections to stop the experiments; thus, he too is victimized. Rather, on the other hand, although he appears visually in only two medium shots in this sequence, dominates the sequence verbally. His brief visual appearance, in which he efficiently takes notes and asks questions in his detective role, makes him less vulnerable and more detached than Messelson. Rather's control of the narration through voice-overs grants him prominence. His visual presence in two medium note-taking shots contrasts sharply with an uncertain Dr. Messelson, whose confusion is made more apparent in tight close-ups which are not used to display Rather.

In addition to the superiority of the classical detective to other characters, a related aspect of the detective formula emerges: the transformation of a serious crime into a game.[30] Both Rather and Messelson use the word *puzzle* in reference to Nevin's death. The metaphor of death as a game or puzzle again directs attention in the narrative to the detective's ability to reason and "play the game" better than other characters. When the reporter does indeed solve the puzzle, his role as narrative hero is solidified. Both sequences featuring the two doctors suggest comparison to television's Lieutenant Columbo, also a classical detective, in which the detective solves puzzles by outwitting characters who are either more formally educated or from a higher social class, but they lack the well-informed common sense of the detective.

Sequence 4, the longest sequence, is the central one in the segment. It contains twenty-five separate shots and runs three minutes, forty-two seconds. This sequence offers a reconstruction of the crime and the presence of the detective sorting clues, identifying villains, and framing the narrative conflict between institution and individual. Significantly, during this sequence Dan Rather's voice again dominates; it is the only voice we hear. The sequence reconstructs the crime and reveals what Doctors Wheat and Messelson could not uncover, or "didn't know"—how the bacteria infected Edward Nevin. The domination of Rather in the voice-over and on-screen narration not only establishes his credibility as a reporter, but also allows him to present evidence as the detective. Although he makes an allusion to "recently declassified Army documents" in order to demonstrate the purpose of the test, he does not credit any document or person as the source of his information. Apparently, the viewers are to assume that the intrepid reporter single-handedly discovered the evidence and pieced it together for the audience.

This central sequence opens with shots of crowds along unidentified city streets. In the voice-over narration accompanying these shots, Rather describes "millions of Americans . . . used by the government as unwitting guinea pigs." As the camera pinpoints individuals in the crowd—an old man, teenage girls, a young woman, and a policeman—Rather continues to build his case against the government. The policeman becomes the unwitting representative of government authority as he controls the crowd on the curb. As he gives the signal to go, Rather's voice-over announces: "So, 19 civilian targets were chosen to practice on." Rather's verbal-only presence here endows him with detached superiority. It is significant that the reporter-detective is present verbally but not visually. Had he narrated the segment among the people in the street, his distinction from them would appear muddied, a potential "victim." As a well-informed social type endowed with insights not afforded to generic laypersons-on-the-street, Rather remains above the street, his disembodied voice controlling the narrative.

Next, the sequence recreates the crime, with producer Harry Moses reenacting the role of "villain" surrogate for the government. Moses plays a government agent who intentionally dumps bacteria into the New York subway system. It is significant that Rather does not perform the recreation of the crime, which would have clouded his role as detective hero. In this reenactment of the army's clandestine operation, the dramatic tension between honesty and deception is played out through a light-dark metaphor. Rather's voice-over is associated with shots of innocent, unsuspecting people on the street in the bright light of day. In contrast, Moses, as the "army operative," descends into the dark recesses of the subway system to undermine innocent people on the streets above. To further enhance the villainy and deception of the government in this sequence, the bacteria is released from a shattered light bulb. Whereas "light" is associated here with the above-ground, innocent crowd shots, the government convolutes that symbol and uses it to deceive.

Rather next appears visually in the following scene far from the street crowds and noise as a lone figure aboard a boat on a gloomy, overcast day in San Francisco Bay. Then, a dramatic, sweeping aerial shot zooms in on Rather, now a lone figure atop a building high above the city. In both scenes his trench coat costume compliments the foggy, mysterious San Francisco background. His isolation from the crowded street scenes again reinforces his portrayal as the de- tached, superior detective. Unlike producer Moses, who dons a dis- guise, dodges the crowds, and travels underground, Rather needs no disguise, avoids the crowd, and travels upward. Rather, now visible, recreates and reveals in these dramatic shots what really happened to Edward Nevin. His lone presence compliments the achievement of his presentation and explanation of the crime. As Rather indicts the army and other federal agencies, these institutions remain visually and verbally absent, juxtaposed with Rather's visual presence as he retells the story of the secret tests and government villainy.

Sequence 5 offers eleven shots and lasts one minute, twenty sec- onds. The sequence builds to a narrative climax as Rather's evidence introduces a "star witness." This sequence traces the discovery by Edward Nevin III, the title character's lawyer-grandson, that the government tests were connected to his grandfather's death. A San Francisco subway station sequence here contrasts with the earlier sequence where *60 Minutes* recreated the crime. Whereas a disguised Harry Moses descended the dark subway stairs to recreate the crime, Edward Nevin's grandson, "a young trial attorney who had been specializing in medical malpractice cases," ascends the subway stairs into the light to reenact his part in the revelation of the crime. Nevin III offers this dramatic retelling in a voice-over while the visuals reenact his discovery on the subway when he came across a story in the San Francisco *Chronicle* in 1976 that first linked his grand- father's death to the secret government experiments: "As a trial lawyer, as someone who deals with these kinds of cases, I looked at it without surprise but with a detached sort of objective view, a professional looking at something within his field. I then discovered

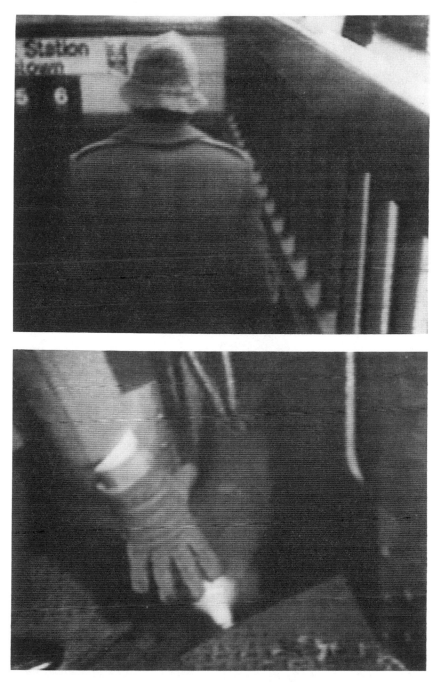

In this two-shot series, *60 Minutes* producer Harry Moses recreates the role of a government agent who drops a light bulb filled with an apparently benign bacteria into the New York subway system. (© MCMLXXX–CBS Inc. All rights reserved.)

High above San Francisco, Dan Rather in this dramatic two-shot series tells
how the government secretly collected bacteria samples that allegedly killed
Edward Nevin. (© MCMLXXX–CBS Inc. All rights reserved.)

that the one person who died as a result of these experiments was Edward J. Nevin, a retired San Francisco pipe fitter who died in Stanford Hospital on November 1, 1950. That was my grandfather."

The varied visual treatment of Nevin III, who is shot in close-ups, medium and long shots, and Rather's surrender of the voice-over narration to Nevin favorably identify him on equal ground with Rather. The final narration here—"That was my grandfather"—further strengthens the positive role Nevin III plays in the story and reaffirms the virtues of domesticity. The substitution of Nevin as narrator works because both Nevin and Rather support similar virtues of family, honesty, individualism, and sensitivity. The continual positive visual treatment of characters—particularly Rather and Nevin III—juxtaposed with only the mention of the bungling government strengthens the conflict between honesty and deception. The individual characters continue to shed light on evidence while the absent institution remains in the dark.

Sequence 6 also contains eleven shots; it runs two minutes, nineteen seconds. This sequence introduces us to specific victims who have also suffered from the crime. Evidence from the characters and the detective directly link the government, as villain, to Edward Nevin's death. Opening with Edward Nevin III describing his hurt, anger, and shock when he found out about the government tests, the sequence establishes the younger heroic Nevin as a vulnerable character in contrast to the detached, emotionally steady detective. This portrayal of Nevin III contrasts with an earlier scene in which it appears that Nevin III might displace Rather as hero in the narrative. An opening tight close-up features Nevin III admitting to his emotional reaction. The next shot grants Nevin III more visual space in which to operate, and therefore his accompanying verbal narration indicting the government is given greater credibility. A background office setting behind the lawyer features law books and adds expert legitimacy to his part in identifying the villain in the narrative.

The next shot brings back the reporter-detective in a voice-over, and Rather identifies the villain as the Pentagon, which will not face him: "It refused our request for an interview." Pronouns here italicize the dramatic tension: the impersonal "it" further depersonalizes the institution, while "our" implicitly includes us as viewers in league with Rather on his quest for truth. The institution as villain is supported by the visual track—an aerial shot of the distant Pentagon building. Rather does not name the individuals whom he tried to contact at the Pentagon. The disembodied Pentagon edifice is juxtaposed with Dr. Wheat, who calls the crime a "fascinating coincidence" and reveals evidence concerning the army's test and Nevin's death. Rather and Wheat provide details of the crime as their narration indicts the Pentagon, which remains aloof and unresponsive in the distant aerial shot.

The second part of this sequence introduces two new characters— Edward Nevin's son (the grandson's father) and daughter, Mrs. Bray. The son accuses the government of "attacking" his father, while the daughter establishes Edward Nevin's special individuality and family orientation. Nevin's son first appears in a long shot, walking with the grandson on a farm. The pastoral shot marks a powerful contrast to the remote Pentagon two shots earlier. Next we meet Mrs. Bray in her living room. The farm buildings, woods, and rustling leaves in one group of shots combine with shots of vases, a doily, a photograph, and a frame, and point up the contrast between these characters' individuality and the impersonality of the Pentagon. Mrs. Bray appears in a tight close-up, distraught over her father's death and recalling his virtues. She discusses her father's "pride" in being an American and the "wonderful heritage" Edward Nevin left behind: "We're a remarkable family." The distinctiveness of family is further enhanced by the emotion (supported through the intimacy of the close-up) that the son through his anger and daughter through her tears bring to this scene. In addition, the narration and visuals offer two relatively powerless characters who cannot understand why the powerful government of their country killed their father. The oppositions posed in this sequence appear unreconcilable, but they prepare the way for narrative resolution in the concluding sequence.

Sequence 7 offers thirty shots in extremely quick takes in one minute, eighteen seconds. It is in this sequence that the reporter mediates the central dramatic tensions embedded in the narrative. This sequence is the denouement of the mystery, the villain is charged and the final pieces of evidence fall into place. A rapidly paced and edited Nevin family Christmas reunion opens the sequence, accompanied by a Rather voice-over, and the editing rhythm gradually slows to match the final on-screen appearance of Edward J. Nevin III, who vows to advocate his grandfather's case in court. The abrupt editing and cluttered frames of the twenty-seven reunion shots are the video counterpart to a photo album and establish a strong domestic sense. Rather confirms the individuality of these people by identifying the various "clans" in the extended Nevin family. He juxtaposes narration about the peace and joy of the Christmas setting with voice-overs about the family's fight against the institutions responsible for Nevin's death. With Christmas carols and family conversation running underneath his off-screen narration, Rather proclaims: "For all these people—all 65 living descendents of Edward J. Nevin—have filed suit against the Army, the Navy, the Department of Defense, and the United States of America for the wrongful death of the founder of this extended Irish-American family."

Once again, the strong visual presence of the family opposes the notorious institutions which remain—as they have the entire segment—faceless and menacing but about to meet their match. The final shots of Nevin's grandson and his on-screen narration pit the integrity of the individual—"I'm Edward J. Nevin III"—against the deception of the government—"You do not test in secrecy. . . . We have to know." The key feature of this sequence is the transformation of a group of "victims," emotionally hurt by this experience, into a united force ready to take on powerful organizations. The contrast between the last shot in sequence 6 featuring Edward Nevin's daughter in tears and the triumph evident in the Christmas celebration and the grandson's final challenge confirms the transformation.

Dan Rather functions as power broker in the final sequence by initiating the shift in control from military might into the hands of individuals united as family. The introduction of the value of family initiates narrative closure and apparently resolves the conflict between the caring, individual members of the Nevin family and the insensitive, institutional Pentagon. But with attention here devoted to family to solve this particular narrative, Rather and *60 Minutes* ignore other kinds of general collective action that a society can take to check the imbalances of power in a democracy.

Restoring Moral Order

A major function of the *60 Minutes* mystery formula displays heroic reporters straddling tensions between individual and institution, safety and danger, honesty and injustice. They emerge from these dramatic situations by either resolving the crime or at least presenting viewers with a well-informed, commonsense interpretation. Explicit in this resolution is the moral affirmation of values such as family unity, democracy, individualism, capitalism, honesty, loyalty, populism, and justice. In "Neighbors" (3/13/88), which is also a movie title, Harry Reasoner tells a story about a crack cocaine operation in a middle-class neighborhood in Florida. Despite continuous complaints from neighbors, the inefficient police have been slow to act on their behalf. As the neighborhood's moral advocate, Reasoner confronts a police representative from the local organized crime division: "You take a community of single family houses, owners living in them. Respectable people, taxpayers and so on—with many of them in a whole square block complaining, and complaining, and complaining. I can't think of a jurisdiction in the U.S. where that wouldn't get you a search warrant." Reasoner's commonsense portrait of this Florida neighborhood is grounded solidly in Middle America. His appeal to police authorities is a moral one that demands they take action in behalf of these citizens.

In "Titan" (11/8/81), in which the transgressions are again government ineptitude and insensitivity, the detective narrative offers tension through a victimized character, a former Air Force sergeant reprimanded by his superiors after he tried to investigate a toxic leak and fatal explosion in a U.S. missile silo. According to the ex-sergeant, "I went down there for God, my country, the flag, my job—everything—I didn't go down there for any other reason. I gave them my all. And what did I get from them [the Air Force]? A letter of reprimand. . . . What about the little guy?" *60 Minutes* affirms the ex-sergeant's status as victim by juxtaposing him to the Air Force, once again an absent villain, who like the Pentagon in the Nevin segment, "absolutely refuses to answer any questions." The reporter repairs conflict between the individual and bureaucracy by siding with the innocent, unsuspecting victim. By affirming honesty and loyalty as individual virtues antithetical to bureaucracy, the story reveals the Air Force as institutional rogue.

The previous segments and the Nevin narrative demonstrate an important subconflict in most *60 Minutes* mysteries: the presence of victims, heroes, and the *60 Minutes* reporter and the absence of villains or menacing institutions. Presence versus absence generally takes two forms on *60 Minutes*: institutional representatives refuse to be filmed, taped, or interviewed, or they simply are not interviewed by *60 Minutes* even though their omission is built into the story as narrative conflict. The absent villain generally represents some form of shadowy business, government, or labor institution. In "Distressed" (5/3/81), for example, a story about a flourishing Florida county listed by the Department of Housing and Urban Development as an economically distressed area, no top HUD bureaucrat would grant Morley Safer an interview. He tells us that one institutional representative said: "No way will I sit down for an interview." *60 Minutes* then introduces a General Accounting Office report that criticizes HUD for using twenty-year-old statistics to determine distressed areas. Safer's narration, filmed outside the HUD building, displays the agency as a big, insensitive, inefficient bureaucracy under no individual's control.

"What Killed Jimmy Anderson" (3/2/86) is another detective story about W. R. Grace, "one of America's largest corporations . . . facing charges it poisoned a Massachusetts community" and "caused the outbreak of childhood leukemia that killed" a young boy fourteen years earlier. Like the Pentagon in the Nevin segment, the Grace plant appears in distant aerial shots, and Ed Bradley tells us later in the segment: "For more than a month, Mr. Grace declined our request for a video taped interview on *60 Minutes*. No other company spokesman would be interviewed, cither. . . . Then on Wednesday, Mr. Grace said he would agree to a *60 Minutes* interview if it was live and unedited. We declined his offer." Once again the villain is absent, kept away in part by a *60 Minutes* editorial policy to control its narrative. In contrast, the reporter's presence in these segments, as our well-informed representative, affirms values of efficiency, justice, and common sense against the inept, unjust, and garbled countervalues of disembodied bureaucracies.

What empowers detectives with the special ability to find clues and resolve problems? James Fernandez argues that a cultural "mission of metaphor" is to move the "subject" of the metaphor, in this case the reporter, "into optimum position," the position of the classical detective.[31] In both *60 Minutes* and classical detective fiction, such optimum position rests in the character traits of superior intelligence and detachment. Like Sherlock Holmes, the reporters appear in control of the situation and above any kind of personal involvement in the crime under investigation. Reporters assume a more positive place in the story than villains or inept institutions, the counterparts to the bungling and inefficient police of mystery fiction. Their portrayals as individual characters—as heroic loners (rather than institutional representatives of CBS News)—grant them a superior moral location in their stories. The *60 Minutes* reporter recognizes "the real" and "what is going on here."

The device of apparent detachment works partly as a ruse to conceal the overt moral stance of the reporter, but as Mary Mander contends, "In every news story, morality or a moralizing impulse is present."[32] Indeed, both Don Hewitt and Mike Wallace refer to *60 Minutes* narratives as morality plays. In a program titled "Looking at *60 Minutes*" (9/27/81) a panel of experts met with Hewitt and Wallace to discuss ethical dimensions of the program's investigative practices. Hewitt was asked by a vice president from Mobil Oil to account for why *60 Minutes* does not do "good" stories, that is, stories that vindicate an apparent villainous individual or institution. The following exchange occurred:

> HEWITT: If we find out something is counter to the public perception of it and is really a good thing rather than what the public thinks is a bad thing, yes, I'm sure we would do that [story]. . . .
>
> JEFF GREENFIELD (then media critic at CBS): When I see an investigative story on *60 Minutes*, I know there's something wrong there because I have become accustomed to never seeing a show where nothing wrong happens.
>
> BOB GREEN (reporter, editor and former president of Investigative Reporters and Editors): Isn't that the purpose of this program to expose things that are wrong . . . ?

It is unclear how Hewitt gauges "public perception" of right and wrong. He admits, "I never look at research figures. I have no idea who's out there."[33] For Hewitt, once again, the bottom line is the story and his own sixth sense about what constitutes a good news drama. In spite of the apparent detachment of reporter-characters, just by virtue of selecting certain kinds of experience to tell stories about and by presenting that experience as dramatic conflict, *60 Minutes* and its reporters engage, as do all reporters in all news narratives, in implicit moral judgments about what is right and wrong, good and evil, normal and deviant.

The *60 Minutes* reporter, as detective, champions individualism and integrity in the face of heartless (and often faceless) bureaucracy. As the sociologist Robert Bellah and his colleagues note in *Habits of the Heart,* historically the detective first appeared as a popular cultural hero "when business corporations emerged as the focal institutions of American life. The fantasy of a lonely, but morally impeccable, hero corresponds to doubts about the integrity of self in the context of modern bureaucratic organization."[34] Depicting *60 Minutes* reporters as individual loners, apart from a team of producers, researchers, and editors who construct the story, apart from the powerful CBS media corporation, endows them with status akin to our other fictional heroes. As the constraints of the narrative formula mask the reporters' own institutional identities, they also prevent *60 Minutes* from revealing how other institutions are constructed and sustained by other teams of individuals. The portrayal of reporters as intrepid detectives isolates them from their own institution at the same time it enhances their story status as power brokers for individualism and clarifiers of narrative mystery.

News and Therapy: Moral Meanings and Tough Questions

4

> When will I learn? The answer to life's problems aren't at the bottom of a bottle. They're on TV!
>
> —Homer Simpson

> How [can] you survive in the Cosmos about which you know more and more while knowing less and less about yourself, this despite 10,000 self-help books, 100,000 psycho-therapists, and 100 million fundamentalist Christians.
>
> —Walker Percy

> Sometimes television is a theater, sometimes it's a cinema, sometimes it's a sports arena, sometimes it's a newspaper, and sometime's its a chapel. And sometimes when there are national moments of distress, America calls on Peter Jennings, Tom Brokaw and Dan Rather to minister to the needs of the nation. They don't go to Jerry Falwell. They don't go to Pat Robertson. They don't go to Cardinal Cook.... The first time it happened ... Jack Kennedy was killed in Dallas. They all came to the set and they held hands and the whole country bound up its wounds by holding hands in front of the television set. They went to church in front of television.
>
> —Don Hewitt

Like the detective but for different reasons, the expert therapist, too, has assumed a position of privilege in our culture.[1] The development of the therapist's social influence also can be traced to the turn of the century during turbulent sociocultural shifts from religion to science, from country to city, from scarcity to abundance, and from self-sacrifice to self-realization.[2] The analyst emerged from these adjustments as a prominent promoter of what Jackson Lears calls the "therapeutic ethos," offering renewal of "a sense of selfhood that had grown fragmented, diffuse, and somehow 'unreal.' "[3] Analysts gained legitimacy, in part, by an ability in general to solve problems, by riding the coattails of prestige bestowed upon medical science, and by positioning individuals at the center of modern life. As Warren Susman has observed, "One of the things that make the modern world 'modern' is the development of consciousness of self."[4]

In their analysis of modern therapy in *Mental Health in America,* Veroff, Kulka, and Douvan contend that "Psychoanalysis (and psychiatry) is the only form of psychic healing that attempts to cure people by detaching them from society and relationships. All other forms—shamanism, faith healing, prayer—bring the community into the healing process. . . . Modern psychiatry isolates the troubled individual from the currents of emotional interdependence and deals with the trouble by distancing from it and manipulating it through intellectual/verbal discussion, interpretation, and analysis."[5] So in the shift to bureaucratic consumer capitalism, just as the detective emerged as hero—as testimony to rugged individualism—the therapist, too, offered respite from the increasing demands of bureaucracy and the pressures of the self cut adrift. Quoting Susman, "It is further a striking part of the turn-of-the-century decade that interest grew in personality, individual idiosyncracies, personal needs and interests."[6]

Around this time several crises and problems signaled society's need for expert analysis and therapy. These included, according to Lears, urbanization, which introduced the "anonymity of the city"; technological advance, which brought "prepackaged artificiality" along with "unprecedented comfort and convenience"; institutionalization, which created "an interdependent national market economy" and cut people off from ties to the land and "primary experience"; and secularization, which displaced religion and isolated people from the ritual of tradition.[7] Analysts stepped into these crises to try and restore a sense of individuality offering "harmony, vitality, and the hope of self-realization." The analyst-therapist grants, and continues to grant, cures for and mediations of modern cultural tension. As sociologists Robert Bellah and his colleagues point out, "the very term therapeutic suggests a life focused on the need for cure."[8]

Significantly, there is a crucial link between the therapeutic and common sense. Roy Schafer argues that the practices of psychoanalysis take the "precritical assumptions" of common sense as a starting point. He regards such sense as a crucial repository of "mythology, folk wisdom, colloquial sayings, jokes, and literature, among other cultural products": "[A]s Freud showed repeatedly, there are relatively few significant psychoanalytic propositions that are not stated or implied by these products."[9] Respecting common sense as a "storehouse of narrative structures," Schafer claims that psychoanalysis over time has "refined" common sense and elevated a stock of archetypal "leading narrative structures" to the realm of certainty: "Psychoanalysis does not take common sense plain but rather transforms it into a comprehensive distillate, first, by selection and schematic reduction of its tensions and ambiguities and, second, by elevating only some of these factors (such as pleasure versus reality and id versus ego) to the status of overachieving principles and structures."[10]

In their sociological interviews with therapists, Bellah and his colleagues note that most respondents emphasized that their own outlook on analysis "was more oriented to achieving 'practical results' than to theoretical consistency or allegiance."[11] Again the utilitarian function of therapy shares common ground with common sense. The reconfiguration of "refined common sense" by some schools of psychoanalysis, although more consciously systematic, shares with journalism a belief in the power of language and narrative to reconstruct accurately the crucial dimensions of human experience.

The therapeutic dimension of news, often masked by the common-sense ways reporters talk about their profession, is nevertheless a vital element of the news process. Instead of discussing news as therapy or psychoanalysis, which resides too closely to the categorically taboo realm of the subjective, journalists refer instead to news analysis or interpretation—although they mark this off from hard news. Championed on the print side by Walter Lippmann during the earlier part of this century,[12] the analyst's role in broadcast news dates from early radio.

In the 1930s a major battle developed between radio journalism and the established powers of print which tried to stop radio from gathering and reporting news.[13] Entrenched in and protective of its doctrinaire practices in neutral, factual reporting, print tried to saddle radio with the "inferior" role of news commentary—the explicit explanation or interpretation of experience. Mainstream reporting marked its territory, deciding to protect its claim to facts and the neutral model. By conceding radio the role of commentary, the press for a time guarded its factual domain.

Yet many journalists at this time thought that interpretation, and not a greater effort to celebrate objective fact-gathering techniques, seemed a more valuable economic strategy in competing with the new medium. A few editors realized that interpretation in print was a way to compete with radio's superior ability to report breaking news quickly. In 1938 Curtis MacDougall noted a trend toward "combining the function of interpreter with that of reporter after about half a century during which the journalistic ethic called for a strict differentiation between narrator and commentator."[14] In 1933 the American Society of Newspaper Editors also supported the idea of interpretive journalism as a way to process social complexity and resolved to "devote a larger amount of attention and space to analytical and interpretative news and to presenting a background of information which will enable the average reader more adequately to understand the movement and the significance of events."[15]

Noting that objectivity and factuality should be the dominant models for journalistic practice, Lippmann, the conscience of American journalism after World War I, acknowledged the role of interpretation in the press. He ranked three press responsibilities: (1) "to make a current record," (2) "to make a running analysis of it," (3) "on the basis of both, to suggest plans."[16] Journalists and readers since have made commonsense distinctions between the neutral model and one alternative—editorial opinion or background interpretation, that is, reports performing explicitly as social analysis. The two models are regarded as categorical opposites: one model is objective, the other is not. This distinction over time has been conventionally crafted by professionals. Because the difference between them is muddier than first appears, the two are clearly marked and assigned particular pages in most American newspapers lest readers confuse them. Yet both engage in commonsense reconstructions of experience. And despite what defenders of the neutral model argue, both are interpretations of selected experience, both symbolic representations of social realities.

There is agreement that the rise of interpretive journalism, in part, grew out of intricacies posed by World War I—especially that war's overt propaganda—and the Great Depression. As a result of "drab, factual, objective reporting," MacDougall contends that "the American people were utterly amazed when war broke out in August 1914, as they had no understanding of the foreign scene to prepare them for it"; he adds that newspapers also failed to prepare readers for the Great Depression.[17] Edwin Emery argues that "the rise of interpretive reporting was the most important development of the 1930s and 1940s" because it represented a viable way for journalism to therapeutically address "the New Deal years, the rise of modern scientific technology, the increasing interdependence of economic groups at home, and the shrinking of the world into one vast arena for power politics. . . ."[18] Finally, Frank Luther Mott suggests, "The increasing complexity of the economic, social, and international news forced, by the thirties, some retreat from the ideal of purely factual news which had prevailed in American reporting for over fifty years."[19] In other words, journalism, through analysis, took a therapeutic turn in a world grown increasingly enigmatic and depressed.

Continuing European immigration, the aftermath of the war, the extended depression, and Hitler's threat to global stability helped analysis take root in forms such as radio commentary, political columns, news magazines, and the first "docudramas." Thus, in the 1930s the stage was set for new forms of journalism to emerge and older forms to revive. When the depression struck, editorials made a strong comeback.[20] More significant, however, was the development of the political column. Literary and humor columns existed before the war, but the political column was a new form. More than 150 syndicated columns developed between 1930 and 1934 alone.[21] Journalists began more and more to see themselves as analysts and interpreters of the world.

It was amid the press-radio war of the 1930s and the controversy over interpretation's place in print journalism that radio commentary flourished. Lowell Thomas delivered the first daily radio network news analysis for CBS on September 29, 1930, and attacked Hitler's rise to power in Germany.[22] By the end of 1931 there were six regular network commentators, and by the beginning of World War II there were twenty.[23]

As political columns and radio commentary evolved, the weekly interpretive news magazines *Time* (1923) and *Newsweek* (1933) developed. In 1931, *Time,* founded by Henry Luce and Briton Hadden, helped sponsor radio's *The March of Time*—"the prototype of many broadcast programs—dramatic and documentary, fact and fiction."[24] (There was also a different "screen magazine" or newsreel version of *The March of Time* which ran in theaters from 1935-51.) This radio program, the first so-called "docudrama," featured actors recreating the roles of current politicians and celebrities and reenacting news events of the day.[25] Luce himself argued that the split between news and story was an artificial one. He recommended that newspapers drop the distinctions between editorials and factual news accounts, suggesting that front pages consist of "intelligent criticism, representation and evaluation of [those] who hold offices of public trust."[26]

However, newspapers did not surrender their front pages to analysis during the 1930s. Lippmann believed that commentary and interpretation were misdirected without the foundation of facts and a "current record": "The really important thing is to try and make opinion increasingly responsible to the facts."[27] Still, objectivity as an ideal had shifted in the early 1930s. According to Schudson, "In the 1890s reporters rarely doubted the possibility of writing realistically; in the 1930s even journalists committed to objectivity acknowledged that objective reporting was a goal beyond reach—the perils of subjectivity were well recognized."[28]

Although occasional stories which spotlight analysis over description find their way onto most front pages of contemporary newspapers, interpretation as a model never gained a status equal to the neutral, descriptive model; it is generally relegated to the editorial and op-ed pages and to the Sunday morning ghetto of network news programs. After World War II, interpretation, in fact, especially on radio, diminished substantially.[29] Not until the 1950s with the impetus from McCarthyism, the Korean War, the international development of atomic power, and tension with the Soviet Union did reporting as analysis resurface in any substantial form in the new medium of television and the CBS series *See It Now*, precursor to *60 Minutes.*

The Analyst Formula

In addition to *See it Now*, a second important model for *60 Minutes* was *Life* magazine, another 1930s creation of Henry Luce.[30] Essentially a larger, pictorial version of *Time*, *Life* interpreted the world through visual images with stories that also ranged from "hard to soft." Unlike the mystery formula, which fits best into the common-sense designation of hard news, a second pervasive narrative formula on *60 Minutes* offers flexibility in which stories run the gamut from "the heavy to the light, from warmth to menace."[31] Within these narratives reporters perform as analysts offering insights into or cures for contemporary tensions. In general, the reporter assumes two roles in these *60 Minutes* analyst segments: that of the historical or social commentator and that of the psychoanalyst or therapist. And in any given analyst narrative the reporter may perform both roles. In each case, however, the reporter is, first, an interpreter who recasts, rearranges, and retells the stories of others. Such narrative interpretation, Roy Schafer suggests, is the essence of analysis:

> [People] tell the analyst about themselves and others in the past and present. In making interpretations, the analyst retells these stories. In the retelling, certain features are accentuated while others are placed in parentheses. . . .
>
> The analyst's retellings progressively influence the what and how of the stories told. . . . The analyst establishes new, though often contested or resisted, questions that amount to regulated narrative possibilities.[32]

In their examination of contemporary therapy, Bellah and his colleagues also see important connections between therapeutic narratives and the self trying to fit into community: "Therapy, which often acts to take apart one's life history so as to 'liberate' one from it, can, on the other hand, help us recover the narrative unity of our lives woven through family ties into the social tapestry of communities situated in a given time, place, and culture."[33] In segments of *60 Minutes*, reporters perform such analysis when they construct "life history" narratives about the individual and communal experiences of others.

One result of the reporter's analytical prowess is to endow these historical narratives with closure. The desire for closure in narrative, as Hayden White argues, is a desire for a moral viewpoint: "The demand for closure in the historical story is a demand . . . for moral meaning, a demand that sequences of real events be assessed as to their significance as elements of a moral drama. Has any historical narrative ever been written that was not informed not only by moral awareness but specifically by the moral authority of the narrator?"[34]

The affirmation of values or morality, both explicitly and implicitly, is a major motif on *60 Minutes* where, as in other forms of historical storytelling, "narrativity. . . is intimately related to, if not a function, of, the impulse to moralize reality."[35] Mary Mander extends White's arguments to the news process, contending, "at the heart of the practice of reporting the news, of translating real events into narrative, lies a moral impulse. That is to say, the practice of journalism rests in an ongoing discrimination between what is right and wrong, what is good and what is evil."[36] Each day those journalists most captivated by the apparently neutral mode implicitly make decisions and carry out assignments bound to moral news judgments.

The *60 Minutes* therapeutic narrative manifests the impulse to moralize reality in mediating three key dramatic tensions: success versus failure, tradition versus change, and the personal versus the social. While the tension between personal and social realms is a variant of individualism-versus-institution theme present in the mystery formula, the different terms call attention to the more general nature of this tension as it is worked out in the analyst formula. In the detective narratives, the institution typically is a government or business organization. In the analyst segments, in constrast, bureaucracies give way to a broader notion of society, a set of borders and rules that an individual character must confront. In the mystery stories, characters serve primarily as a function of plot, and their individual behavior and attitudes are rarely explored in depth. In the analyst segments, a single character generally is the focus of a fourteen-minute story. Whereas detective segments include on the average eight to ten characters who are named and interviewed, in the analyst segments two main characters are usually featured, the subject of the story and the reporter.

Four distinguishing characteristics of the analyst formula include the role of the reporter (1) as social or psychological analyst, endowing the narrative with closure and moral meaning, (2) as intimate confidant, (3) as foil to villainous characters or promoter of heroic characters, and (4) as inquisitor, asking tough questions.

Social and Psychological Analysts

On *60 Minutes* the reporter performs as social commentator, analyzing and interpreting historical, political, economic, and cultural trends in relationship to an interview subject, the major character in these narratives. For example, in "Martin Luther King's Family at Christmas" (12/24/68), Mike Wallace tells a story about King's family and analyzes the effect of King's death on the civil rights movement which in Wallace's words is "leaderless" and "rudderless" without King. Wallace's role in this segment is not so much to analyze historical events as it is to offer a narrative that explains the present and predicts future directions of social phenomena.

In another example, "New York Yankee" (5/3/81), Harry Reasoner offers social commentary on Yankee owner George Steinbrenner, who is characterized by Reasoner as "almost impossible to work for." He "can't hit, run or throw, but boy can he talk," Reasoner tells us. The reporter offers insights and forecasts trends regarding labor-management relations in baseball. Reasoner predicts ominously that Steinbrenner "should be heading toward another successful season—but don't bet on it." Reasoner's analysis implicitly rejects negative aspects of Steinbrenner's character (egocentrism, physical mediocrity, and self-indulgence), aspects that run counter to the commonsense virtues of Middle America.

A second analytic role features the reporter more explicitly as therapist. Moving away from public events and issues, here the reporter probes the private, emotional world of the characters in order to reaffirm values. Again in "Martin Luther King's Family at Christmas," Wallace diagnoses the emotional states of the King children by asking how they are adjusting to their father's assassination. The narrative then affirms the ability of the private family to overcome the chaos and conflict inherent in a public assassination. Wallace also serves here to help viewers come to terms with the tragedy and enigma of assassination by placing chaos within the comforting boundaries of narrative.

Another example, "The Shah of Iran" (10/14/76), allows Wallace to practice some confrontational psychology by reading to the Shah from his CIA psychological profile: " 'A brilliant but dangerous megalomaniac who is likely to pursue his own aims in disregard of U.S. interests.' " Wallace asks the Shah, "Should I go on?" and then concludes the sequence with narration that analyzes the Shah's mental features by juxtaposing them implicitly with positive virtues such as humility and egalitarianism. In "Anderson of Illinois" (2/17/80), Morley Safer overtly displays the therapist persona when he conducts a kind of verbal Rorschach test on 1980 presidential candidate John

Anderson: "For an underdog, Anderson is a gentle soul who does not speak harshly of his rivals, even when you play the candidate game with him. . . . I'll give you a name, and you give me an answer. Ronald Reagan?" Safer offers three more names to complete the test. In so doing, Safer constructs a story that implicitly supports Anderson's alleged kindness and modesty as values for everyday life.

Occasionally, the reporter-therapist will make a diagnosis or lead us in that direction. "A Wild and Crazy Guy?" (4/10/88) offers a "soft" profile of comedian-actor Steve Martin. In explaining his serious and comic moods, Diane Sawyer playfully suggests, "The split in Martin's personality is about as wide as it gets. You just can't believe this mild-mannered museum intellectual is the same guy who does those outrageous things." In "Tammy" (10/2/83), a "hard" story about a young prostitute and her father, Reasoner's series of probing questions suggest those of a social worker or sex therapist: "So, you were a little scared, maybe a little humiliated, but . . . the money was real?"/ "When you broke [your father's] rules, was it a way of getting back at him?"/ "What were her feelings, as far as you know, about sex?"/ "How does a father deal with that, with that kind of news?" In this story, the reporter probes the emotional states of the interview subject in search of a cure for a larger social problem.

The Intimate Reporter

A second characteristic of the analyst formula features the reporter as a character with personal likes and dislikes, as confidant of the interview subject. One visual instance stands out, a scene from "Lena Horne" (12/27/81) where Ed Bradley and Horne walk hand in hand across a busy New York street. Although not always portrayed as vividly, reporter intimacy also surfaces in other analyst narratives. In "Madame Minister" (9/19/82), actress and Greek cultural minister Melina Mercouri takes Harry Reasoner "on a date" to a Greek nightclub. In "Mister Right" (12/14/75), Mike Wallace, in a sweater and jacket, interviews presidential candidate Ronald Reagan during a jeep ride on Reagan's California ranch. And in "Over the Hill" (2/5/84), an interview with members of the Senior Health and Peer Counseling Center in Santa Monica, California, Wallace confides in the group and reveals his age—"Uh-huh. I'm 65." In these examples the analyst persona displays a more involved personal stance in the narrative that sets the stage for the imposition of moral order as the narrative reaches closure.

Occasionally, the greater intimacy of the therapy segments places the reporter in a position to call overt attention to his role as a reporter, as surrogate for Middle-American viewers. The following exchange takes place between Wallace and Palestinian Liberation Organization leader Yasir Arafat:

WALLACE: What do you think Americans think of you?

ARAFAT (pause): The people?

WALLACE: Yeah, the people.

ARAFAT: I am a man trying to find a place for my people under the sun.

WALLACE: You don't think they think of you as a terrorist? You don't think they think of you as a—

ARAFAT (interrupting): Yeah, you see George Washington has been mentioned as a rebel. De Gaulle has been mentioned by his enemies—

WALLACE (interrupting): But you understand Yasir Arafat is not regarded in the same way as George Washington or Charles de Gaulle for whatever reasons.

ARAFAT: Who said it?

WALLACE: I say it. I'm a reporter. And I think it's sensible . . .

ARAFAT (interrupting): Yes, sir.

WALLACE: And I try to report accurately.

Not only does Wallace speak for us in this segment ("Yasir Arafat," 2/19/89), but the lively conversation with Arafat, who questions Wallace's interpretions, also opens the analyst to a more self-conscious stance about his reportorial role in constructing sense.

A visual device that personalizes the reporter also comes into play in the analyst segments. In contrast to the detective formula in which the reporter is typically shot no closer than medium range, in the analyst formula the camera zooms in considerably closer in reaction or question shots with the interview subject. For example, in "A Wild and Crazy Guy?" Sawyer, who accompanies Steve Martin to an art museum, is also featured in close reaction shots in an interview scene in Martin's living room. In "More Than a Touch of Class" (4/7/74), the interview with Glenda Jackson in a London pub, Wallace appears three times in close-up shots and in one extreme close-up where part of his forehead is cut off; in none of the detective narratives featuring Wallace is the shot composed this tightly.

Subject as Hero or Villain

A third characteristic of the analyst segments, the treatment of characters as heroes and villains, also involves the use of visual space. Interview subjects in these narratives are treated as either representatives of mainstream values (heroic) or marginal countervalues (villainous). In certain segments, the interviewee receives equal visual space with the reporter. These narratives generally portray the subject heroically, that is, the interviewee appears also as an enforcer of, or model for, basic values. For example, in "Extremism in the Defense of Liberty" (7/20/75), Karl Hess, who has "progressed" from his job as Barry Goldwater's "arch-conservative" speech writer to inner-city social reformer, receives visual space similar to Morley Safer, who appears mostly in waist-up medium and long shots.

When an interview subject appears as a deviant from mainstream virtues and a polarizer of tensions, the camera denies visual space (this is also true for victims, those who are caught in gray areas between tensions they cannot resolve). For example, in "The Shah of Iran," Wallace battles the Shah in an interview that features symbolic conflict between American democracy and a foreign dictatorship. The villainous Shah appears almost totally in extreme closeups that, at times, cut both his forehead and chin from the frame. Wallace, featured in nearly forty shots in this segment, receives much more visual space. In most shots we can see the reporter's hands at work in the frame, demonstrating that Wallace is in more control of the space around him. And it is Wallace who affirms American ideals in the face of the Shah, who stands for foreign, tyrannical countervalues.

Another visual technique that separates heroic from villainous or victimized subjects involves the camera's depiction of private artifacts, a device that personalizes interview subjects. In "The Empress" (5/18/75), for instance, a profile story of the then Empress of Iran, shots create a contrast between public ceremonies and private, more intimate moments featuring the empress with her children at a birthday party. Other shots in this narrative also help resolve a conflict between public and private through familiar glimpses of a living room featuring family artifacts that portray the empress as a model of simplicity, modesty, and motherhood in spite of her regal position and wealth. By contrast, the camera generally ignores the private, personal lives of villains. In "The Shah of Iran," for example, we do not see him with his children, at birthday parties, in an intimate living room, nor are we told stories from his youth. The questions and the visuals focus not on the private but on the sociopolitical nature of his alleged public, anti-American, anti-democratic postures. And although these two segments treat wife and husband very differently, narrative boundaries hide these differences and pack them off to a region outside the report.

Reporter as Inquisitor

A final characteristic of the analyst formula features provocative confrontational questions that generally probe deviations from values. The reporters display this characteristic by confronting and questioning characters who are portrayed, at least during a part of the interview, as representing countervalues. In "General Ky and Big Minh" (10/21/71), for example, Mike Wallace asks General Ky if he plans to overthrow the South Vietnamese government. "No coups on your mind?" Wallace asks as he confronts Ky on questions on disloyalty, anti-democracy, and deception. In "Anderson of Illinois," Morley Safer challenges the 1980 presidential candidate on his plan to cut federal spending: "Well, so what are you saying? Abandon the cities?" At the end of this narrative, Safer couches the "tough" question in negative comments made by other reporters: "It's kind of interesting . . . the perception of John Anderson. For example, this Washington *Post* headline is 'Dream Candidate Going Nowhere.' Tom Wicker, a liberal columnist in the New York *Times,* says the man running on either side can't win. Conventional wisdom? Leo Durocher says nice guys finish last. What do you say to all that?" Safer here implicitly seeks moral closure; he wants Anderson to take a stand in relation to common sense.

Generally, the provocative question allows the reporter to express moral indignation against people and positions that violate common-sense values. For example, in "Invade Nicaragua?" (10/27/85), Mike Wallace berates the young chief of staff of Nicaragua's military for naively excepting weapons from the Soviets. Wallace asks the Sandinista commandante if the Soviets "want a piece of the revolution," and he responds, "No. I don't know what they want. . . ." Wallace reacts as our surrogate, "Come on! You know they're not doing it just out of the goodness of their hearts." As analyst, Wallace here attempts to straddle tensions between communism and democracy, and he re-centers the narrative on the side of democratic ideals. A major function of the provocative question sequences, which are often featured in other *60 Minutes* formulas, locates the reporter in the middle, between us and them, between private and public tensions. Indeed, as Ian Connell has noted, "The 'hard,' 'tough' style of interviewing . . . was legitimized as an attempt 'to get at the facts' on behalf of the public. This adoption of a 'watchdog' role on behalf of the ordinary voters also led to the attempted identifications with 'us,' and the attempts to articulate the kinds of questions that 'we' would ask of 'our' powerful representatives if 'we' only could."[37] In the analyst formula, posing tough questions includes the viewer in the reporter's point of view, clarifies narrative tension, and sets the stage for mediation.

The Case of the Probing Analyst

A segment that illustrates the analyst formula is "What Became of Eldridge Cleaver?" (5/18/75, Appendix C). William McClure and Paul Loewenwarter produced the narrative; Mike Wallace is featured as the reporter-analyst interviewing the former Black Panther party leader, who at the time of the interview was living in exile in Paris. This segment runs ten minutes, fifty-seven seconds, and contains seventy-two shots.

Sequence 1 contains two shots and runs thirty-seven seconds. As historical analyst, Wallace offers an opening viewpoint on violence and the place of the Black Panther party amid the culture of the 1960s: " 'Violence is as American as cherry pie'—a black revolutionary said it in the sixties as black violence hit our major cities and law and order sometimes became police brutality. It was the black Panthers who were the most militant of all blacks then, a gun-toting cadre self-appointed to protect the black ghetto, they said from the white 'pigs.' And Eldridge Cleaver was then the most vocal of the Panthers."

This sequence sets up a number of key narrative oppositions between white and black, past and present, and normalcy and deviance. The convoluted use of the Middle-American "cherry pie" slogan dramatically sets the stage. As social critic, Wallace identifies the Black Panthers as the "most militant of all blacks" during the sixties, and Cleaver as "the most vocal" Panther. The tightly cropped photo of Cleaver just to the right of Wallace in the frame also suggests the close scrutiny to which Wallace will subject Cleaver in this probing narrative. Wallace makes a case that the Panthers of the 1960s were associated with "gun-toting" and violence, concepts outside the boundaries of commonsensical, established cultural activity. There is the suggestion here that "black violence" *caused* "police brutality" and disrupted the normal order of society. Following this opening statement, Wallace then foreshadows two possibilities for Cleaver's present state of mind—he may still think as he did in the 1960s or he may be "cured."

Sequence 2 is the first of three flashbacks from a 1970 segment, which serves as the past, in juxtaposition with scenes in this 1975 narrative, which represent the present. Sequence 2 contains eleven shots and runs one minute, forty-seven seconds. It opens with a bit of detective work as Wallace in trench coat takes us back to the scene of Cleaver's shoot-out with the police. He establishes Cleaver as a criminal fugitive. This sequence presents a late 1960s' version of Cleaver as a villain who threatened Middle America. Shifting to his role as analyst, Wallace represents us in this sequence as he asks Cleaver in 1970 about the meaning of his violent rhetoric and what effect it might have had on "the American people." A key visual shot in the segment features Cleaver sitting with his wife and child as he holds up the clenched fist of the child in a "power to the people" salute in this apparent portrait of an American family gone bad. Wallace's voice-over then offers a list of Cleaver's threats of physical attacks on government leaders. The main function of this flashback scene is to establish Cleaver in 1970 as a villain who subverted commonsense notions of normalcy. Cleaver's role is underscored by the length of time he is shot in tight visual close-ups with the top of his head and bottom of his chin cut from the frame. At times, the camera takes a low-angle approach to him, which strengthens his menacing rhetoric; at other times, given that his space is so restricted, his face appears to jump out of the frame during his animated discussion in which he is shown in extreme close-ups. Visually, Cleaver seems out of control.

Wallace, however, is shot here in medium and over-the-shoulder shots that give him more control over his place in the narrative. His voice-over commentary dominates; Cleaver does not speak until nearly two minutes into the narrative. In opposition to Cleaver, then, Wallace looks and sounds "normal." The narrower focus and visual presentation support Cleaver's "deviant" position. The foreignness of Cleaver's 1970 politics is further strengthened in the visual shots of street scenes and veiled women in Algiers (his new home after his self-imposed exile).

Sequence 3 lasts one minute, forty seconds, and has ten shots. It continues Wallace's narration, updating filmed footage from the 1970 segment. Wallace as historian acquaints us with the Black Panther movement since Cleaver fled the United States. As analyst, Wallace continues to portray Cleaver in a negative fashion, implying that he was a coward for fleeing while other "law-abiding" Black Panthers served prison terms. The Panthers who did not "flee" have now been purged of their deviance by answering to the normal American system justice. Shots of jailed or dead Panthers juxtaposed with earlier shots of Cleaver free in Algiers underscore Wallace's narration. This sequence ultimately portrays the radical Panthers who "remained home" as the norm in contrast to Cleaver, who looks doubly deviant for abandoning his fellow revolutionaries, who Wallace interprets as a "small, demoralized, beleaguered group" in Cleaver's absence.

The second part of the sequence reveals Wallace critiquing Panther activities in the 1960s and early 1970s as "brainwash indoctrination." The visual representation features a young black teacher leading a class of children; they are using Cleaver's own 1960s slogans ("Pick up the gun," "off the pigs"). The visuals support Wallace's indictment by placing the children in the extreme bottom frame of a number of shots, with the teacher and posters of black revolutionaries looming over them. Another shot presents a young black girl with a blue ribbon in her hair raising a clenched fist; Wallace's voice-over narration in this sequence refers to "brainwash indoctrination about the pigs." The visuals also undermine the credibility of the teaching session by showing two black girls, distracted and apparently too young to understand what is going on, fighting with each other. Earlier Wallace's narration had undermined shots of the Panther "serving the people" slogan with voice-overs about police shoot-outs and other acts of deviant behavior by the Panthers. Although this

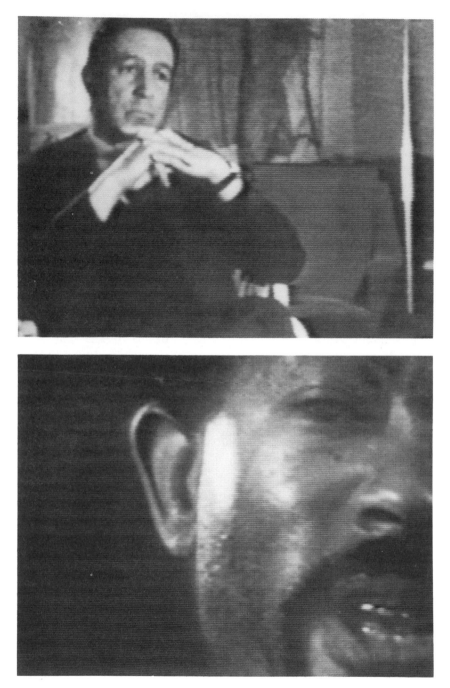

In this two-shot series, detached analyst Wallace, champion for the common-sense of normalcy, sits in marked contrast to the "deviant" Eldridge Cleaver, framed so tightly at times that his head occasionally lunges off the screen. (© MCMLXXV–CBS Inc. All rights reserved.)

sequence features on-screen narration from the teachers, Wallace's voice-overs dominate and undercut the "indoctrination." After shots which show a teacher talking favorably about Black Panthers Huey Newton and Bobby Seale, Wallace's narration interrupts the on-screen voice in order to tell us that these "heroes" are really only common criminals who stand in opposition to centrist norms. Wallace's verbal authority in this sequence ultimately suggests that what he offers is truth or actual knowledge about the history of the Panthers, whereas the teachers sympathetic to the Panthers offer only rhetoric and indoctrination. Visuals that show distracted and disruptive children further support, by contrast, Wallace's stability and normalcy as well-informed social analyst. In a subtle way, he also becomes the heroic individual matched against the deviant and doctrinaire "institutional" organization that constitutes the Panthers.

Sequence 4, a flashback sequence recapping Cleaver's life in the late sixties and early seventies, lasts one minute, fifteen seconds, and contains ten shots. The sequence continues Wallace's analysis of the Panther party and updates us about more Panthers who have served prison sentences while Cleaver has enjoyed "freedom" in exile. Concomitantly in this sequence, Cleaver poses explicit and major tensions from his viewpoint, between freedom and oppression, between liberation and imperialism. In an interview setting, Cleaver associates himself and black people with middle-class values of freedom and individuality, while at the same time suggesting that the U.S. government and the upper classes represent the "fascist, imperialist, social order." Visual background artifacts of black artwork and black families personalize Cleaver and support his narration. Cleaver is portrayed more frequently in a full head shot rather than in tight close-ups; greater head room evokes a sense of control and stability in contrast to the unstable and constrained feeling that the tight head shots conveyed in the earlier interview. Social critic Wallace, however, has the last word and undercuts Cleaver's position with his accounts of a Panther plane hijacking and Cleaver's "wearing out his welcome" in Algeria.

The last two shots in the sequence also contradict Cleaver's narration and reinforce Wallace's point of view. The visual shots that support Wallace, first, feature the "alien" Algiers street scene, and second, frame Cleaver in a tight close-up with the camera zooming in as Wallace's voice-over puts Cleaver in perspective at the end of the sequence. Wallace's narration and analysis dominate this sequence in which Cleaver is briefly permitted to espouse support for a competing set of commonsense values. Wallace takes over at the end of the sequence, however, by discrediting Cleaver for condoning the hijacking. Wallace's credibility as a legitimate reporter-analyst is supported here again by the association of his narration with America, truth, and commonsense knowledge. The rhetoric of Cleaver, an illegitimate fugitive now a citizen of a foreign land, pales in comparison to Wallace's well-informed position.

Sequence 5 brings us to present time—in this case, 1975. The sequence contains fifteen shots and lasts two minutes, twenty seconds. This is the narrative's transition sequence in which the deviant positions of Cleaver are made explicit and the therapeutic norms that Wallace sets up are affirmed. Geographically, the scene shifts from mysterious Algiers to the familiarity of Paris and its Western cultural landmarks. Wallace refers to a "graying Eldridge Cleaver" by which he means both Cleaver's age and his rejection of issues as merely black and white. Visually, the militant posters and intense portraits of black leaders from the 1970 footage have been displaced behind Cleaver; a zebra skin now hangs on the wall. Verbally, the "fascist, imperialist social order" of sequence 4 has become "the system" in sequence 5. Cleaver admits that "the system" solved the Nixon administration problem without the kind of violence Cleaver once advocated, although he argues that the system worked because of the "pressure" that he and others exerted.

As analyst, Wallace diagnoses and verbally resolves the difficult tensions posed earlier in this narrative by eliciting from Cleaver an admission that his "deviant" tactics were not necessary. Resolution continues when Cleaver addresses his personal therapist as "Mike," and when he reveals a lack of "knowledge" about handling a "political situation" through nonviolent tactics. Visual support for Cleaver's transformation comes in his increased access to visual space as this interview with Wallace unfolds. Starting in sequence 4, when we learn of the Algerian government's unhappiness with Cleaver and his support of hijacking, up through the middle of sequence 5, Cleaver is portrayed usually at close range, with forehead, chin, or both chopped from the frame, whereas the more detached reporter-analyst is revealed generally in waist-up, medium-range shots. However, beginning with the shot in which Cleaver first eschews violence

A "graying" and "cured" Eldridge Cleaver, "no longer a black symbol of resistance," receives a bit more visual space toward the end of the narrative. (© MCMLXXV–CBS Inc. All rights reserved.)

as a revolutionary tactic, Cleaver is granted more of the same kind of space Wallace receives—medium and full-head shots—through the rest of the sequence. His access to greater space allows his hands to move within the frame, and we see his "liberation"—his cure— from the confining space of earlier shots and earlier rhetoric. His former deviant positions are in the process of healing. Cleaver is now in better control of the space around him. The *60 Minutes* therapy is working, and Cleaver is becoming "normal."

Sequence 6 contains fifteen shots and lasts two minutes, forty-six seconds. The segment opens by juxtaposing the family man, a now-serene, "graying" Cleaver strolling the streets of Paris in the shadow of a cathedral, with flashback images of Cleaver shooting at the police and raising his child's fist in a black power salute. The outdoor shot of Cleaver and his wife along the Left Bank contrasts with the bullet-ridden, burned-out house Mike Wallace showed us in sequence 2. The relaxed, pipe-smoking author in a medium to long shot at his typewriter contrasts sharply with the 1970 version of Cleaver. The 1975 Cleaver confronts the ghosts of his past deviancy. He tells

Wallace he wants to "come home"; he's ready to stand trial and go to prison like other Panthers before him. In the sequence's climax, Wallace as analyst-confessor has Cleaver "renounce" violence and communism. Cleaver now apparently associates freedom with the United States rather than with the foreign countries that supported his exile. He confesses that "the system" works, that "our institutions, rather than be destroyed," need to be "perfected" and "developed." Cleaver now asserts that adherence to middle-class norms (patriotism, freedom, peace, home, and family) will empower the individual in the battle with imperfect and powerful institutions. Deviance from those norms—as Cleaver advocated in the first three sequences— apparently cannot resolve social tensions.

A final key mediation involves Cleaver's affirmation of his "true home"—the United States. His authentication of home comes about because of his return to standard norms and his renunciation of past behavior. His show of patriotism at the end of the sequence mediates between the 1970 Cleaver, deviant revolutionary, and the 1975 Cleaver, normal citizen. Wallace, as both confessor and therapist, pronounces Cleaver repentant, cured of his deviance—"no longer a black symbol of resistance to white capitalism, imperialism."

Sequence 7 closes the narrative in one brief shot that runs thirty-two seconds. Wallace tells of the death of Cleaver's father and that Cleaver cannot "come home" for the funeral. Wallace also provides historical analysis and updates of the present group of Black Panthers. His sudden switch from Cleaver's personal loss and disappointment to the social change and "success" of the Panthers offers a symmetrical moral closure—the Panthers following Cleaver's own penitent course. Instead of the violent revolutionaries referred to in the opening sequence, analyst Wallace reports on a "changed outfit," now "working" and "muted." They too are apparently cured, "nonviolent" reformers hard at work "inside the system." The Panthers' adjustment from deviance to normalcy obscures Cleaver's personal loss and closes the narrative with a comforting image, parallel to Cleaver's own repentance and return to normalcy.

In this analyst segment, as in the exemplary detective narrative, the reporter sorts out positive virtues from their apparent negative counterparts, thereby endowing the narrative with common sense and moral meaning: Cleaver must pay a price when he oversteps the bounds of a society's rules and that once that price is paid, society forgives.

Conflicts between person and society, tradition and change, which shape many analyst segments, are often resolved through the presence of a character whose moral code once deviated from centrist virtues. Wallace introduces the concept and value of repentance in order to resolve opposition between the concrete entities of the story, a radical Cleaver and the Black Panthers versus established government leaders, and the abstract concepts that both sets of characters represent: revolution and status quo, deviance and normalcy, change and tradition. The transformation of Cleaver's idiosyncratic experience into the myth of prodigal son resuming his place in society requires that Wallace oversee the struggle between opposed sets of moral values. It is not merely the introduction of the concept of repentance that resolves this particular narrative, but the performance of Wallace domesticating deviant attitudes, curing the patient, and comforting a Middle-American audience.

Realizing the Self

Within the formula frame, the therapy narratives call for resolution of central social as well as narrative tensions. As in the detective segments, a chief mission of the reporter is to resolve fundamental, emotional, and conceptual oppositions. In "Martin Luther King's Family at Christmas," for example, Mike Wallace mediates a struggle between life and death in the closing sequence: "Martin Luther King left a legacy for all of us, but we cannot fail to understand especially at this Christmas season. But he left us, too, Coretta King." Mrs. King then discusses "creative suffering" and argues that despite the tragedy "it doesn't mean we will sit around and bathe in our grief." Wallace, as curative mediator, celebrates the presence of Coretta King and her family as a solution to the enigma. As I have suggested, other narratives also offer the family as a solution for social as well as personal conflicts and suffering. Resolution and moral meaning for the audience in these segments are enabled through the probing, guiding questions of the reporter-therapist.

In other segments, the reporter is harder on the interview subject but with the similar effect. "Man of Honor" (3/27/83), for example, is a story about greed, corruption, and murder—integral parts of mythic stories about the Mafia. Mike Wallace confronts alleged Mafia leader Joe Bonanno about mob killings: "Who orders a hit? Who orders a killing?" Wallace spends much of the narrative asking similar questions that reveal criminal values and attitudes antithetical to Middle America. Yet in the final sequence—a Bonanno family Christmas dinner—tension dissolves as virtues of family, tradition, and religion displace earlier dramatic confrontations. Bonanno's final words end the sequence: "God bless you." And in those words deviance merges with middle-class normalcy.

The Bonanno and Cleaver segments both offer a metaphorical framework for transforming the abstract and less familiar categories of deviance and normalcy, tradition and change, into the more concrete and familiar terms of a dramatic news narrative. Within the structure of the analyst formula, mediation—indeed therapy—transpires as reporters rescue the mysteries of human experience from apparent contradiction, thereby endowing the narrative referent with meaning and sense.

There are moments in certain analyst segments that are revelations of the intricacies of human experience, that stand back from the contradiction and allow it to exist. "The Enemy" (3/19/89) features such a moment. Morley Safer introduces this analyst segment about North Vietnamese soldiers who fought against the United States during the Vietnam War: "More and more American veterans . . . are returning to Vietnam—confronting the enemy—not merely out of curiosity but as therapy to lay to rest the ghosts of that war." Safer then shifts the focus to a powerful interview-therapy scene, offering the following exchange about the war between Safer and a former Viet Cong soldier, now an English teacher in Vietnam:

> SAFER: Did you ever have any doubts about why you were there?
> TEACHER: Never—
> SAFER: Was there ever a time or day when the whole thing just made no sense at all to you?
> TEACHER: One day when I was terribly ill—I suffered from malaria— I didn't think about death then but I felt terribly lonely—on the hammock, in the rainy season, deep in the forest.

Safer probes here, but he also listens. Instead of playing up political tensions between us and them, the narrative catches up the theme of an individual caught in war. As this soldier-teacher poignantly reconstructs his stories of the past, his nightmares, his fear of the jungle, juxtaposed with American soldiers who retell their stories and dreams, Safer leads us to common ground—not necessarily the terrain of shared political values or middle-class norms but of self.

In *Habits of the Heart,* Bellah and his colleagues attribute to the therapist what are also features of the contemporary reporter: "For all its genuine emotional content, closeness, and honesty of communication, the therapeutic relationship is particularly distanced, circumscribed, and asymmetrical. Most of the time one person talks and the other listens. The client almost always talks about himself and the therapist almost never does. . . . The therapist's authority seems to derive from psychological knowledge and clinical skill, not from moral values. The therapist is there not to judge but to help clients become able to make their own judgments. The therapist is, nonetheless, even in not judging, a model for the client."[38] Although moralizing may be more explicit in the relationship between *60 Minutes*'s reporters and their "clients" (on-screen interview subjects), reporters cherish—as do many contemporary professionals—their ability in democracy to lead us to judgments that we can make ourselves based on the stock of well-informed knowledge they provide.

In the greater intimacy of the analyst narratives, there is also both a closeness and a distance; reporters reveal very little about themselves while interview subjects reveal much. This asymmetrical relationship is not problematic for most reporters, just as it is not problematic for many therapists, since they believe—and we believe with them—that distance endows them with a richer skill in seeing the "way things really are."

In our culture, even the most conventional news serves a therapeutic function by marking off boundaries between deviancy and normalcy, sickness and wellness. In the choices conventional reporters make regarding crime and corruption narratives, there are embedded implicit moral judgments that help readers and viewers sort out those experiences that either affirm or deviate from their own values. John Cawelti argues that formulaic stories, whether front-page news reports, *60 Minutes* analyst narratives, or classical detective fiction, allow the audience to survey "the boundary between the permitted and the forbidden and to experience in a carefully controlled way the possibility of stepping across this boundary."[39] So the murder story on page one of the Detroit *Free Press,* the Mike Wallace interview with a Mafia leader or a Black Panther, the *Co-*

lumbo detective story share in maintaining the thin moral distinction between the normal and the deviant, the permitted and the forbidden—a moral line that serves common sense.

Just as the detective hero emerged in contemporary America as a standard-bearer for individualism, therapists and all their modern spin-offs—including well-informed reporters—take up the battle against bureaucracy, deviance, and the undermining of self. But increasingly, both professional postures suggest a jagged break between the heroic individual and the villainous institution. And rather than provide ways to repair this break, our contemporary narrative formulas intensify and solidify the gap as natural, as part of common-sense knowledge. And the *60 Minutes* analyst formula in particular—by isolating interview subjects and focusing attention on individual characters and reporters—points to few ways to examine or recover the individual's standing within institutions in this era of bureaucracy.

In a society dominated by the values of individualism, news as therapy finally supports the existing social order by facilitating people's adaptation to "the way things are." With this prevailing centrist order accepted as a constant, as it is in the Eldridge Cleaver story, *60 Minutes* in these analyst narratives frequently views problems only as individual ones which affirm or deviate from a taken-for-granted center. In their critique of therapy and individualism, Bellah and his colleagues warn us about the limits of the therapeutic context: "What is not questioned is the institutional context. One's 'growth' is a purely private matter. It may involve maneuvering within the structure of bureaucratic rules and roles, changing jobs. . . . But what is missing is any collective context in which one might act as a participant to change the institutional structures that frustrate and limit. Therapy . . . lacks any public forum."[40]

The potential of *60 Minutes* is that it presents the therapeutic spectrum of news in the public forum of television. Its narrative news formula, however, too often defines the public dimension only in terms of the personal idiosyncrasies of its characters—in terms of Eldridge Cleaver's individual problems—rather than leading us to a larger critical forum on the institutional frameworks that frustrate an Eldridge Cleaver and all of us trying to make common sense and "recover the narrative unity of our lives."[41]

News and Adventure: The Quest for Authenticity

5

> Those [*60 Minutes* reporters] are the white hats, and every week they ride off into the twilight looking for the black hats, doctors who rip people off, phony cancer institutes, car dealers who are cheating. It's a western.
>
> —Burton Benjamin

> I hate the word "documentary." No one wants to read a document. For God's sake, who wants to watch a documentary? Bill Moyers did a thing called *CBS Reports: Illegal Aliens.* It was great, but it should have been called *The Gonzales Brothers,* and the ads should have shown the immigration service chasing two wetbacks through the back alleys of Los Angeles.
>
> —Don Hewitt

> Television is not, to my way of thinking, primarily a means of communication. It is rather, a means of transportation, whereby its vast audience can be instantly transported to various world stages where history is enacted.
>
> —Edward R. Murrow

60 Minutes works, according to Don Hewitt, because it is about the "adventures" of five reporters. The perception of *60 Minutes* as adventure, as a Western, suggests images of reporters, often on unfamiliar ground, overcoming obstacles to accomplish some moral mission—a feature of any good adventure narrative. John Cawelti lists a rich variety among adventure formula plots and themes: "the triumph over injustice and the threat of lawlessness in the western; the saving of the nation in the spy story; the overcoming of fear and the defeat of the enemy in the combat story."[1]

The adventure story formula in *60 Minutes* offers a new variation of the hero: the reporter as tourist, a well-informed wayfarer traveling the world in search of drama. The same sets of nineteenth-century historical conditions that prepared the way for the analyst also contributed to the importance of the tourist to twentieth-century culture. Urbanization and secularization, the "prepackaged artificiality" of modern technology, fractured the ties to "primary experience" and tradition.[2] These changes initiated a twentieth-century search for the past, for lost identity, for *real* experience.

In tracing the bureaucratization of America, a strong link exists between the resistance to impersonal institutions and a general restlessness in the human spirit that drives us to travel and adventure. Marking the turn of the century as the greatest period in wayfaring between Europe and America, within America that same period saw substantial movements from country to city, and from East to West.[3] Enigmatically, these two directions ran counter—one movement toward a modified open frontier and manifest destiny, the other toward the civilizing potential, the technological marvel, and the monetary promise of the city. Among other things, we sought space, freedom, power, property, money, safety, security, identity, status, and ultimately how and where we fit within the larger social order. Beginning in the 1950s, the move to (and meaning of) the suburbs symbolically mediated the tension of an America traveling in two directions: the claiming of open space just outside the city with expressway access to civilization, yet in a place at the edge of farmland. And just beyond, wilderness and the natural. It is not mere coincidence that the middle classes located themselves comfortably at the crossroads of this middle ground.[4]

In *The Tourist,* Dean MacCannell defines modern tourists as wayfarers, adventurers, and "sightseers, mainly middle class, who are at this moment deployed throughout the entire world in search of experience."[5] Tourists implicitly seek resolutions for contradictions between nature and civilization, humanity and technology, tradition and modernization: "For moderns, reality and authenticity are thought to be elsewhere: in other historical periods and other cultures, in purer, simpler lifestyles." Our preoccupation with the real, with the natural, and with the nostalgic represents part of the contradictory and "conquering spirit of modernity."[6] We can see the contradiction daily in the commercials that dominate television featuring synthetic products posturing as real and natural. These twin adjectives saturate American advertisements, which, despite the alluring claims and the nostalgia for premodern times, describe processed and manufactured products.

This substitution of the manufactured for the natural, the image for the real, is a major theme in Daniel Boorstin's *The Image: A Guide to Pseudo-Events in America.* Boorstin connects practices in both conventional news and contemporary tourism to the "pseudo-event," a "new kind of synthetic novelty which has flooded our experience." In modernized, commercialized, technologized America, we have apparently changed the meaning and spirit of adventure—in both news and tourism—to unspontaneous, calculated pseudo-events, to "contrived experience that somebody is trying to sell us."[7] Boorstin too is nostalgic for a premodern sense of adventure, for authenticity and tradition, for real news-gathering and real traveling: "One of the most ancient motives for travel . . . was to see the unfamiliar. Man's incurable desire to go someplace else is a testimony of his incurable optimism and insatiable curiosity. We always expect things to be different over there."[8]

Despite Boorstin's critique of modern journalism, the touristlike pursuit of authentic experience also anchors the practice of reporting, particularly the less conventional forms such as investigative and literary journalism. According to Dean O'Brien, "journalists, also in search of authenticity, travel from one source, event and sight to another," trying "to penetrate the markers and the 'staged authenticity' of front regions (news releases, government hand-outs, pseudo-events) to reach genuine back regions."[9] Contemporary reporters try to break through what they regard as those "front regions"—the theatrical rhetoric of politicians, the publicity brochures of business, and the manufactured dispatches of government bureaucrats. Like well-informed tourists, reporters also search for the authentic; they want to penetrate artificial facades in order to write or air reports that reveal "the way it really is."

60 Minutes heightens the drama of this quest by locating its adventure stories in one of two locales: in the familiar American heartland or in the more exotic settings of foreign countries. Both narrative types intriguingly reverse the pattern of movement in the early part of this century. Instead of Europe-to-America, *60 Minutes* travels back to Europe and to exotic places beyond; instead of country-to-city, *60 Minutes* visits small-town America. Both types seek to recover a lost cultural center by retracing old paths and rediscovering the traditional and the natural. As viewers, we vicariously accompany reporters in this quest to get beyond the artificial and back to the real. Just as the detective seeks to resolve problems between honesty and injustice, between safety and danger, the adventure hero of *60 Minutes* repairs contradictions between nature and civilization, between tradition and modernization, between the familiar and the exotic, and between the self and society.

The Adventure Formula

The adventure stories of *60 Minutes* display several recurring characteristics; they portray the reporter-tourist (1) acting as our surrogate in exploring and describing the new or unfamiliar, (2) searching for authenticity by trying to recover the past, the natural, and by smashing through the facade of contemporary civilization and technology, and (3) confronting villains, usually portrayed as either bureaucracies, alien values, or modernity itself (often in the guise of modern Americanization).

The segments that portray the reporter-tourist in Middle America often begin by affirming their dramatic structure. For example, Dan Rather as our surrogate, in jeans, travels the country in "Wildcat Trucker" (2/22/76). He begins the narrative, "There's a new brand of folk hero around these days—the wildcat trucker. Like the cowboy and the gold miner and the aerial barnstormer of an earlier era, he's taking his place in Americana." Again in "Charity Begins at Home" (2/4/79), a story about a town that "takes on the state of New Jersey over the issue of welfare," Morley Safer takes us on a tour of small-town America. Locating the story in the world of fiction, Safer as narrator begins the tale: "This is one of those *Our Town* kind of stories, and if you were writing it as fiction, there are certain things you'd have to include" such as an "ice cream parlor" and a "hardware store." He adds, "The tale we have to tell is one of those late twentieth-century American dramas."

Other segments explicitly connect traditional virtues with these heartland locations. Safer illustrates this connection at the beginning of "The Gospel According to Whom?" (1/23/83), a story about church donations used to fund political causes: "A fairly typical Sunday morning in a fairly typical town. Americans are still among the most church-going people in the world. . . . Logansport [Indiana] is Middle America and proud of it."

Acting as Surrogate

In describing a guiding myth of modernity, MacCannell notes that "the position of the person who stays at home in the modern world is morally inferior to that of a person who 'gets out' often" because "authentic experiences are believed to be available only to those moderns who try to break the bonds of their everyday existence and begin to 'live.' "[10] To an extent, television news mediates the tension experienced by those of us caught in the routine of everyday life. News can take us on an adventure—to unfamiliar locations outside our homes.

In their more exotic travels, *60 Minutes* reporters function in part as tour guides, who accompany us to foreign places and remind us of "reality and authenticity elsewhere."[11] For example, in "1000% Inflation" (3/12/89), a story about the growing disparity between rich and poor in Brazil, Mike Wallace renders this exotic place familiar as he tours the streets of Rio de Janiero. He sits beneath a shade umbrella, beer in hand, listening to street musicians; he then describes the soaring cost of living. In a light blue shirt and white cotton slacks, he strolls through an open market questioning vendors about the cost of bread and fruit. Against the spectacular backdrop and postcard peaks of the Rio hillside, he addresses us in a navy polo shirt about what is happening in this foreign place. Accompanied by a Catholic missionary, he treks up the steep back alleys of a "shanty town," and we learn firsthand about the decrepit conditions of Rio's marginalized classes. In contrast, in plaid sport shirt and light summer trousers, our reporter-tourist strolls along a Rio pier with a wealthy local businessman against the setting of lavish yachts. In the short span of a thirteen-to-fourteen-minute narrative, *60 Minutes* has interpreted and transformed this different place, taking us to real locales and authenticating Brazilian experience.

In another example, "Paris Was Yesterday" (4/22/73), Wallace dines at a Parisian cafe and narrates a sightseeing tour about old and new Paris; he becomes our surrogate, rendering this unfamiliar place accessible and familiar. Again in "Oman" (8/24/80), a story about a U.S. military base in the Mideast, Wallace dons shorts and relaxes with a newspaper at poolside. In voice-over narration, he comments about his role in the narrative: "Even Americans aren't especially welcome as tourists," a comment that implicitly includes us in partnership with Wallace—our adventure story hero—as he dares to tour exotic lands.

Searching for the Natural

"How to Live to Be 100" (7/5/81) illustrates another feature of the adventure-tourist formula. Here Morley Safer investigates the longevity of a particular community of Russians, attributing their endurance to an authentic lifestyle not covered over with layers of modernity. The reporter lists the community's rules and values: "food from earth, not from a can; hard physical labor, not the so-called leisure years, and above all an unbreakable belief in family life that makes age more important than youth or wealth." A visual counterpart to his narration features a 107-year-old man bathing in the natural setting of a cold mountain stream. Similarly, in "Yanks in Iran" (1/2/77), Mike Wallace talks to disappointed American citizens who had come to Iran on a failed search for identity and authenticity. One character, who has decided to leave Iran after eight years, tells Wallace about other Americans who "think they're coming to the promised land." Shots of traditionally dressed Iranians and plain white homes oppose shots of modern billboards and a sound track of radio advertising for Pepsi, 7-Up, and Caterpillar tractors. The disgruntled character then discusses the expenses, drugs, "smog, noise, cars," and other symbols of modernization that have disrupted the Americans' quest. These explicit symbols of artificiality pose a set of countervalues to the commonsense traditions of moderation and pastoralism.

In the less exotic heartland tales, part of what is accomplished is not only the authentication of the reporter's presence, but also the verification that these places display genuine small-town markers and symbols: the ice cream parlor, the hardware store, the meeting hall, the church, the diner, and main street. The established authenticity and individuality of the small town then is contrasted with the artificiality and impersonality of the institutional city. For example, the opening of "Away from It All?" (8/1/76) establishes a quest for an authentic experience that apparently can be found only in a small-town setting. The reporter here asks if we ever had the feeling that we "wanted to get away from it all—pollution, taxes, pressure." Shots of neon signs and congested urban streets, the symbols for the indifferent big city, are then contrasted visually with shots of a lake, a church, an inn, barns, horses, and a waterfall in Dairy, New Hampshire.

Confronting Aliens and Modernity

A major conflict in these adventure segments, particularly the foreign segments, pits near against far or us (the United States) against them—a narrative conflict often used in fictional spy stories, in adventure movies like *Rocky IV*, in sports stories about the Olympics, or in Persian Gulf news reports. Here generally the villain is some "backward" or alien set of values. In "Yugoslavia" (2/17/80), for example, Dan Rather interviews a foreign couple who affirm Middle-American values in contrast to the apparently more repressive, centralized values of communism. This narrative portrays a view of socialist Yugoslavia as a U.S. ally modeled on our own culture. Rather tells the Yugoslav couple, "It strikes me, as you talk, that your life here is very much like middle-class life in the United States or England." *60 Minutes* then reveals a scene in a Yugoslav nightclub with the couple out for an evening of dinner and dancing. With "When the Saints Go Marching In" playing in the background, Rather offers this voice-over narration: "The scene is Korcula. It could be Saturday night in Kalamazoo. Dancing to American jazz music mixed with Yugoslav rock. In many other important ways, this is happening in Yugoslav society."

With this narrative, *60 Minutes* merges the themes of its exotic foreign land and American heartland formulas. The characters in this story support consumerism and speak proudly of newly purchased middle-class conveniences. These individuals from a foreign country appear heroic through association with values of democracy, individualism, and capitalism. The Soviet Union, as the agent for villainous communism, emerges as a distant institutional force (visually unrepresented in this story). As villain, the Soviets lose the support of individuals, or at least the support of this couple who, in spite of life in a communist society, apparently prefer American virtues and commodities.

Whereas in the foreign-place segments, the villain is typically foreign values or modernization, in the heartland stories the villain is more often an institution (located in the artificial city rather than the natural country). In "New York Is Falling Apart" (2/19/89) the villain, the decrepit city and its maze of malodorous and run-down tunnels, opposes the victimized citizens who must endure the city's sprawling decay.

This direct attack on the modern city as villain, however, is rare on *60 Minutes*. More typically the city or some other nefarious institution remains absent in the narrative. Rarely represented visually (as in the mystery segments), the city and its countervalues become menacing in their absence. For example, in "Rural Justice" (2/22/76), the absent values of the urban legal profession oppose the law and order code of small-town South Carolina magistrates. Contrasted with the "big city" legal system (which demands that rural magistrates hold law degrees) are these small-town judges, one of whom moonlights as a night watchman. In emphasizing the importance of humility and individualism, this rural judge tells Morley Safer that he refuses to wear a judicial robe because "it would scare people," and he wants to "make them feel at home. . . . I take this little magistrate's job to heart." While five rural judges are portrayed visually, no one from urban legal institutions appears in this segment. The concrete presence of individual magistrates, who connote intimacy and hospitality, contrast here with the law profession. Reinforced by its menacing absence, the urban legal system connotes unfamiliarity and hostility.

A final aspect of this adventure formula emphasizes modernization-bureaucracy and its role in concealing or destroying authentic experience. In "Seward's Folly" (9/1/74), for example, sprawling U.S. oil companies represent modern Americanization as villain. Synonomous with inauthenticity, "big oil" — as Morley Safer calls it — has brought urban problems such as prostitution to the formerly virgin Alaskan wilderness. Safer speculates that corporate "big money" will undermine the simpler, "natural," traditional values affirmed by native "fishermen and hunters."

The tensions between individual and institution, humanity and technology, also play a significant role in the heartland narratives, helping structure our readings of these adventure tales. "Dirty Water" (12/16/84) tells a story about the Prudential Insurance Company allegedly depleting and polluting the water system in a northwest Indiana community. Harry Reasoner dramatically frames the conflict between the "praying mantis" technology of Prudential's fertilization machines and the local farmers and families who see the technology as "a soulless and ominous *Star Wars* creature threatening their heritage, their land, their livelihood."

The Adventures of the Roving Reporter

An exemplary segment that illustrates the tourist formula is the rebroadcast and updating of a segment titled "Rolls-Royce" (6/22/80, Appendix D). Originally aired in 1971, this tourist-in-a-foreign-land narrative was produced by John Tiffin. Morley Safer stars as the reporter who visits the Rolls-Royce automobile plants in England. This segment runs fourteen minutes, ten seconds, and contains 111 separate shots.

Sequence 1 lasts thirty-two seconds and contains Safer's opening address to viewers. It introduces a then-versus-now conflict by comparing ingredients that have changed since the segment was last aired. Safer as present-time narrator describes the discrepancy between what a Rolls-Royce cost in 1971 and what a Rolls costs in 1980: "When this story about Rolls-Royce cars was first broadcast nine years ago, we said the cheapest Rolls sold for $24,000, the most expensive for $50,000. Here's what inflation has done: the cheapest is now $85,000 and the most expensive $156,000. But enough talk of money. This story is about quality."

These juxtapositions between the cheaper, simpler 1971 car and the more expensive 1980 car are crucial in setting up positive associations with the past and negative associations with the present. Later in the segment these associations become explicit as Safer argues for virtues associated with tradition and nature, and against their negative counterparts—modernization and civilization. Significantly here, Safer draws attention away from "money"; the segment never takes up the question of who can and cannot afford a Rolls. The reporter strategically adjusts the focus of narrative conflict to tradition-change ("This is a story about quality"); tensions between the upper class who buy the cars and the workers who build the cars remain embedded and unexamined.

Sequence 2 contains nine shots and lasts fifty-eight seconds. The sequence is dominated visually by workers at the Rolls-Royce plant in England and verbally by Safer's voice-over narration. The sequence continues the then-now tension revealed in the introduction and establishes a conflict between British and American values.

Visually, the workers at the Rolls plant in England dominate this scene while Safer's voice-over narration controls the discourse. Safer tells us that the Rolls is apparently the "last of the great handmade cars," and close-up shots of workers carefully hand waxing and tending to parts of a Rolls support the narration.

The key verbal conflicts for the narrative appear, however, when Safer introduces tensions between General Motors and Rolls-Royce, between Henry Ford and Henry Royce. Royce and his "handmade" Rolls represent British tradition, while Henry Ford and GM signify American modernization and its "plastic" assembly lines. In a tribute to care over speed, the reporter notes that "in its best week" Rolls workers produce fifty-three cars, whereas GM makes "21,000 cars in a single day." Although Safer is functioning primarily as social analyst, he does give us our first "tour" of the Rolls-Royce plant and introduces, in the last shot, the major "character" in the story — the Rolls-Royce. The identification and introduction of the car, but not the factory workers, suggest their subordinate position to the car in the narrative. Detailed shots of workers closely attending the Rolls are verbally contrasted to the large, impersonal assembly-line impression of an American automotive plant. General Motors stands for the concrete embodiment of the big, indifferent corporation in contrast to the individual Rolls workers who are portrayed as personal attendants to each Rolls in the plant. As noted in the other *60 Minutes* formulas as well, the villain is often visually absent.

Sequence 3 is the central sequence in this segment, running five minutes, thirty-six seconds, and containing forty-two shots. The first scene establishes the reporter as tourist by displaying Safer driving a car and visiting a junk-yard in order to set up the first major visual opposition — the lack of durability, the "junk" nature of society set against the durable, timelessness of the Rolls. As Safer drives, he recites a line from Willy Loman in Arthur Miller's *Death of a Salesman:* "Once in my life I would like to own something outright before it's broken. I'm always in a race with the junkyard." As he recites, Safer maneuvers the car into a junkyard where he sets up a major visual tension — the lack of durability, the "junk" nature of society, versus the durable timelessness of the Rolls-Royce. Just after Safer steps from the nondescript, obsolete car and walks to the foreground, in the background a powerful machine dramatically descends and crushes the car as we watch with Safer. He tells us,

Morley Safer dramatically comments on the "junk nature" of contemporary society and "the fate" of our own cars as another generic auto becomes obsolete in the background. (© MCMLXXI–CBS Inc. All rights reserved.)

"And this will soon be the fate of the car you're driving today." With machine crushing machine behind him, Safer describes the effects of modernization on authentic experience: "The trouble really is that nothing these days is built to last. . . . We live most of our lives in a junk society. Our durables aren't very durable. But when something is built by hand out of materials given by nature, old-fashioned pride is maintained."

This scene is then juxtaposed with the sleek beauty of the Rolls and the intimate attention given by "the old-fashioned pride" of individual workers at the Rolls plant. Safer, in a voice-over and in contrast to the grim Willy Loman, reads next from an Oliver Wendell Holmes poem, "The One-Horse Shay,"[12] about a handmade carriage:

> So the deacon inquired of the village folk
> Where he could find the strongest oak,
> That couldn't be split nor bent nor broke—
> That was for spokes and floors and sills;
> He sent for lancewood to make the thills;
> The crossbars were ash, from straightest trees;

The panels of white-wood, that cuts like cheese,
But lasts like iron for things like these; ...
Step and prop-iron, bolt and screw,
Spring, tire, axle, and linchpin too,
Steel of the finest, bright and blue;
Thoroughbrace bison-skin, thick and wide;
Boot, top, dasher, from tough old hide
Found in the pit when the tanner died.
That was the way he "put her through."
"There!" said the Deacon, "naow she'll dew!"

The poem is juxtaposed with detailed shots of Rolls workers. Safer foregrounds the nature side (oak, lancewood, ash, white-wood, bison-skin, and tough old hide) of this conflict with civilization. His voice-over supports shots of factory workers using natural materials that compare favorably to the tradition presented in the nineteenth-century "schoolboy poem," as Safer calls it. The entire second part of sequence 3 contrasts dramatically with the junkyard scene that has now been overpowered by the presence of the Rolls workers and their natural materials.

After the poem, Safer opposes the "local craftsmen" of Rolls-Royce against the "tyranny of machines" and the "big automotive plants" that apparently represent the worst of twentieth-century American industry. In one shot an unnamed Rolls worker scratches the ear of a pet cat in a scene that looks more like a backyard garage than a large auto plant.

In his Rolls factory tour, Safer interviews one worker, who discusses the natural materials—the "timber and metal"—that he works with and looks with disfavor upon the "stamped-out" Detroit cars. Safer, who describes the Rolls auto factory as a "cottage industry" in contrast to the sprawling technology of an American auto plant, questions a Rolls worker: "Well, what's the difference between this and a stamped-out car?" The man responds, "Well, a stamped-out car is just a stamped-out car, isn't it? I mean, anybody can build them." In continuing the indictment of the U.S. car industry, Safer asks, "How would you like to work in one of the big auto plants and run a machine that simply punched out one of those doors every ten seconds?" The worker responds, "Well, I think it would bore me within two or three hours. . . . I'd sooner use my hands and make it myself." The American auto industry symbolizes bureaucratic, negative dimensions of modernization. A contemporary villain, it holds values counter to the traditional craftsmanship that Safer finds in another modern corporation but one that preserves pre-modern values. It is important here that *60 Minutes* spotlights the American *institution* as villain and not *individual* American autoworkers; this would complicate the elegance of *60 Minutes*'s narrative viewpoint.

Once again the Rolls workers embody the concrete representation of caring individuality, while the visually absent "big plants" stand for depersonalized technology. The verbal references to timber and metal concretely represent the natural and authentic—positive virtues in the adventure formula. On the other hand, references to the "stamped-out" cars from the Detroit assembly line stand for the negative countervalues of crass artificiality and heartless progress.

As the tourist-surrogate in this sequence, Safer asks simple questions about how things work in the plant. He searches for authenticity, which he finds in the natural materials, and efficiency, which he finds in the Rolls workers. However, what Safer does not ask the worker who builds the car is whether he could buy the car. The narrow narrative focus on the individual competence of the worker limits expanding the meanings of this exchange to its class dimensions.

As the Rolls-Royce takes on human and animal characteristics, tension between worker and technology, self and society, nature and civilization diminishes. In the narration, the Rolls is described as having "a personality" and a "pedigree." A laboratory technician, who looks like a veterinarian or general practitioner, probes the Rolls with a stethoscope. The director of the plant mentions the car's "three or four month gestation period," and Safer compares the plant's testing facilities to an "incubation ward." In Safer's narration and in the visual counterparts, the Rolls—a technological product of a bygone civilization—nevertheless takes on human or animal features. Machine becomes person. The technological becomes the natural.

To strengthen this transformation, the personalization of individual workers is minimized so the elite Rolls itself can dominate as the major character. By humanizing and substituting the car for its upper-class owners, *60 Minutes* directs attention from the social disparity between workers and elites. Although many workers are seen, none is specifically identified; they remain generic "local crafts-men." Only the managing plant director, David Plastow, is identified by name; he is also presented as "the youngest of the craftsmen" which serves in addition to diffuse labor-management tensions which offers another implicit contrast to the Detroit auto industry.

Sequence 4 lasts two minutes, twenty-one seconds; it features twenty-six shots. While Safer's voice-over verbally prevails in all but the last five shots of this sequence, Rolls-Royce cars—blue, white, silver, and black—visually take control of the frame, appearing in twenty-two of the twenty-six shots. The sequence opens with Safer's slightly irreverent reading from the Rolls-Royce chauffeur's hand-book. Shots of individuals identified only as chauffeurs again support the car's role as the dominant character.

Sequence 4 also demonstrates a shift from the production of cars at the plant to their consumption by owners and drivers. While sequence 3 features shots of Rolls-Royces in parts and pieces as they are produced, sequence 4 features twenty-two shots of various fin-ished cars. Implicitly continuing the car-as-character metaphor, the narrative suggests that the car has passed from its inchoate beginning at the plant—its "birth"—to its maturation as a finished product. Again the continuity of Safer's narration provides a smooth transition from part to whole, from production to consumption, as the reporter moves the narrative itself toward a sense of completion.

The second part of sequence 4 focuses on both the durability and tradition of the Rolls, and Safer's reference to "the familiar complaint of depreciation" conjures up the American auto industry and again sets it against the appreciation of the Rolls. Safer's narration informs us that despite the age of many Rolls-Royces, "nothing is dated about them." They transcend time, style and modernity. The Rolls thus simultaneously mediates the conflict between tradition and change, between appreciation and depreciation. The continued treat-ment of car—star of this narrative—as character also repairs con-flict: "Letting the car down is somehow unpatriotic," and owners begin "to care about how . . . the car is looked after."

Sequence 5 lasts one minute, fourteen seconds, and has seven shots. The sequence reestablishes Safer as tourist continuing his visit to the Rolls factory, "a British institution with an almost mythical tradition," and rebuilding the tension between tradition and mod-ernization. He visits two office managers, one in charge of spare

Mr. Trimming efficiently locates from the anti-computer card catalogue the record of the oldest Rolls still being driven. (© MCMLXXI–CBS Inc. All rights reserved.)

parts, the other in charge of records. Whereas the car is personified in the narrative, the role of the managers is again deemphasized. Safer refers to the two men in this scene only by their last names and calls them "pillars of the institution." On the other hand, Safer personalizes the Rolls plant with a reference to the "bowels of the factory." The "pillars" metaphor mythologizes the workers at the same time the "bowels" metaphor personalizes the car and elevates its status in the narrative.[13]

The visual counterparts to this narration offer a cluttered, lived-in office setting where records of every Rolls ever built are kept in a library card catalogue. The presence of this traditional filing system contrasts with the absence of a modern, apparently efficient, computerized American office. In the scene's climax, the records manager named Trimming—at Safer's request—puts on his glasses, walks down a cluttered aisle straight to a 1927 file, and pulls out the card on the oldest Rolls still being driven. He reads: "Miss L. Overend. Delivered on the 9th of June, 1927." Both past-present and tradition-modernization tensions are obliterated in Trimming's efficient act.

Sequence 6 includes twenty-six shots and lasts three minutes, thirty seconds. This concluding sequence features the reporter's journey to just outside Dublin, Ireland, where tensions are resolved and his search for authenticity ends. Safer visits Lutitia Overend, the ninety-one-year-old owner of the oldest Rolls still in operation. She verifies the durability and tradition of the Rolls; she has owned the same one for forty-four years. She also testifies, as owner, to the importance of the natural, of the handmade, over the technological—recalling the factory scene where the Rolls was built by hand by local craftsmen. She supports the "crank handle" method of starting the car over the "automatic"; she greases ·the car herself in thirty places ("takes five actions of the hand").

The narrative takes a complex turn here as Lutitia Overend criticizes the *new, modern* Rolls for its technical complexity ("lots of components . . . just thrown . . . together"). Safer supports her charges by comparing a new, modern Rolls—shown in city settings—to "something out of Detroit in the fifties . . . fallen victim to the fickle hand of modernity." Visually the scene further authenticates Overend's Rolls through the appearance of the reporter-tourist with Lutitia Overend driving her car in a country setting. Safer here identifies Detroit, the city, and modernity as villains, and the natural, pastoral tradition of the Rolls-Royce as potential "victim."

Through Safer's display of the Rolls's survival, these conflicting ideas are mediated. The 1927 Rolls persists even in the face of the new, modern Rolls, which in some ways has "fallen victim" to Detroit and modernization. Miss Overend gently strokes the steering wheel and ascribes a "personality" to her car: "treat it as you would an animal or person. Have sympathy with it . . . help it along." The technological again becomes the personal, as the focus on the individual car masks broader class divisions and social inequity. Overend, whose class standing is not at issue in this story, complains only that the new Rolls is not "half as dignified" as her 1927 model.

The final shot presents Safer updating the story since its original broadcast nine years earlier. His closure to the segment again suggests the metamorphosis of machine to person as the 1927 Rolls displaces Miss Overend. He announces, "Lutitia Overend died a few years ago. The car, however, is still going strong." The survival of the car bridges past and present, life and death. The car-as-person metaphor provides narrative resolution as the machine becomes an individual

Tourist-reporter Safer travels to Dublin and visits with ninety-one-year-old
Lutitia Overend, then the owner of the oldest working Rolls. This 1927 car,
a major character in this adventure story, "outlives" Miss Overend. (©
MCMLXXI–CBS Inc. All rights reserved.)

and takes on a life of its own, sustaining virtues of tradition, authenticity, and nature in the face of technology, modernity, and artificiality.

A Sense of Place

As the "Rolls-Royce" segment illustrates, the conflict between tradition and modernization saturates the adventure narratives of *60 Minutes*. In these segments there is a dramatic search for authenticity, for a sense of place. In modern societies overrun by technology, the search is not often as easy as in "Rolls-Royce." For example, in "Paris Was Yesterday," Mike Wallace and Janet Flanner, who wrote from Paris for *The New Yorker* for fifty years, recall the Paris of the 1930s. Flanner comments, "Paris was more gracious in its pleasure—more customary. You knew who you were." This personal vision contrasts with arresting shots of modern Paris overrun by litter, junkyards, crowds, and fast-food signs; modern buildings are "bogus new towers . . . hatched by vipers" that lack the majesty of the authentic Eiffel Tower.

While tension between tradition and modernization generally features events, issues and ideas in opposition, nature opposed to civilization marks a clash of locale where natural settings oppose artificial cities. "The Oil Kingdom" (6/9/74) depicts a tour of Saudi Arabia. Shots of nomadic tribes herding sheep in the desert compete with crowded city street scenes and modern oil rigs. Nature—visually portrayed by the desert, animals, and nomadic tribes—combats civilization, visually portrayed by a modern city and oil rig technology. In such *60 Minutes* narratives, symbols for nature often emerge as affirmations of simplicity, purity, and pastoralism. Nature is seldom viewed as complex, wild, and menacing, but only a positive, premodern counterpoint to the evils of modernity.

In addition to the explicit narrative conflict, what is ultimately mediated in this and other tourist segments are tensions between place and space, and between time and space. The reporter as tourist takes us to a previously unfamiliar environment, and through verbal narration and visual representation, transforms the insecurity of space into a place, a now-familiar, concrete setting that we, as viewers, visit and come to know. Wayfaring reporters, our surrogates, locate themselves in the unfamiliar and through the narrative transform an unknown space into familiar place, thereby allowing us to feel, as in the case of adventure narratives generally, that we too know how to distinguish authenticity from artifice, villains from heroes, virtue from vice.

Solving the tension between time and space is more problematic. We know, for example, that narrative time represented in a given fourteen-minute *60 Minutes* narrative might, in fact, stand for real time that developed over five or six weeks of researching and shooting a story, and may extend even further back as the narrative reconstructs histories of certain events, places, and characters. We also know that in the process of picking camera distances and shot angles, *60 Minutes* producers choose to show us some places and not others. This reconstruction and re-presentation of temporal and spatial dimensions accommodates the limits imposed by narrative formula.

The use of the adventure narrative in *60 Minutes* shares with the novel a particular way of ordering and delineating time and space. The Russian linguist M. M. Bakhtin, in his analysis of the novel, argues that an effective strategy for solving time-space problems is to situate the narrative "on the road" where dramatic encounters occur: "On the road . . . , the spatial and temporal paths of the most varied people—representatives of all social classes, estates, religions, nationalities, ages—intersect at one spatial and temporal point. People who are normally kept separate by social and spatial distance can accidently meet; any contrast may crop up, the most various fates may collide and interweave with one another."[14] So in "1000% Inflation," Wallace, on the road in Brazil, dramatically juxtaposes the poor and the rich, who may never really encounter one another but who become narratively linked on *60 Minutes* as we cut back and forth between privilege and poverty. And Morley Safer, on the road in "Rolls-Royce," forges a narrative bond among a ninety-one-year-old Dublin woman, Rolls-Royce factory workers, and ultimately the viewers at home—again none of whom may have actually encountered one another—but whose paths interweave through the collapsing together of time and space in the reporter's adventure and in our experience of that adventure.

On the road in the novel—and this may be extended to the literary and novelistic qualities of *60 Minutes*—"the spatial and temporal series defining human fates and lives combine with one another in distinctive ways, even as they become more complex and more concrete by the collapse of social distances."[15] For, Bakhtin, then, the travel or road metaphor, although it can function to limit meanings within narrative borders, may also enrich them. With class distance between rich and poor apparently overcome in "1000% Inflation" and geographic distance between Britain and America overturned in "Rolls-Royce," *60 Minutes* potentially offers a way to measure varied and idiosyncratic experience (experience we may only get from television's ability to collapse distance) against the middle ground of common sense, against the well-informed perspective of the *60 Minutes* reporter.

In his assessment of tourist experiences, Erik Cohen makes an important distinction between the role of the pilgrim and the role of tourist as counter impulses in modern travel: "Pilgrimages and modern tourism are . . . predicated on different social conceptions of space and contrary views concerning the kind of destinations worth visiting and of their location in the socially constructed space; hence they involve movement in opposite directions: in pilgrimage from the periphery toward the cultural centre, in modern tourism, away from the cultural centre into the periphery."[16] In *60 Minutes* both impulses are represented. The heartland segments reveal a return to both a pre-modern cultural and geographic center, toward natural, known and familiar virtues. The foreign segments, on the other hand, invoke a spirit of exploration into the unknown, an adventure out to mysterious lands and the cultural periphery.

The power of *60 Minutes* resides in the ability of its two road formulas on any given Sunday to accommodate either impulse. Our wayfaring reporter—both a pilgrim *and* modern tourist—then has the mastery to bring multiple realities together at a single point in time and space, allowing us to look, to judge, and even to take exception to the ways in which experience is appropriated to suit the needs of a narrative in search of the middle ground. Sometimes that ground is defined through location at the center, in the heartland. But just as often that center is defined from the periphery as our surrogate reporters travel to distance places and match the experience against their own and our common sense.

News and Arbitration: Managing the Social Margins   6

> There's a fine line between show biz and news biz. The trick is to walk up to that line and touch it with your toe but don't cross it. And some people stay so far away from the line that nobody wants to watch what they do. And other people keep crossing the line.... But there has to be a line because the line is called truth. And the difference between what we do is, we tell true stories and other people tell make believe stories.
>
> —Don Hewitt

Near the turn of the century, not only the New York *Times,* but also progressive intellectuals like John Dewey believed in a version of the science model for journalism and what it could do for American democracy. As James Carey notes of the progressives' realistic reverie: "Scientific reporting was a vision for a future organization of society based on the new dynamics centered around the telegraph. The news report of the future would supersede literature, and the literary consciousness, of the past. It was to be tied to an irreducible, statistical order of facts documenting the state of the social organism."[1] In countering the romanticism, uncertainty and subjectivity of art, some progressives maintained that printing technology, the telegraph, and the railroad in combination with this new "scientific attitude" would foster "a new form of social intelligence, achieved through the workings of the newspaper, which would establish an integrated republic and an ordered social life."[2]

In 1920 in *Liberty and the News,* Walter Lippmann also envisioned the scientific method—the "valid fact" and "disciplined experiment"—as a way for journalists to make sense of the complexity of the times, the aftermath of a world war, the elusiveness of facts, and the problems of subjectivity.[3] Two years later in *Public Opinion* Lippmann suggested, "As our minds become more deeply aware of their own subjectivism, we find a zest in objective method that is not otherwise there."[4] Lippmann sought a metaphor for journalism that would help reporters remain detached even as they immersed themselves more deeply in the experiences they covered.

One reportorial posture that attempts to minimize this gap between involvement and detachment, between the literary and the scientific, between subjectivism and objective method, is the stance of the well-informed reporter arbitrating conflict. Within this stance reporters align facts with objective method and values with the subjective domain.[5] Through the convention of routine journalism, they conceal overt ideological distinctions and moral choices by overwhelming readers and viewers with details and description—with facts. In a democracy then, conventional wisdom suggests that it becomes the responsibility of the news audience, not the reporter's, to judge and make appropriate value stands. The well-informed reporter's responsibility extends only to adhering to the common conventions and traditions of the trade—"getting the facts"—not to the experiences themselves or to explicit moral judgments about those experiences.

Yet we know that a newspaper story about a teenage murder or a drug raid in not *naturally* news; it is news because historically such behavior has been judged by journalism as deviations from Middle-American norms. And news is frequently about distinctions between what is normal and what is deviant in a democracy. Nevertheless, the common sense of journalism dictates that reporters guard the border that separates the techniques of gathering "natural" facts from the contamination of what reporters morally value. Yet the selection of the murder or drug story as news is a moral rather than a neutral selection. The celebration of neutral conventions, however, masks the moral impulse in the news.

The referee posture in journalism represents the exemplar of the well-informed reporter who in news stories must straddle facts and values often to make common sense of opposing points of view. To perform this balancing act—between fact and value, between competing positions—the reporter, as referee, commands a hierarchy of discourse that privileges certain kinds of knowledge.[6] In representing the voices and views of the well informed, *60 Minutes* reporters, in attempting to maintain a neutral stance, present experience as four competing yet intertwined voices of knowledge: well informed, common sense, expert, and nonsense.[7]

The discourse of the well informed orders and orchestrates this hierarchy by setting the stage for each *60 Minutes* segment. Although closely allied with common sense, what separates this level from other types of news knowledge is the reporter's control over each level and his or her masterful arbitration of competing levels. In his essay, "The Well-Informed Citizen," Alfred Schutz defines the kind of knowledge relayed by reporters as "socially derived knowledge" — that is, knowledge which necessarily originates from experiences we cannot have first-hand. Socially derived knowledge — which makes up the bulk of what we know — results from the transformation of abstract experiences outside our own into the concrete narrative frameworks of others who witness or interpret that experience for us. Significantly, Schutz uses four reporter metaphors, including "the eyewitness," "the insider," "the analyst," and "the commentator," to explain how socially derived knowledge is transmitted in a culture by well-informed citizens.[8]

This well-informed plane of knowledge is the terrain of reporters. Here they draw boundaries, marking off an issue and groups of characters as residing within or outside the domain of common sense. Mike Wallace, for example, begins the "The Kongsberg Connection" (4/10/88) by admonishing "greedy" corporate interests in two foreign countries: " 'The Kongsberg Connection' is the story about how a greedy Norwegian company—Kongsberg—conspired with an equally greedy Japanese company—Toshiba Machine . . . to sell highly sensitive technology to the Soviets, technology that helped make Soviet submarines quieter, harder to detect underseas."

In addition to the narrative reconstruction of this experience that most of us could not witness first-hand, the well-informed reporter explicitly addresses the issues of commonsense boundaries in his confrontation with a former Kongsberg executive, Bernard Green, who has admitted to conspiring with the Soviets:

> GREEN: Are we going to trade with them [the Soviets] or not? Because if you're going to trade with them, you're going to help them in some way or another.
> WALLACE: Militarily, we're talking about . . . one thing's to sell them refrigerators, another thing's to sell them NC-2000s [computer submarine technology].
> GREEN: You really don't know where is the borderline.
> WALLACE (in next scene): Where to draw the line? What to do about

all this? Well, on a side street in Paris there is an outfit set up by the U.S. and its allies that is suppose to prevent greedy Western businessmen from selling advanced technology to the Soviets.

Wallace tells us that this watchdog "outfit" is "toothless" as he continues to color in the story with the stuff of socially derived knowledge—visual images, on-screen narration, and voice-overs. Eventually, he castigates the Norwegian business for its violations of commonsense borders; the company is based, after all, in a country whose own government continually patrols its geographical borders to guard against threats from Soviet submarines.

From their command posts as well-informed citizens, *60 Minutes* reporters explicitly speak common sense. These two levels in the knowledge hierarchy are intricately bound together. By way of contrast, in shorter television news packages, reporter narration carries common sense implicitly. More often common sense is typically represented in the familiar person-on-the-street interview. Someone, selected not for expertise but for ordinariness, is asked to voice an opinion about a newsworthy event or issue. When presented in the context of a news narrative, such interviews take on the ambience of consensus. A single interview subject often stands in for a larger community of Middle-American viewers. Consequently, in stories presenting controversies, a lone interview or sound bite often determines which of the competing definitions of the situation is perceived as "correct," as common sense.

The discourse that dominates the next level in the news hierarchy is that of expert knowledge. Reporters seek out appropriate experts who provide enough conflict to sustain the news narrative. So, in addition to his own well-informed voice, Wallace in "The Kongsberg Connection" seeks out a variety of politicians and investigators to outline then flesh out the conflict. They add their expert voices to the pool of knowledge that the well-informed reporter then arranges and presents anew. These news characters are from the land of specialized knowledge. The language of this realm is frequently "jargonese" and often has to be decoded and translated into common sense by the well-informed reporter.

The civic treasures of specialized knowledge include access to privileged information and state secrets. Located outside the borders of common sense, specialized knowledge is generally possessed by authorities involved in state security (industry regulators, military analysts, law enforcement officers, and intelligence agents) or professionals in various arts and sciences (mathematics, music, medicine, and higher education). Walker Percy defines modern experts as "the true princes of the age": "*They* know about science, *they* know about medicine, *they* know about government, *they* know about my needs, *they* know about everything in the Cosmos, even me. *They* know why I am fat and they know secrets of my soul which not even I know. There is an expert for everything that ails me, a doctor of my depression, a seer of my sadness."[9] By italicizing *they,* Percy acknowledges the fundamental division in contemporary society between the have and have-nots of special expertise. Reporters as well-informed citizens once again are called upon to mediate between the realm of the expert "them" and the rest of the commonsense "us."

Experts lend to journalism one of its most cherished conventions—the respectability that comes with the trappings and posture of science. Experts allow journalists to distance themselves (the pose of "scientific objectivity") from experience by placing the burden on those who are quoted. Jonathan Alter argues that on a national level the pool of experts, whom he calls the "usual suspects," is often confined to a privileged few: Gloria Steinem on feminism, Carl Sagan on science, Alan Greenspan on economics, John Naisbitt on the future, Henry Kissinger on diplomacy, and William Bennett, a former education expert turned drug expert. Alter says of expert sources in general that "the impression conveyed is of a world that contains only a handful of knowledgeable people." He blames directly the constraints of deadline and the inability of national journalists to break free from convention: "The favored few who make the most quoted list are generally aware of how good they have it. They realize that their public exposure is a result not only of their own abilities, but of deadlines and a failure of imagination on the part of the press."[10]

Beyond the outskirts of common sense exists a type of "knowledge" that is more fully representative of the have-nots of modern life. Frequently marginalized in the news hierarchy and best described as the realm of nonsense, this is a place of "superstition and gullibility," of fools and lunatics, of archaic and absurd ideas, of illogical and irrational ways of being.[11] A large chunk of nonsense consists of obsolete knowledge. Although once accepted as common sense, obsolete knowledge is no longer an ingredient in social consensus. For example, where we once inhabited a flat earth, now the world is round; where we once used leeches to purify bad blood, now we reduce cholesterol and eat oat bran (witness Kellogg's "Common Sense Oat Bran" cereal commercial). Although obsolete knowledge is still a part of folklore in many cultures, it has largely been processed out of common sense.

In today's news stories, nonsense spans a broad spectrum. On one hand, nonsense may be just a lack of common sense. In this context, expert jargon, which lacks the accessible, utilitarian imperative that marks common sense, may overlap with and serve as nonsense. A 1989 *Newsweek* review of the latest James Bond film provides an overt example of journalism taking to task an academic's interpretation of Bond movies; the reporter-reviewer, Jack Kroll, then translates the "expert" version into a more familiar, conventionally "wise" review:

> So you think the James Bond stories are simple spy-sex-shoot-'em-up stuff? Well, they've long been fertile ground for heavy-headed critical types, one of whom has applied to the Bond works "a Levi-Straussian analysis of a series of binary oppositions which . . . provides the structural coordinates for the system of ideological meanings. . . ." Such academic gobbledygook makes you wish you had a *Licence to Kill,* which happens to be the title of the new Bond movie. This, the 16th Bond, is a pure, rousingly entertaining action movie which makes it clear that "binary oppositions" are good guys vs. bad guys and "ideological meanings" are us vs. them.[12]

On *60 Minutes,* Andy Rooney's concluding essays and reports also hold up the buzzwords of specialized knowledge to common-sense scrutiny. In "Bugs Are a Negative Factor" (3/19/78), a story whose title is a line from a scientific report, Rooney arbitrates a conflict between the worth of a jargon-filled, government-sponsored $900,000 feasibility study about a Montana wilderness area and the "common taxpayer" who has to spend hard-earned money for unreadable, unusable studies. Rooney, the voice of the common man, tells us, "Isn't this part of the gobbledygook that justifies people asking for more money from Washington — making it sound like something it isn't?"

More often, however, nonsense resides just beyond the border, far from the inaccessible language of experts. This is the bleakest side of nonsense, the marginal realm of the homeless, drug addicts, criminals, the mentally ill, the third world, terrorists, foreign dictators, or the "revolutionary rhetoric" of radical groups like the Black Panthers. Their voices are seldom heard in the news; instead these views are "socially derived," filtered through expert interpretations or through the common sense of well-informed reporters. Take for example this comment by the ubiquitous George Will, well-informed citizen *extraordinaire* with a *Newsweek* column plus a regular spot on an ABC Sunday morning news-talk show. In a mid-1980s appearance on ABC's *Nightline,* Will identified certain kinds of homelessness not just as marginal but as "illegal": "Therefore, there is a simple matter of public order and hygiene in getting these people somewhere else. Not arrest them, but move them off somewhere where they are simply out of sight. . . ."[13] Often translated by reporters, the unheard voices of nonsense are frequently labeled as them pitted against us—an "us" which includes reporters and the implied contingent of Middle-American viewers and readers.[14]

The Arbitration Formula

Of all the formula variations on *60 Minutes*, news as arbitration most closely identifies this broadcast with the conventional journalistic split between detachment and involvement, facts and values. This *60 Minutes* formula remains most clearly aligned with traditions of orthodox journalism. And although the other formulas display the well-informed reporter who manages the hierarchy of discourse, this role is most pronounced and performed in these particular segments in which a number of features separate the reporter-as-arbiter from other formulaic roles: (1) posing as detached observers, (2) deferring to experts, (3) accenting dialectical rather than expository structure, (4) abandoning the search for an unequivocal villain, and (5) presenting clouded narrative resolutions.

Striking a Neutral Pose

Managing the hierarchy of news knowledge is a tricky business best carried out on *60 Minutes* by the reporter in the guise of a referee. First, the reporter assumes the role of a more conventional television journalist, similar in some ways to the role Ted Koppel plays on ABC's *Nightline* or the role Robert MacNeil and James Lehrer play in their hour-long PBS report. In this role there is a greater attempt to appear detached. At times, the reporter's role is further minimized in that visually he or she appears in far fewer shots compared to the other formulas (although voice-over narration still dominates these segments). For example, in "Social Security?" (3/2/75), "Guns" parts 1 and 2 (9/18/77; 9/25/77), "Remember Pearl Harbor?" (12/3/78), and "Earn It!" (12/16/79), the reporters appear in fewer than ten shots per narrative (in other formulas, the reporter is generally featured in anywhere from twenty-five to fifty shots).

Characteristic of the more detached role is Morley Safer in "Guns." He appears in this segment on a rifle range with members of the National Rifle Association. Instead of donning a more casual outfit and taking his turn on the range in a detective segment—as did Dan Rather in "Hired Gun" (5/2/76)—Safer remains the detached, well-informed, and well-dressed reporter—in suit and tie as he walks past the NRA shooters.

Bowing to Experts

In these arbitration narratives, there is also a tendency for the reporter to defer to expert interview subjects who have been brought in to document two sides of an apparently controversial issue. For example, in "What Happened in Laos?" (3/30/71), Mike Wallace announces in his introduction that *60 Minutes* went out to "round up some expert military reaction" to discuss U.S. military strategy in Laos in the early 1970s. A retired French general and a retired British air force vice-marshall are interviewed for their analyses. Similarly, in "To Live or to Let Die" (3/2/75), two doctors, one the "chief of a newborn intensive care unit," are brought into the narrative to comment on whether healthy parents should allow their babies born with severe birth defects to live. While these experts surface in other *60 Minutes* formulas, in the arbitration segments there is a greater tendency for experts to provide knowledge while the reporter-referee merely inquires.

Illustrating the Argument

A third characteristic of the referee formula foregrounds dialectical rather than expository structure. Whereas strong contradictions inviting resolution are posed within a narrative framework, more dramatic features are backgrounded. Displacing scenes such as crime reconstruction or villain confrontation are the abstract, issue-stated oppositions themselves posed as the central feature of these segments. Reporters instead are positioned between the two sides of an argument, where they referee competing levels of knowledge. They toss the issue into the air in the opening introduction, and the two sides—the two sets of characters—go at it.

In "What Happened in Laos?" for example, Wallace sets up the dialectical structure in his introduction: "Was the Laos operation a success or a disaster? Americans are not the only ones arguing about it. Friends and allies are trying to assess it too." Wallace introduces the two foreign military experts who take opposite sides in tensions between success and failure, U.S. and foreign, peace and war. In "To Live or to Let Die," the rights of severely handicapped newborn babies are opposed to the rights of their parents who want to lead "normal" lives. This dialectic structure then frames tensions between deviant and normal, religion and science, emotion and reason, parent and child, life and death, and personal and social through which the ideological contest is articulated.

Discarding the Villain

Unlike the other three formulas, the arbitration segments feature the genuine absence of an unequivocal villain. In these narratives the villain's role is muddied—sometimes even missing because in most of these segments there is no strong conflict between individual and institution. These segments pit either two large institutional positions or two sets of individual positions against one another. This obscures the major conflicts featured in most *60 Minutes* segments and displays either both or neither as villainous positions, again a dialectical feature.

Villains are scarce indeed in the arbitration narratives. In "To Live or to Let Die," sets of individuals at odds over the rights of children versus the rights of parents come into conflict, but no sure culprit emerges. In "What Happened in Laos?" an individual representing one government debates an individual representing another government. While the notion of institution lurks in the background of many of these narratives, the institution's role as transgressor is less clear.

In "A Question of Mercy" (4/16/89), Ed Bradley arbitrates a powerful story about the rights of AIDS victims to choose death versus the illegality and moral implications of euthanasia. Bradley interviews a man, representing the "Safe Passage Group," who assists AIDS victims in their own suicides; the man is caught between a society which legally views his help as murder, and his own conscience which permits him to offer relief to AIDS victims. In one key interchange Bradley suggests, "This isn't the kind of country that accepts your viewpoint readily." In defending his stance, the man responds, "That's not Joe Middle America somewhere—that's me."

This segment, like other arbitration narratives, is explicitly about social margins and gaps, about what Joe Middle America will tolerate and what he will not. Does this character represent common sense or nonsense? Is he a villain or hero? The reporter's role is to take us to the precipice, show us either side, and let us judge.

Clouding the Narrative

A final characteristic of the referee formula highlights the lack of clear resolution. Often in these segments, only the reporter-referee's mediating presence amid the conflict offers any narrative closure. For example, in "What Happened in Laos?" it is unclear at the end whether the U.S. mission in Laos was a failure or a success. The reporter referees the conflicting ideas and positions but makes no attempt at moral closure in the last scene, which features one of the experts attacking U.S. military strategy. "To Live or to Let Die" also offers no emphatic solution. The segment features two sets of parents discussing their severely handicapped children. Once couple says, "We have no hope"; however, later Mike Wallace in voice-over narration offers another viewpoint: "Where there is life, there is hope." He then narrates the dilemma of another husband and wife who want their child to die yet are trying to keep him alive. In the end, the reporter-referee offers no explicit moral meaning as closure.

In "Earn It!" Dan Rather comments on both sides of the issue. He summarizes the values of the criminal pay-back program that would relieve overcrowded prisons and give victims monetary compensation directly from the criminal. At the same time the reporter points out nonsensical aspects of the program: it discriminates against the poor, takes jobs away from noncriminals, fails to instill the fear of punishment in criminals, and fails to slow down the crime rate. Again the closure offered in this segment appears in the presence of the well-informed reporter as arbiter straddling and surviving the dialectic. And although the mediation is clouded in these stories, at home in the safety of our family rooms, we survive with the reporter, protected from troubling stories where the worst realities do not quite seem to cohere.

The Tale of the Reporter at the Margin

An exemplary segment analyzed to illustrate and explain the arbitration formula is "Why Me?" (5/18/75, Appendix E). Joseph Wershba produced the narrative; Morley Safer serves as the well-informed reporter in a story about the seniority rights of white workers at a security firm in conflict with black workers and affirmative action. The segment runs thirteen minutes, forty-two seconds, and contains 126 shots.

Sequence 1 is a single shot that lasts fifty-two seconds, by far the longest unbroken shot in this narrative. As referee, Safer tosses the issue into the air at the outset posed in front of the magazine backdrop featuring the producer's byline:

> When it comes to a job, seniority is a sacred word. Seniority means the longer you've held a job, the more security you have, especially if you have a strong union to protect you. Last hired, first fired. And last hired, first fired usually means blacks, women and other minorities are the first to go. With the Civil Rights Law of 1964, the government told all of its private contractors and business in general: Put minorities on the job and keep them there. But civil rights leaders are complaining that only a few employers are doing that; and where they are doing it, white workers are complaining it's discrimination in reverse. . . .

Safer introduces the major dramatic tensions that organize this narrative, including white against black, majority against minority, and labor against management. In this segment black workers and white both present competing versions of common sense. These characters embody in the narrative the central issue—minority hiring practices versus seniority rights. Safer also identifies the central question: "Why a white with seniority is being laid off, and a black with little seniority is being kept on?"

Sequence 2 switches place to the Nevada setting of the Energy Research and Development Administration (ERDA), formerly the Atomic Energy Commission, where nuclear tests are monitored and where a company named Wackenhut operates security. It contains forty-five shots and lasts three minutes, twenty-two seconds. Safer alone appears in the first four shots at the control center of ERDA to establish historical background and to show us—in his words— "the field of battle" upon which the ensuing conflict will play out.

In this sequence Safer totally dominates both on-screen and voice-over narration. Other than ambient background noises, only a guard checking identification interrupts Safer's verbal control. Given that one characteristic of the referee formula presents a detached, apparently neutral reporter, this sequence, in which Safer commands both the early visuals and the entire narration, is crucial in endowing the reporter with the authoritative voice of the well informed. Such a voice appears in control of the facts and therefore in control of reality, even in this narrative in which the conflicts often seem overwhelming and irreconcilable.

This sequence continues the conflict laid out in the introduction. Unlike conventional news, *60 Minutes* and Safer explicitly define the moral impulse in this narrative; they chose ERDA precisely because the issue up for arbitration is juxtaposed with the more epic tension between nature and civilization: "Quite frankly, we chose this site because of its exotic background: right here where our genius for harnessing nature and our genius for destroying this planet live side by side." Safer then poses the tension that will unfold against this exotic backdrop—"the right of a man to get a job, and the right of another man to protect his job." As he prepares to referee the battle, Safer acknowledges that these two sides are on a "collision course." Supporting this narration, the first visual representation in which Safer does not appear features a close-up of an ERDA security guard loading a gun. The tone is dramatically set for the tense battle we are about to witness. Visuals of the Nevada desert and mountains provide stirring and concrete counterpoint to the symbolic tension of white versus black, authority versus servitude. The moral impulse affirms and celebrates the natural setting—undisturbed, peaceful, and simple compared to "civilized" people (and their technology) who supply the world with tension, turmoil, and misunderstanding.

The second half of the sequence abuts Safer's narration about

ERDA operations, contract clauses, and collective bargaining against a collage of visual images of black guards at work with white guards. One shot juxtaposes a group of apparently inexperienced black workers milling around with a more experienced white guard expertly checking ID passes at an ERDA entrance. Safer compares old hiring practices with the new practices established by the Civil Rights Law of 1964 as he illustrates the "collision course," not only between black and whites, but also between changing times and traditional practices.

Sequence 3 provides the central chunk of the narrative, revealing Safer strategically positioned opposite four black and four white security guards. This sequence runs five minutes, fourteen seconds, and contains fifty-one shots. It begins with Safer, as detached reporter, relinquishing control of the narration (almost five minutes into the story and after forty-six shots) to the discussion among the eight guards. As referee, Safer flips the issues back and forth in his on-screen and voice-over inquiries:

"What do you say to that?"
"He makes a good point. How on earth do blacks ever get seniority?"
"What do you have on your side?"

Safer attempts a neutral but well-informed pose by challenging assumptions made by each group of guards. First, he asks the white guards if they "have a responsibility" to help correct the history of hiring injustices done to blacks over the years. Later he asks the black guards if it is "fair" and "just" that a black worker with only "60 days . . . or even five years tenure" be allowed to keep his job. True to the referee stance, Safer does not offer a view regarding his own responsibility but remains faithful to convention and merely describes these competing views of common sense. Majority and minority workers are continually juxtaposed throughout the remainder of the sequence, overwhelming us with the white-black nature of this presumably two-dimensional controversy.

Just as a professional referee in an amateur wrestling match interrupts the bout when action drags, Safer occasionally prods the participants to pick up the pace of the narrative. He says to the white guards, "Is it possible, do you think, that this whole fight . . . is a red herring, a cover-up for old-fashioned racial discrimination?" And to a black guard, he counters, "Mr. Stewart, do you think that

In a reaction shot, Safer strikes a neutral pose and listens to security guards debate competing commonsense positions regarding seniority rights and affirmative action. (© MCMLXXV–CBS Inc. All rights reserved.)

this contract, this blue book here, does amount to reverse discrimination?" Both questions prompt those on either side of the precipice. Safer's role as referee reaches the climactic stage during an intense argument over racial prejudice among the competing guards. Safer tries unsuccessfully to interrupt and clarify different positions, but the sequence closes with a long shot of the eight participants, voices spilling into one another—like the station house in a *Hill Street Blues* melodrama—and raised in anger.

The tensions in this section of the story appear irresolvable as each side makes a case as the victim of injustice while portraying the other side as the transgressor. As referee, Safer jockeys back and forth in search of a middle ground. Well informed, Safer asks the white guards if they have "the law, justice, tradition" on their side, then later asks those same guards if their position is not just "a cover-up" for prejudice.

Reminding us of its fluid nature, Safer first aligns common sense with law and justice in this scene, then turns around and teams it

60 Minutes orchestrates and Morley Safer referees the battle between evenly matched workers—four white and four black. (© MCMLXXV–CBS Inc. All rights reserved.)

with racial injustice. Likewise, Safer asks the black guards about the "injustice" done to a white worker with seniority who is suddenly displaced by an "inexperienced" black worker. The black guards stand for change in common sense, while the white guards uphold tradition. The issues are murky because from the white viewpoint change is associated first with injustice to whites, while tradition champions fairness and right; but from the black vantage change represents justice, while tradition is associated with a dominant white power structure that discriminates against blacks. Both sides fight for their definition of the boundaries of common sense, dramatically demonstrating the precious and precarious complexion of this symbolic territory.

Sequence 4 is brief, lasting one minute, six seconds and containing seven shots. Safer introduces another character, the security firm's manager of operations, Wallace Hawkins, who Safer tells us has "to tread neutral ground in the dispute." This neutral position identifies with the reporter-referee's own inability to solve the tensions. The

127

sequence continues to present the narrative as "both sides of an unresolvable predicament." Like Safer, Hawkins refuses "to take sides." When Safer asks him to choose, he tells the reporter, "I don't wish to comment on that, Morley." While this sequence also fails at narrative resolution, it does introduce the potential of an institutional villain. Because the government requires the security firm to adhere to affirmative action, and because the government is responsible for the current law, *60 Minutes* could suggest that the government is to blame for the bind. However, characteristic of the referee formula, the potential of the government to emerge as culprit does not materialize.

Sequence 5 runs one minute, four seconds, and also has seven shots. The visuals continue to feature shots of black guards and white guards at work. Safer also introduces us to a government representative, Bernard Menke, "a federal labor relations expert" who reframes the narrative as conflict between winning and losing, employer and employee: "As you know, unions can win it, and they can lose it. . . ." When this expert suggests a resolution to the problem of a "hard-won" seniority clause and introduces the mediating term "compromise," Safer reasserts the moral complexity of the issue: "Some compromise for a man with ten, twelve years of seniority! How is that a compromise? It's a sellout." The reporter's moral outrage, while seemingly uncharacteristic of the arbitration formula, distinguishes Safer as both our surrogate, standing up for men who may lose their jobs, and as narrative catalyst, initiating dramatic action. Characteristic of the arbitration segments, however, Safer defers to the government expert whose redeclaration for compromise closes the sequence: "No party achieves all of the objectives that they would like to achieve."

Sequence 6 contains thirteen shots, runs one minute, three seconds, and reasserts the black-white tension, but now with families, rather than individual workers, symbolically opposed to one another. *60 Minutes* affirms the apparently incurable nature of the problem in a variety of juxtaposed shots featuring white neighborhoods and black. Safer comments on the visual tension of the next eight shots: "and this is what we're really talking about—black workers who've come up through a lifetime of racism, perpetual victims of last-hired, first-fired, who've managed to build families and home and a life like this one in North Las Vegas. And we're talking about white

60 Minutes seeks the common ground of "family" as the program juxtaposes shots of Las Vegas neighborhoods—one black and one white. (© MCMLXXV–CBS Inc. All rights reserved.)

people who live in communities like this in Las Vegas, who have children and playgrounds and homes like these, and who can lose them if they lose their jobs."

This sequence manages to suggest who is not the villain. Earlier both white workers and black workers, as representatives of tradition and change, were portrayed as potential villains in the central sequence in which Safer arbitrated arguments among the guards. Here, however, Safer mediates opposition by establishing both groups as victims caught in a bind. The middle-classness of neighborhood and family scenes for both blacks and whites supplies a temporary common ground. The concluding shots of the contrasting neighborhoods display a kite falling to the ground, a visual, poignant counterpart to the failure to achieve narrative resolution.

The nature-civilization tension featured in an earlier sequence re-emerges as a foil to the confusion and enigma of the black-white conflict. The opening shot in this sequence reveals the Nevada atomic test site, which represents the negative countervalues ushered in with civilization in contrast to the desert and mountains, which represent the values of natural serenity. As the camera shows us a dirt road cutting through barren landscape, Safer notes, "The sheer background gives you the shivers: aspirations and discrimination and reverse discrimination and nuclear fusion all mixed up together."

In the mystery narrative discussed in chapter 3, the family served as a mediating third term to resolve conflict between individual and institution. In this narrative, however, while middle-class families displace individual workers, other tensions remain unmediated. Even the government's role as bullying villain is undercut by the appearance of a "government expert" who sympathizes with "anybody who's facing a loss of their job."

Sequence 7 provides narrative closure by returning Safer to the scene of his opening narration. The brief sequence lasts forty-five seconds and contains one shot. While Safer does not provide clear resolution, he does go back to the control room at ERDA to take charge of the narration again. The reporter does not provide resolution of the black-white tension, but reframes the conflict around tensions between practice and theory, between the personal and the social. In this closing narration, Safer creates and introduces an unnamed singular worker—"a fella out there" (identified as neither white nor black)—and pits the common sense of this fictional character against impractical theoreticians: "The problem is as ancient as the question 'why me?'—a question no collection of judges or philosophers or gurus will ever be able to answer. . . . High-falutin' logic means nothing to a fella out there who's worked hard all of his life. . . ."

Safer dispels tension by sacrificing "an answer" for "a job," by siding with the worker over theory and logic. He supports virtues of common sense, family, and individualism. The use of a single, colorless, unidentified worker who stands for all workers shifts the narrative away from black-white, tradition-change tensions. The personal worker triumphs over the social sphere of judges, philosophers, and gurus; common sense conquers expertise. The fictional worker becomes the symbol for heartland values ("worked hard all of his life, never discriminated against anyone, has a family to support and a job to protect") in a struggle in and against a nonsensical bureaucratic order. It is not merely the introduction and affirmation of common sense that close this narrative, but the presence and performance of Safer straddling gray areas between tradition and change, between black and white, and then championing a middle ground.

Finding Common Ground

At one level of meaning, *60 Minutes* reporters are clearly caught in these arbitration narratives between competing points of view. This reportorial strategy is anchored in the both-sides-of-the-story convention of journalism, or what Edward Epstein has called the "dialectical model."[15] This model assumes that such complex issues as election-year politics and abortion generally can be represented by two viewpoints, giving the appearance that issues are two-dimensional rather than multifaceted.

In solving the problem of a reporter caught in an ideological bind, *60 Minutes* depends on the dialectical model to more easily transform experience into narrative tension. In a rare hour-long referee segment "Guns" (4/5/81, rebroadcast from 1977), which aired shortly after the assassination attempt on Ronald Reagan, Morley Safer converted the sticky, tangled issue of gun control into a two-dimensional battle between members of the National Rifle Association and anti-gun lobbyist Nelson Shields. Although Safer presents a multitude of opinions from the NRA, they are brief, generally depersonalized, and scattered throughout the segment. Shields, on the other hand, is personalized, quoted directly a number times for long stretches in the narrative. We see him making speeches, working in shirt sleeves at his desk, and calling on lawmakers. In the story, Safer, apparently a detached referee, figures prominently in reverse-question shots juxtaposed with visuals of Shields. Safer is seldom portrayed visually with the unidentified and generic NRA members.

Although this narrative cannot explicitly resolve the gun control issue, implicitly it celebrates the heroic individual against the nefarious institution. What is ironic is that the institutional NRA position supports the individual's right to bear arms while the individual Shields calls for broadening social and collective responsibility that should take precedence over individual rights. The irony and contradiction, however, are concealed outside the bounds of the arbitration formula.

In spite of the appearance of detachment in the referee formula, in two ways *60 Minutes* and its reporters claim privileged positions in and control over these narratives: through editing and narration, they construct the narrative and control its possibilities, and through greater distance from the conflict, they locate themselves in an advantageous place between both sides of a marginal issue where they — like Koppel and MacNeil-Lehrer — can set one side against the other. Within the confines of this structure, *60 Minutes* reporters alone administer the boundaries of common sense; they alone appear to find the common ground from which to view the situation completely.

Combination Formulas

Although I have identified exemplary examples of certain *60 Minutes* formulas, a more accurate interpretation suggests that these formulas and reporter poses are generally used in combination. That is, the reporter in any one narrative might perform as detective, as analyst, as wayfarer, and as arbiter. Generally, it is in these segments that the referee can be found — in combination with other formulaic roles. There are few "pure" referee narratives on *60 Minutes* because reporters customarily do name villains and offer moral closure. More frequently, the referee stance combines with other postures on *60*

Minutes, as in, for example, referee-analyst and referee-tourist performances.

Referee-Analyst

In this formula, the reporter generally arbitrates a controversial issue, appearing to remain neutral and relying on expert testimony. However, what distinguishes these narratives from a purer referee formula is the analyst persona also adopted by the reporter at some point during the segment. Consider "Joe Clark" (3/6/88). Harry Reasoner, on one hand, analyzes the title character, an authoritarian principal in a tough New Jersey high school. On the other hand, Reasoner referees a larger debate between this principal's individual right to be unconventional and other individuals who want him to obey the "laws of the land." This narrative is once again about social margins. As analyst, Reasoner provides intimate glimpses into the psyche of this bat-wielding, bull-horn-toting principal who had become the subject of a major motion picture and *Time* magazine report. As referee, the reporter mediates a larger struggle between idiosyncratic personal style and common social expectations.

At times abandoning the earlier detached referee posture, the reporter in these combination formulas supports one side of a controversy over another. Another example is "In This Corner Weighing 2000 Pounds" (10/27/70). Reasoner, an overt referee-announcer here, pits U.S. automakers against the foreign small-car industry. The very title and the following sample of Reasoner's opening narration employ a boxing metaphor to characterize the Volkswagen: "In this corner wearing plain trunks and weighing 1850 pounds, priced at $1,899—the all-time small-car champ, that gargantuan midget from Germany—the Volkswagen Super Beetle." A bell rings and we hear cheering. After Reasoner introduces the rest of the competitors, he announces, "and may the better vehicle emerge victorious."

While experts—executive managers from Ford, General Motors, Volkswagen, and Toyota—are interviewed, Reasoner switches from his explicit referee persona to analyst. His iconoclastic commentary places him squarely in the foreign imports corner: "America practically invented low cost production of automobiles, but Germany and Japan have stolen the small car market out from under America's nose." Later Reasoner admonishes the American auto industry when he suggests, "America may have destroyed Germany and Japan on the field of battle twenty-five years ago, but in recent years Germany and Japan have been wiping the field with us in the small-car market." Reasoner concludes with the "jump ball" statement that both foreign and American models are selling well, but he "calls a foul" on the U.S. industry for expensive options that drive up prices.

At times, the narration and visual depictions in these combination segments offer two apparently irresolvable points of view. Characteristic of the referee formula, the dialectical rather than expository structure of these narratives emerges in the foreground. The reporter's role as a character fades a bit more into background. However, the referee turns analyst at some point in these segments and endows the narrative with explicit moral meaning, a central feature of the analyst formula. In the case of the foreign car segment, Reasoner favors the side of the foreign automakers, whose efficiency, modesty, work ethic, discipline, moderation, and common sense reflect the virtues that *60 Minutes* affirms and promotes week after week. Reasoner criticizes the U.S. auto industry for failing to live up to the values that apparently made the American auto industry an international force—values which have since been abandoned and rediscovered by foreign competitors. Reasoner's moral clarification provides the narrative with a mediation of tension as it both chides the American auto industry to reclaim its heritage and offers support for the traditions of Middle America.

Referee-Tourist

In this combination formula a controversial two-sided issue is presented against the background of either a foreign or American landscape. In other words, the reporter becomes both tourist in the environment and referee at the center of an issue. In "Birds, Bees and Ballots" (12/9/69), for example, Harry Reasoner's opening narration sets up the issue: a school's responsibility to provide sex education versus traditional family and religious values which hold that the responsibility of sex education belongs to individuals, not institutions.

The setting is Renton, Washington, a small town near Seattle. The reporter states that there is "no more explosive issue" that "tears communities apart" than the issue of sex education. Set against street scenes and tours of Renton, this segment also features the muddied narrative structure and unclear resolution common to the arbitration formula. The reporter, as surrogate tourist, visits schools, churches, and town meetings. Characteristic of the heartland narratives, a search for authentic American attitudes guides this segment. As in the other combination formula narratives, however, the reporter shifts between his role as tourist and his role as referee. Characteristic of other arbitration segments, no clear resolution is provided in the concluding scenes. As neutral referee, the reporter makes little attempt to offer a solution; instead he tells us, "Bitterness is so deep, it's hard to see how the split in Renton is going to be healed."

In a second example, "Las Vegas by the Sea" (9/1/74) features opponents of statewide gambling in New Jersey pitted against proponents who see Atlantic City gambling as a means to provide the state with money for urban renewal. As is characteristic of the arbitration formula, the dialectical argument is featured over expository narrative elements: three characters who oppose gambling are interviewed and challenged by three other characters who favor gambling. As in "Why Me?," once again competing views of common sense are presented. Characteristic of tourist segments, reporter Mike Wallace is featured riding in a golf cart and strolling on the Boardwalk, functioning as surrogate vacationer and revealing glimpses of Americana. Typical of the referee formula, there is no obvious villain in this story. Wallace's concluding narration offers closure that appears to support both sides. He points out that although gambling could indeed exploit the poor in New Jersey, it could also save the deterioration of Atlantic City. As our well-informed citizen, the reporter arrives at his own common ground which intersects the competing positions.

Unlike the referee-analyst narratives, which feature the reporter offering moral meaning and favoring a particular side of an argument, in the referee-tourist segments the dialectical issue posed is not clearly resolved. The reporter-tourist personas in these segments function as our surrogate as they take us on tours, not only of particular locales, but also of places that feature apparently irresolvable controversy and intrigue. They define the periphery of these issues and thereby bring us back to the center.

David Thorburn has categorized the kind of centrist storytelling that takes place on 60 Minutes and network television as "consensus narrative."[16] Thorburn poses his interpretation against a vertical "top-down" cultural reading which sees consensus merely as a synonym for the dominant ideologies of a culture. Thorburn wants to rescue the notion of consensus by invoking an alternative, horizontal model of culture. He sees consensus narrative operating across different times and cultures—in "the oral-formulaic of Homer's day, the theater of Sophocles, the Elizabethan theater, the English novel from Defoe to Dickens, . . . the silent film, the sound film, and television during the Network Era."[17] The moral imperative or "assignment" of consensus narrative, then, "is to articulate the culture's central mythologies, in a widely accessible language, an inheritance of shared stories, plots, character types, cultural symbols, and narrative conventions. Such language is popular because it is legible to the common understanding of a majority of the culture. . . ."[18]

In their roles as moral arbiters, the reporters of *60 Minutes* advocate a mythology or consensus narrative that makes sense of contradictory experiences and manages the margins of our society. The program affirms that individuals through adherence to Middle-American values can triumph over institutions which deviate from central norms: allegiances to family, common sense, honesty, education, religion, capitalism, health, democracy, competition, work, loyalty, duty, fidelity, moderation, fairness, team play, efficiency, simplicity, authenticity, discipline, modesty, humility, security, cooperation, and ingenuity.[19] The term *middle* in middle class signifies arbitration of a variety of contradictory tensions: us and them, public and private, liberal and conservative, nature and culture, tradition and change, and, most significantly for *60 Minutes*, individual and institution.

News and the Myth of Individualism

7

> At its most basic, individualism is the pursuit of personal freedom and of personal control over the social and natural environment. It is also an ideology—a set of beliefs, values, and goals—and probably the most widely shared ideology in the U.S.
>
> —Herbert Gans

> But individualism has come to mean so many things and to contain such contradictions and paradoxes that even to defend it requires that we analyze it critically, that we consider especially those tendencies that would destroy it from within.
>
> —*Habits of the Heart*

> Newswork emphasizes the primacy of the individual. . . .
>
> —Gaye Tuchman

The stories of *60 Minutes*—held together by reporters performing as detectives, therapists, tourists, and referees—take viewers in and out of the problems of everyday life. On any given Sunday, *60 Minutes* as cultural production recruits viewers in the process of building, challenging, and maintaining a commonsense perspective on American society. In other words, *60 Minutes* constructs a largely Middle-American mythology—a mythology that celebrates the dignity of the *self* in the face of bullying bureaucracy and sinister *others*.

I use myth here not in its narrower pejorative sense, but as a central sense-making process at the heart of any culture—defining its people, its organizations, its norms, and its tensions. The main task of mythology is to provide a society with a stock of stories that hold out the possibility of confronting and suspending the conflicts and contradictions of everyday life.[1] In a world where experience at times defies our individual common sense, cultural myths search for a way to make and impose sense. And each Sunday *60 Minutes* takes on the tensions in contemporary America and wraps them in the security of its familiar and mythic formulas.

Shortly before he died in 1987, Joseph Campbell complained to Bill Moyers on PBS that one of the problems with contemporary America, unlike pre-modern cultures, is that we lack a central mythological system that would help explain and incorporate the increasing complexity wrought by advanced capitalism, impersonal technologies, and creeping bureaucracy.[2] And while Campbell may have been essentially right about the absence of a nurturing mythic system, I argue that if there is a central, single myth sustaining contemporary America, it is found, among other places, on television—and in television's fierce affirmation of American individualism.

In their 1985 sociological study of American individualism, *Habits of the Heart,* Robert Bellah and his colleagues define two general components to the "numerous, sometimes contradictory senses" of American individualism: one, "a belief in the inherent dignity and, indeed, sacredness of the human person" and, two, "a belief that the individual has a primary reality whereas society is a second-order, derived or artificial construct. . . ."[3] But their definitions and accounts of individualism generally ignore its promotion in mass media, especially television, the leisure and cultural pursuit located near the center of many of our living rooms, and therefore near the center of the lives of most Middle Americans. Instead, devoting minimal attention to television, *Habits of the Heart* exudes a predictable, elitist, expert distrust of television's role in democracy. Bellah and his colleagues vaguely categorize American television as part of the "culture of separation," highlighting its "disconnectedness" to reality, its "extraordinary discontinuity," and its failure to support "any clear set of beliefs or values."[4] If *Habits of the Heart* is right on these points, at the very least this important study fails to grasp how television mimics the actual disconnectedness and discontinuity that are a part of everyday life—from news reports on Sudanese starvation to comic advertisements for meatier dog food, from the self-indulgent pulse of MTV to the self-righteous warning of television evangelists.

Like *Habits of the Heart,* television, in its own way, and in spite of its connection to commodity commerce, also seeks meaning, sense, and affirmation of the "sacredness" of the individual. The mythic impulse on television searches to resolve fundamental, archetypal conflicts between good and evil, tradition and change, nature and culture, and individual and institution. Not only does television offer a generally intelligible vision that affirms individualism in the face of bureaucratic tyranny, but it also often does so through the coherence, continuity, and assurance of its formulas—through its adventures, its mysteries, its melodramas, and its news.

And nowhere on television is individualism as celebrated as it is on *60 Minutes*. In the more than 120 episodes featured in its 1979-80 season alone, a season when *60 Minutes* ranked as the most watched show in America, no fewer than forty segments carried titles either naming or nicknaming individuals featured in those segments. A sampling: "Jesse Jackson and Billy Graham" (9/16/79), "Castro" (9/30/79), "Edward Rubin, M.D." (10/21/79), "Pavarotti" (11/4/79), "Marva" (11/11/79), "The Ayatollah" (11/18/79), "Roy Innis" (11/25/79), "The Sheik" (12/23/79), "Big John" and "Roy Cohn" (both 12/30/79), "George Who?" (1/13/79), "Bette Davis" (1/20/79), "The Death of Edward Nevin" and "Anderson of Illinois" (both 2/17/80), "Citizen Loeb" (2/24/80), "Bobby Knight" and "Barry Goldwater" (both 3/9/80), "Libya's Qaddafi" (3/23/80), "Anne Lindbergh" (4/20/80), " 'Here's . . . Johnny' " (4/27/80), "Fellini" (5/11/80), "The Establishment vs. Dr. Burton" (5/18/80), and "A Man Called L'Amour" (6/1/80). While part of the narrative reflex in all news routinely limits meanings to stories about particular characters, the *60 Minutes* reconstruction and foregrounding of experience around dramatic characters place the program at odds with the myths of science which anchor more conventional reporting.

Studying mythic dimensions in news reveals clues, however, about how both conventional and dramatic journalism organize experience. Myths are not merely apocryphal stories associated with earlier cultures but are vital contemporary creators of meaning and value.[5] John Hartley in *Understanding News* contends that modern myths allow "a society to use factual or fictional characters and events to make sense of its environment" and "endow the world with conceptual values. . . ."[6] News, then, and *60 Minutes* are in the business of making myths.

In focusing on the narrative formulas of *60 Minutes*, I necessarily have turned my attention to the roles reporters play as contemporary messengers of myth. These individual and public roles constitute important social metaphors that act to clarify the abstract and make known the unfamiliar. In his study of British television, Roger Silverstone asserts that the metaphorical power in myth relies on the "transformation of conceptual categories: raw and cooked, full and empty, inside and outside, young and old. As one becomes the other, as the abstraction is given concrete form, the world can be spoken of and it can, if only provisionally, be understood." Television in general performs for society the role that metaphor plays in myth: "Television's effectiveness consists in its ability to translate the unfamiliar into the familiar and to provide frameworks for making sense of the unintelligible."[7]

The reporters of *60 Minutes* are powerful—often heroic—performers in the American drama. As individuals, they act to resolve tensions between the familiar and unfamiliar, between the known and the unknown, and ultimately between the images of their own stories and the represented world.

Within human experience, as Edmund Leach argues, "there are certain fundamental contradictions . . . with which all human beings must come to terms," and "myth provides a way of dealing with these universal puzzles."[8] Because most of us cannot live suspended between these contradictory forces (life-death, nature-culture, old-young, permanence-change), the myths of our religions, our science, our literature, and our news help us confront and suspend the tension. Myths and *60 Minutes* constrain the uncertainty of experience by casting it into the familiarity of story.

Like all storytelling, *60 Minutes*'s narratives incorporate the mythic rhythms of the birth-life-death cycles of human experience within the beginning-middle-end patterns of narrative construction. In contemporary America we most often tell stories featuring individual-society and private-public conflicts. *60 Minutes* tells stories that categorize and sort personal identities from the social milieu—stories that tell us who we are. These stories of individual self lie "at the very core of American culture," and, with all their contradictions, are "closely linked to middle-class status," to a common center.[9]

The narratives of *60 Minutes* feature the myth of individualism at its core—a core which redefines all sorts of experience in terms of its own center. Following are retellings and interpretations of contrasting *60 Minutes* segments which demonstrate the power of individualism resting at the heart of commonsense, middle-class virtues. The pull of this myth brings us back to center amid modern anxieties over human suffering, burgeoning technology, corporate complexity, and bureaucratic indifference.

Individualism in the Mainstream

Although I have generally concentrated on the four major formulas in the *60 Minutes* repertoire, the more than twenty-year history of the program is much richer and more complex than can be accounted for herein. As I suggested in chapter 6, reporters seldom perform only *one* role in any individual story. Often a reporter may act as detective, tourist, narrator, social critic, historian, prosecutor, therapist, and referee in various narratives. In fact, the reporter might enact three or four different roles within the same story. One commonality, however, among the goals of all of these well-informed social types is to bear witness to American individualism.

"Mister Right" (12/14/75) serves as one representative performance of the multidimensional reporter in his examination of individualism. In this segment that pre-dates the Reagan presidency by five years, Mike Wallace interviews then Republican candidate Ronald Reagan against the background of his California ranch. In his opening narration, Wallace, as the reporter-tourist, frames the story as a vacation: "*60 Minutes* elected to spend some time with Ronald and Nancy Reagan at home in California." In one scene Wallace, Ronald, and Nancy Reagan (a long-time friend of Wallace's), deep in conversation, lean over the ranch fence as horses graze in the background. Another interview scene features Wallace in sweater and windbreaker riding with Reagan across the countryside in a jeep. Together they analyze the everyday mood and politics of the country.

The choice of setting here suggests an authentic American experience—a Western ranch, home to a former movie star who in his films celebrated the mythology of the Western hero. *60 Minutes* intersperses clips from old Reagan movies throughout the segment. At one point, Wallace asks him about his presidential plans and whether he could beat Hubert Humphrey in 1976. Reagan says, "I'd sure give it a good country try," disclosing that his own values apparently rest in the land, in rugged rural settings, away from artificial and big-city modernity.

As he tries to make sense of this particular individual, Wallace also surveys the ranch and identifies Reagan's social privilege: "You've got it made." He then wonders why Reagan would abandon this place in the country where his values apparently rest for the turmoil and callousness of Washington bureaucracy. In aligning himself with the center, Reagan denies both personal ambition and right-wing, off-center views. Instead, he talks of his sense of duty ("Life begins when you begin to serve") and how his friends persuaded him to seek high office. His responses to tangled moral questions such as the death penalty ("I'm in favor... because it saves lives") and abortion ("I can't get over that you're killing someone") offer uncomplicated, declarative clarity as they seek a center along the muddy conservative-liberal continuum.

At strategic points in the interview, Wallace—as cross-examiner—begins to challenge Reagan with the accusations that he is off-center: a "button pusher," who "frightens some folks," who "doesn't understand the problems of human beings," and has a "reputation of being insensitive to people at the bottom of the heap." Wallace begins defining for Reagan the parameters of individualism if he indeed wants to serve as our president.

Here, Wallace masterfully explores our dominant American myth and, according to John Fiske, its chief paradox: "the most widely held communal value is that of individualism. The desire to be oneself does not mean the desire to be fundamentally different from everyone else, but rather to situate individual differences within communal allegiance."[10] So Wallace, paradoxically, explores both the individual qualities that have elevated Reagan to a privileged status beyond the ordinary and demands that Reagan understand and incorporate his individualism within ordinary "communal allegiance." In other words, the segment acknowledges Reagan's individual differences and accomplishments; at the same time, it insists that Reagan be more like "us"—feet firmly planted on common ground.

At another point in the segment, Wallace continues to locate the Reagans' individual values within a broader context. Wallace becomes psychoanalyst and asks the Reagans to play a word association game. He tosses out words and phrases—the death penalty, marijuana, abortion, Ted Kennedy—and asks the future presidential couple to situate their responses on middle ground. At the end of his outdoor interview with Reagan, Wallace in his role as narrator-

In early 1989, Wallace interviewed the Reagans in a special one-hour episode that marked the Reagans' return to "regular" life. (© MCMLXXXIX–CBS Inc. All rights reserved.)

analyst endows the story with the moral meaning of common ties. In speaking for "all of us," Wallace comments that Americans are "disillusioned over politics" and "dishonesty" in government. He tells Reagan on behalf of the viewers: "We're always in trouble . . . no matter who we elect." The reporter serves notice that the value of honesty—the moral, individual antidote to the disease of corrupt, institutional politics—is what we seek in our political candidates.

Fourteen years later, Wallace again interviewed the Reagans just before they were to leave the White House to return to private life in California. In "The Reagans" (1/15/89), a special hour-long analyst segment which features flashback scenes from the 1975 interview, Wallace immediately locates the narrative in the individual rather than the social domain: "Our conversation with them didn't delve deep into foreign policy or budget deficits. Most of our time was spent on their personal insights into what these past eight years have brought them. They talk of their views of the Gorbachevs, both Mikhail and Raisa, of Ollie North and John Poindexter. Mrs. Reagan speaks with some candor of the former White House Chief of Staff,

Donald Regan. They ruminate on the pressures of private life in a public fish bowl."

Wallace spends much of the interview personalizing Reagan. He notes, for instance, that Reagan's morning newspaper ritual starts with reading the comics then moves on to the "serious stuff." Reagan tells Wallace that he is currently reading "George Burns' story about Gracie." Wallace later in the interview calls attention to Reagan's weight training regimen in the basement of the White House. Wallace as analyst here places Reagan's routines in the comfortable context of Middle-American values—enjoying the comics, reading celebrity autobiographies, and staying fit.

While Wallace situates Reagan's individuality within the context of common allegiances, he challenges Reagan to respond to criticisms from the periphery. Wallace calls on Reagan to answer for his administrative policies concerning African Americans: "Can you understand why many feel they have missed the Reagan Revolution?" Reagan deflects attention from broader social trends and consequences. Instead, he tells individual anecdotes that pull us into his personal values and behavior. He recounts his early support of blacks in mainstream professional sports, his hiring of black policymakers during his tenure as governor of California, and his childhood upbringing "in which the greatest sin that would bring the wrath of both father and mother down on me and my brother was prejudice and discrimination." Reagan talks about the "suffering" he endured because he was sometimes located "on the other side" by "some of these [black] leaders." In his defense, he points with pride and humor to his honorary membership in "The Tuskegee Flyers," a group of "great black fighter pilots" who fought in World War II and trained at Tuskegee Institute, "one of the great Negro colleges."

Living up to his introductory promise to focus on the personal, Wallace does not draw Reagan into a debate on chronic national patterns of prejudice and discrimination. At least in this interview, Reagan's understanding and misunderstanding of these issues remain anchored in his individual reality not in broader competing definitions of social realities. Wallace here repositions Ronald and Nancy Reagan on the ladder of social status. Where the Reagans would climb to the top, Wallace pulls them back to the middle.

In defining the Reagans in terms of the center, the Wallace analysis masks an important and persistent contradiction: the kind of privilege and status acquired by the Reagans would normally be at odds with Middle-American virtues of moderation and simplicity. Yet the Reagans achieved an admired, even heroic, stature among a fairly substantial portion of America's heartland, in part because news stories like this one portray them as Middle American despite their privileged social rank.

Individualism at the Margins

In sharp contrast to the preceding segments about the individualism of this privileged California couple regarded increasingly as icons for centrist values, a segment about a homeless woman offers a view from the periphery. Through her transformation in the *60 Minutes* narrative, however, she too arrives at a midpoint on the class ladder.

Joyce Brown became a news character in 1987, when the city of New York whisked her from the street against her will and committed her to psychiatric care.[11] In November 1987, the New York *Times* story began its own dramatic account and interpretation this way: "Lawyers and psychiatrists clashed in a courtroom at the Bellevue Hospital Center yesterday over whether New York City had the right to take a homeless woman from the streets and treat her against her will in a psychiatric ward."[12]

Nearly three months later, *60 Minutes* presented its compelling version in a story titled "Brown vs. Koch" (1/24/88).[13] In this referee-analyst segment, battle lines are erected between competing experts, between personal rights and social obligations, and between normal (commonsense) and deviant (nonsense) behavior. Instead of emphasizing expert conflict between psychiatrists and lawyers, or between government officials and social activists (as conventional television news might), *60 Minutes* transforms the story into an even more personal drama—a dispute between a heroic individual, Joyce Brown, and a meddling autocrat, New York Mayor Ed Koch.

As the Reagans are icons for privilege, Joyce Brown briefly becomes an icon for the homeless. The center of a controversy that referee-analyst Morley Safer of *60 Minutes* calls "an urban fable for our time," Brown animates a clash of contradictory meanings and competing values that strike at the sacred heart of American individualism.

A story about the social problem of homelessness becomes a battle between individual characters, as street person Joyce Brown takes on New York Mayor Ed Koch. Safer narrates and arbitrates. (© MCMLXXXVIII–CBS Inc. All rights reserved.)

Following the knowledge hierarchy in news, Safer introduces the major characters and their social class positions. First, we meet the well-informed reporter who introduces Joyce Brown, victim in the story and now a potential voice for common sense. Next, we meet Koch, official leader of New York City government. A variety of doctors and lawyers parade before us confirming Brown's lucidity or madness. Shots follow of unidentified homeless, representatives of the world of nonsense; and unlike Safer, Brown, Koch, and other experts, they do not speak in this narrative that is also about them.

In spite of her apparently marginal status, Joyce Brown delivers a powerful affirmation of individualism following Safer's introductory remarks: "I am an adult—a 40-year-old intelligent woman. And I don't need Mayor Koch or Bellevue to tell me where I can live." Her opening statement effectively sets up her individual confrontation with autocracy and bureaucracy.

Next, a class battle takes shape between the homeless and, in Safer's words, "the rich people on the upper East Side." At different

146

points in the segment, Safer argues that the city's "Project Help" commits homeless people to Bellevue because they trespass into "high rise, high life territory where you can spend $50 a week to have your dog walked or $450 a month to have your car parked." And Safer skillfully plugs Koch into this class war: "He [Koch] also lives on the upper East Side in this gracious home just off Gracie Square, barely a mile away from Joyce Brown's spot." That spot, Safer tells us, is "literally the pavement" over a hot air vent.

After setting up Koch as a member of the privileged, *60 Minutes* then connects an interview in which Brown claims to be a "political prisoner" with a Koch interview. The mayor smugly but emotionally responds, "Please, this is not the Soviet Union where she's a political prisoner. Is anyone suggesting that Joyce Brown is a political prisoner?" Safer now has his villain. He points to Koch, firmly shakes his finger, and says, "Joyce Brown—Joyce Brown is." Safer, who at times referees this battle between Brown and Koch at a distance, here adopts the role of analyst as he appears to side with Brown's individuality and against the mayor's institutional stand.

As institutional representative, Koch makes his case against Joyce Brown, insisting over and over that Brown, her position, and her supporters are "bizarre," "ridiculous," and "outrageous." But Safer carefully places Koch's arguments in the context of a battle over whether Brown speaks with the voice of common sense or nonsense. In one of the tight close-ups which put her individuality under cramped scrutiny, Brown defends her right to be homeless by affirming personal freedom, the most sacred tenet of individualism: "This is the United States of America—the Constitution—freedom of choice. If that's the way a person wants to live their life, and they're an adult, who am I to say they can't do that."

In trying once again to find communal and consensual ground, Safer asks her to defend her individuality. In sensible tones she explains her "bizarre" behavior. She prefers the streets to living in a shelter because, "Shelters are very dangerous. I've been in one before. The people that you're there with, you don't know, uh, why they're there, what brought them there. Some are insane. Some are criminals. They are very dangerous people. And they're not kept up good." Brown, in vindicating herself, identifies with *us*—and against *them,* the general homeless population. *They,* after all, are very dangerous people. And, now elevated temporarily to star status in

147

Safer at Joyce Brown's "home," a Manhattan sidewalk over a hot air vent, just down the street from Mayor Koch in Gracie Mansion. (© MCMLXXV–CBS Inc. All rights reserved.)

the *60 Minutes* drama, Brown makes it clear that she does not consider herself to be one of *them*.

She also calmly explains why she defecated in the streets: "As far as using the pavement as a toilet, I didn't have access to a bathroom. There were times when I would go to restaurants and ask them, 'could I use their bathroom?' And they would say, 'no, you can't.' Even if I offered to buy something." Finally, when Safer confronts her with the charge that she burned money, she provides another apparently rational response:

BROWN: I only needed $7 to eat per day. I never kept any more than $7 per day because I was on the street and I could be mugged.

SAFER: Is that reason to burn up the money?

BROWN: It depended on the manner in which they gave it to me whether or not I burned it.

SAFER: How do you mean?

BROWN: Well, sometimes they would throw money at me. Just ball it up and throw it at me. Now that's not the way you give people money. Everyone doesn't want to live on the street. But if that's what they want to do, let them do it.

Her testimonial to individualism is intercut with reactions from a sympathetic Safer. And, immediately following this polite interchange, *60 Minutes* punctuates her explanations with a sound bite from one of her ACLU lawyers: "Joyce Brown is rational, coherent, articulate, today, just as she was when she was on the streets. She has a track record of living on the street for over a year, keeping herself warm, providing food for herself, entering the hospital in good physical condition. A person like that simply doesn't meet the civil commitment standards, under the Constitution or under existing law." Her seemingly sane responses to the most outrageous charges undermine Koch, his experts ("five city psychiatrists" who diagnosed her as paranoid schizophrenic), and their position that she inhabits a world of nonsense. Thus, Joyce Brown appears to win the war of sound bites with Koch, emerging as the voice of common sense and standard-bearer for individualism.[14]

In an update of "Brown vs. Koch," which aired one month later in February 1988, Harry Reasoner tells us that Brown has been released by the city of New York. In part because of her celebrity status in the *60 Minutes* story, she now has an apartment, a part-time job, and "a half dozen book and movie offers to sort through.

And last week she lectured at Harvard Law School. The subject—
'The Homeless Crisis: A View from the Street.' " Here, Joyce Brown
takes on trappings of middle- and upper-class success by gaining
social credentials. She has a job and a real address. Her sudden rise
up the status ladder works to reconcile the residue of contradictions
regarding her former marginal standing. In supporting centrist virtues, *60 Minutes* once again prizes the discourse of individual common sense over the institutional discourse of experts and officialdom.

In reclaiming Brown from the domain of nonsense, *60 Minutes*
does not, in any way, also bring other unidentified homeless into
the fold. In Brown's ascent up the hierarchy of knowledge, in becoming an expert lecturer on homelessness, she leapfrogs over the
unidentified homeless, leaving them in the nether region of the other.
They, the homeless, still represent a danger to us—a meaning that,
as Safer reported, is even shared by Joyce Brown at the beginning
of the segment when she responded to her status as a test case for
Project Help:

> BROWN: I was definitely the wrong one that they did pick on . . . (she
> smiles and laughs).
> SAFER (off-screen and laughing): How do you mean that?
> BROWN: Because I'm sane. I'm not insane. And there are thousands
> out there they could have used for a model. I'm the wrong one.

Brown regards herself as a champion for American individualism
and defends her right to choose to be homeless. Her endearing
laughter underscores her role as heroic individual in this drama—
although her words continue to marginalize the "thousands" of
unidentified homeless "out there" as part of the periphery at the
outskirts of common sense.

Joyce Brown's apparent personal triumph suggests in part that
American individualism works. In fact, *60 Minutes* aired a second
update of "Brown vs. Koch" in June 1988 and reported that President Reagan had appropriated the story as both a representative
example of rugged individualism and "the care with which America
deals with its homeless."[15] But as an individual icon for the homeless,
Joyce Brown may not be at all representative. If she is mentally ill,
as the City of New York claimed, she may typify fewer than 20
percent of the homeless; if she is homeless by choice, as her lawyers
and Reagan claimed, she may represent fewer than 6 percent of the

homeless.[16] Joyce Brown, then, may be right; she may be "the wrong one," untypical of America's homeless. Yet paradoxically, over her protest and by virtue of her climb up the class ladder in this news drama viewed by millions, she ascended for a time to the position of individual star—one of George Bush's "thousand points of light."

What distinguished Joyce Brown as the temporary emblem of homelessness for *60 Minutes* was her ability to articulate a commonsense position. Ultimately, as she extolled heartland individualism, her plight seemed less threatening. Through the Joyce Brown story, the news places the apparent deviancy of homelessness, to use the terms of Stuart Hall and his colleagues, "back into the consensus" by "translating the unfamiliar into the familiar world" of the narrative.[17] The *60 Minutes* story restores Middle-American safety and normalcy as Joyce Brown—this marginal representative from another world—reenters and reaffirms our world.

The Limits of Individualism

Both the Reagan and Joyce Brown segments demonstrate how *60 Minutes* attempts to reposition its characters at a central location more in line with a consensual middle ground. In "Mr. Right" and "The Reagans," Mike Wallace has to rescue Ronald Reagan from positions both too far right of center and too high on the social ladder. In "Brown vs. Koch," Morley Safer faces the opposite task as he must pull Joyce Brown up from her homeless standing and deviant antics to a more comfortable, centrist position.

Each of these stories speak to the limits of individualism. In their implicit moral judgments, *60 Minutes* defines marginal activity: scaring people as reactionary "button pusher," ignoring "people at the bottom of the heap," "burning money," and "defecating in the street." Both sets of news narratives suggest that individualism must be responsive to some notion of communal allegiances and consensual values.

What eventually makes the celebration of individualism in *60 Minutes* specifically and in news generally an alluring mythology is the limits it places on other stories and other ways to view and reconstruct experience. On one hand, we cannot deny the power and appeal of stories about individual heroes in an increasingly bureaucratized, corporate culture where it is easy to lose one's bear-

ings. In arguing that myths create individual identities and locate
the hero in the larger social order, myths—in which the hero-seeker
endures rites of departure and initiation—also cross different cultural
borders and transcend time periods.[18] The power of myth is the
ability of its stories and its heroes to make sense across cultures,
space, and time.

On the other hand, however, what do news stories of individual
heroes tell us about how it is to live within the social—not merely
individual—milieu of an unequal, technological, and commodified
America? John Fiske warns that "Clearly the news is peopled by
real individuals, but in representing events through people the news
is following the conventions of classic realism, for it assumes that
the way to construct an understandable and authentic version of the
real is through the actions, words, and reactions of the individuals
involved. Social and political issues are only reported if they can be
embodied in an individual, and thus social conflict of interest is
personalized into conflict between individuals." What happens, Fiske
argues, is that collective, historical, and political contexts are limited
and obscured because "the social origins of events are lost."[19]

The individuals who are chosen over and over to speak in news
reports are a select few. They reoccur in the news because of their
privileged social standing or their individual expert knowledge. As
Fiske writes, "The socially powerful tend to be familiar to us as
individuals, the powerless or the voices of opposition are familiar
mainly as social roles, which are filled by a variety of forgetable
individuals. The elite, who appear repeatedly, bear the accumulated
meanings of their past appearances. Because these are embodied in
an individual they carry greater semiotic weight in our individualistic
society than do the accumulated meanings of 'roles,' such as union
organizer, victim, and so on. The social power of elite persons is
underscored by the narrative power that familiarity confers."[20] And
so whereas we will remember Ronald Reagan because of his privileged status as a major reappearing star in the American drama,
Joyce Brown's fame is fleeting.

Commenting on Brown as a symbol for homelessness, Mike Wallace argues that her choice is related much more to conventional
news criteria, to her easy accessibility, and to her deviant behavior,
than to an attempt by *60 Minutes* to open up and sustain a public
forum on homelessness as a social problem: "She was picked because

she was on the streets of New York, and she was shitting on the street. And because she was an articulate black woman. That's why she was picked. She was available easily, she could be covered a lot, she was doing outrageous things, and she was the center of a small storm . . . in New York, at that moment. And she was a phenomenon. We haven't heard from Joyce Brown in a year, and I doubt that we're ever going to hear about Joyce Brown very much again."[21]

Wallace's observations mark a troubling aspect of *60 Minutes* and news in general. Joyce Brown and other individuals who pass through the frame of narrative news are appropriated for drama only up to a point. Then these characters no longer suit conventions of timeliness, proximity, or deviancy; they no longer fit the narrative. As Fiske suggests, major news stories are primarily about "what disrupts the normal," about deviating from consensus; therefore, there is "little sense of continuous history in news, and few references to previous events."[22]

In addition, the passing of Joyce Brown beyond the confines of *60 Minutes* marks the inability of formula to sustain in a long-range way any dialogue regarding broader community and institutional enigmas. Once an individual character who plays a particular generic role is spent, rather than cashing in the story at the level of the social, *60 Minutes* turns from Brown and banks on other "outrageous" characters who may for a time partially capture, individualize, and dramatize the intrigue of a larger social dilemma.

The most familiar voices in the news, then, represent "a limited range of social positions," usually speaking to and contained within the boundaries of Middle-American common sense. Voices from the periphery that appear too radical or nonsensical, Fiske notes, are generally "not allowed to speak directly, but are reported, that is, mediated if there point of view is represented at all."[23]

Trashing the Institution

60 Minutes and the news finally forge an unspoken trap. This trap captures individualism at the expense of understanding how our large institutions work and how they ultimately control and are controlled by people who are protected within complex organizational and corporate structures—people who may refuse to talk to *60 Minutes*. And, in their absence, *60 Minutes* simply portrays the institution as a narrative villain. In part, the individuals in power who run institutions such as New York City government or the Pentagon understand the constraints of journalistic conventions and hide behind the broad protection of institutional anonymity. The organization may be indicted by the news, but the persons who refuse the scrutiny of the news remain safe. Mike Wallace offers this defense of *60 Minutes*'s treatment of the Pentagon:

> Look, I make no excuses for anything that any of our people do about the Pentagon. The Pentagon . . . is our public servant. We pay their bills. They work for us. I simply don't believe that they have the right not to answer us. . . . And for eight years [under the Reagan administration and Secretary of Defense Caspar Weinberger], they wouldn't talk to us. . . . Well, does that mean we become captives of that, and therefore don't do the stories because they will not talk to us? As a result of which, you'll take a helicopter shot or you'll stand out in front of the Pentagon and say, "Look. We wanted to talk to this individual, and we wanted to ask these questions. They didn't want to answer us."[24]

From the reporter's perspective, Wallace speaks common sense. But in understanding how institutions work and don't work, are we limited only to insider knowledge and a flesh-and-blood interview subject on camera or in quotes? Do reporters—often genuine experts after years of covering particular institutional beats—know things they cannot tell us because of limits imposed by journalistic neutrality and formula? Not only, then, are we denied access to knowledge by individuals who control secrets to understanding particular institutions, but also by news organizations themselves whose very conventions limit access to the meanings of these institutions in contemporary America.

What Edward J. Epstein said of Bob Woodward and Carl Bernstein's now classic *All the President's Men*—and the metaphorical transformation of Watergate into a detective story—continues to apply to journalism and *60 Minutes*: "If the reporter can be established as an intrepid, omniscient Sherlock Holmes, the focus of attention is shifted" away from "the real powers that be."[25] In the late 1970s Epstein argued that most reporters "fail to understand the role of institutions" because of "an unwillingness to see the complexity of bureaucratic infighting and of politics. . . ." Returning to Watergate as a metaphor, Epstein also suggested how myths focused on individuals can limit meanings: "So long as journalists maintain their usual professional blind spot toward the inner workings and conflicts of the institutions of government, they will no doubt continue to speak of Watergate in terms of the David and Goliath myth, with Bernstein and Woodward as David and the government as Goliath."[26] Limited by formula and preoccupied with individual stories at the expense of how institutions work, journalism—even enterprise reporting—continues to confirm Epstein's diagnosis. As Michael Schudson notes, "even muckrakers have typically focused on the hypocrisies and corruptions of government, rather than on underlying assumptions or structures of power."[27]

In fact, the 1980s' Iran arms-for-hostages scandal should have demonstrated the inner machinations of two powerful institutions—the executive arm of government and the Pentagon. Yet through daily journalism this set of complicated experiences more often became the Oliver North Story. A single individual, a relatively minor figure in the organizational configurations of the powerful institutions he served, replaced the presidency and the Pentagon as the focal point for journalistic meanings about this entanglement. And North, despite the legal convictions and fines related to his deception, emerged heroically in some corners of Middle America—indeed labelled "hero" by then-President Reagan.[28] Aided and abetted by the inability of news reports to focus on the social dimensions of this experience, North managed to pass himself off as a victimized individual fighting the menacing institutional inquiries of Congress, the press, and finally the courts. No matter that North was also an underling himself in two institutions. Because of press and public appeal for news stories with individual characters, North became the central symbol in this affair. In both the Watergate and Iran arms stories what often passes in journalism for information is just as significantly affirmation of stoic American individualism.

There is an elegant irony in that news is often criticized by the conservative right for its noisy and nosy social liberalism, yet what is acclaimed by news is the very individualism—the very celebration of "a thousand points of light"—that remains the bedrock of conservative politics. Don Hewitt, perhaps the highest-paid editor in the history of news, in a 1989 New York *Times* editorial writes of his own bind: "Having gotten used to being 'a misguided, bleeding heart liberal,' I woke up the morning after the [1988] election to find that

I was 'an ultra-right wing, Neanderthal conservative' to boot. Journalists have to be one or the other, don't they? But which one am I? A conservative or a liberal?"[29] Hewitt doesn't appear to take a side here. Depending on the individual issue and his own situational ethics, ultimately he can be comfortable in either camp. The editorial continues:

> Maybe I wasn't in school the day they taught it, but I don't understand what's conservative about selling arms to an ayatollah and liberal about wanting to find out how that happened.
>
> I often wonder how an old Hollywood hand like Ronald Reagan could have done that. After all, John Wayne, Gary Cooper and Jimmy Stewart would never have sold guns to the bad guys. I thought America did far too much crowing about its little tin-soldier war in Grenada and showed a lack of backbone when it didn't go into Lebanon and find the terrorists who killed our marines. Liberal or conservative?

Hewitt's words, like the best of *60 Minutes*, signal the "open eye" of common sense that sees through the arbitrary and illusory boundaries of rigid political categories. But Hewitt's other eye is closed. Like a *60 Minutes* narrative, his editorial too is *not* about the failure of social institutions and individuals' existential and collective responsibility for that failure; rather, as in the Reagan or Joyce Brown segments, it's about individual choice and consensus values. Hewitt's "sixth sense" cannot see the same arbitrary, illusory, and uninspected boundary operating *between* conceptions of individualism and social institutions; he believes too in individual not social reality.

Like most of us firmly planted in Middle America, Hewitt and *60 Minutes* honor individual reality as natural, perceptive, and therefore genuine, but chide social realities as constructed, capricious, and therefore inauthentic. Like his program, Hewitt has invoked the powerful mythology of individual choice to mediate and resolve collective and political dilemmas. His commonsense views reveal too why he celebrates the personal journalism of *60 Minutes* over the institutional journalism of traditional network news documentaries.

60 Minutes's stories salute the integrity of the individual and affirm virtues that sustain us in the face of contrary and incomprehensible tension. Hewitt argues that one reason for the program's success rests in his own ties to Middle America: "My strength is that I have the common touch. I don't know why this is, because most of the people I hang around with are pretty elite. But Kiwanians, Rotarians, I understand them. . . . Maybe it's because I grew up in New Rochelle, the small town that George M. Cohan wrote '45 Minutes from Broadway' about. It was very Middle American. . . . My mother was a housewife. We were middle class."[30] Hewitt's "common touch" is common sense. His small-town, middle-class history taps into a fundamental mythic impulse in American culture, a nostalgic yearning to retreat from the large-scale bureaucracies and institutions that might rob our lives of meaning and coherence. We are, each of us, seekers of a moral order—a common ground—that stories so often provide.

60 Minutes, however, is too often blind to a perception of itself as an elite social institution. The reporters—who often appear as heroic loners at odds with bureaucracies—actually work with a large team of *60 Minutes* staffers and work for a large news conglomerate. Given the way *60 Minutes* features and honors its own individual star reporters over the team of producers, shooters, writers, researchers, technicians, and editors who actually construct each story, it is not surprising that the narratives themselves pay such homage to rugged American individualism. Significantly, and ironically, Hewitt calls his operation a "shop" not an institution.[31] The program, however, has indeed become a powerful cultural institution. In addition, these real reporters who, like Don Hewitt, represent a certain elite, East Coast, upper-middle-class value system, affirm in their stories virtues more central to America's heartland. In great part this contradiction is what American television is most often about. Indeed, the most important role that Hewitt's *60 Minutes* "shop" may play in American culture is the construction, maintenance, and repair of a Middle-American mythology that appears to hold us together, to offer a stable center amid our wobbly cultural contradictions.

Like Clockwork: The Search for Center

8

> Turning and turning in the widening gyre
> The falcon cannot hear the falconer,
> Things fall apart; the center cannot hold.
>
> —William Butler Yeats

> The present world is in some sense deranged, the center is not holding. . . .
>
> —Walker Percy

> The search for common moral understandings continues even in the face of the assertion that they are impossible.
>
> —*Habits of the Heart*

The story unfolds in the streets of Cairo. A *60 Minutes* reporter tells us about an alien place, the "city of garbage," within Egypt's capitol. The visuals in these opening shots—troubling to Middle-American consciousness—are difficult to watch. Men, women, and children dig through mounds of garbage in search of food and clothing. These are Cairo's outcasts, trash collectors for Egypt's biggest city. They have built their homes and lives atop the rubble they collect.

We meet Sister Emmanuelle, a French nun who has worked as a missionary among these people for fifteen years. This October 1987 segment is named after her. Diane Sawyer, in rumpled cotton, khaki, and jeans, walks the streets with this remarkable woman, who smiles and offers hope. Sawyer interviews her at home—a one-room shack which Sister Emmanuelle describes as better than any Hilton. The missionary shows us her "shower": a pitcher of water she pours over her head. She counsels an outcast couple about their stormy marriage. She practices her English reading Agatha Christie novels. She raises millions of dollars to build a high school. She lobbies Cairo's leading politicians for better conditions. She teaches Diane Sawyer a dance.

By the end of "Sister Emmanuelle" (10/18/87), a once foreign place has been transfigured—tamed by the *60 Minutes* drama which has made the unknown and the foreign accessible. This ability of *60 Minutes* to tell stories, to make the unfamiliar familiar, the uncomfortable comfortable, represents both the grace and the sin of the most financially successful and most influential news program in American television history. *60 Minutes* both transforms and reforms the world. Through its mystery, therapy, adventure, and arbitration stories, the program enriches by affirming the spirit of heroic individuals—not just Sister Emmanuelle but all of us—who prevail in the face of oppression.

But *60 Minutes* also skews social phenomena; the ongoing experiences of Cairo's outcasts, or the homeless in "Brown vs. Koch," or the security guards in "Why Me?" are not fourteen-minute teleplays. Other mysteries persist outside the boundaries of dramatic resolution and affirmation. The program claims little social responsibility for experiences it reconstructs as news drama. The reporters of *60 Minutes* leave these places to pursue other stories—and we leave with them. We will all be together again next week—same time, different place. We can count on the show to deliver the transformed experience that many of us seek in fiction: the unmasking of villainy, the celebration of integrity, the taming of ambiguity.

News and Social Change

Acclaimed and admired for their performances in independent roles, the reporters of *60 Minutes* periodically do step forward from the pose of heroic yet distant observers of experience. They occasionally act as an arm of social justice on behalf of individuals. In adopting such a social role they extend their performance past the limits and requirements of narrative formula. Mike Wallace, in his autobiography *Close Encounters,* argues that viewers regard the program as a dramatic "unofficial ombudsman": "[B]y the late 1970s . . . I kept bumping into people who jumped at the chance to alert me to some scandal or outrage that was ripe for exposure on *60 Minutes.* They would give me vivid accounts of foul deeds and the culprits perpetrating them, and urge me to take appropriate action: 'You really should look into this, Mike. It's right up your alley.' "[1]

Certainly, a large number of segments conclude with *60 Minutes* serving explicitly as mediating ombudsman—reporters calling for congressional investigations, redressing government oversights, and championing individual rights in the face of bureaucratic ineptitude. One particularly impressive display of its power for social change occurred in 1984. During a fifty-one-day hunger strike on behalf of the homeless, activist Mitch Snyder became an interview subject and story topic on *60 Minutes*. Just a few hours before the interview aired, President Reagan, aboard Air Force One, finally agreed to renovate a homeless shelter a few blocks from the nation's Capitol building.

This story and others portray a heroic press, a fourth estate, monitoring abuses of power, the insensitivity of institutions, and breakdowns in consensual values. Harry Reasoner, upon rejoining the program in 1978, noted at the time: "Now, when people have a problem, something strange or suspicious going on in their community, instead of writing their congressman, they write to Mike Wallace and demand he fix it."[2]

A key dimension of this heroic function is to move people to social action. Morley Safer acknowledges this power of *60 Minutes* in a follow-up report at the end of a December 1979 broadcast: "And an update on our story on Marva Collins, the Chicago school teacher ["Marva," 11/11/79]. That story brought a deluge of mail to both *60 Minutes* and to Marva Collins. A lot of viewers sent her money, money enough for Marva to be able to expand and train other teachers in her no-nonsense method of educating." Although such an update conveys pride in the program's ability to endorse action and change, this is not an explicitly acknowledged goal of the program; it is only regarded as a happy accident, an afterthought—an "update"—rather than a central mission of the program.

More frequently, however, the various updates and concluding "Letters" segment return us to a center, reaffirming an embedded set of virtues. A letter from the September 30, 1979 program, for example, argues too that our bureaucracies are dishonest and inefficient. As Morley Safer comments, "And finally about our story on the government fiasco surrounding a multi-billion dollar plan to store oil in caves and salt caverns, a viewer thought reporting that fiasco was hardly newsworthy. He wrote: '[If] a government project [ever] runs on time, runs smoothly within or near the projected cost and free of corruption, that will be news.' " Again, a letter from the

February 10, 1980 program about a story on the Federal Trade Commission affirms the preeminence of the individual: "It's about time some government agency did what it was set up to do. . . . Look out for the little guy."

In a final illustration, the following two touching letters conclude the December 12, 1979 program and affirm individualism, friendship, and religious ritual in the face of the struggle between life and death. Hosting the "Letters" segment, Safer says, "Far and away most of the mail was about last week's story on the two boys who were helping each other cope with cancer. One viewer said: 'It was truly poignant to see a youngster who should perhaps be tremulously considering his first date coming to grips with his ultimate one in a fashion that would put many of his elders to shame.' And finally, 'With all the pain American hearts are going through at this time . . . [those] two young boys showed there is still some real America left. Merry Christmas!' "

The "Letters" segment on *60 Minutes* represents another important narrative layer built into the program. The letters take on their own dramatic rhythm juxtaposed to one another, affirming and contradicting, teasing and chastising the program. Frequently, the letters serve as overall closure to the dramatic tensions raised in that evening's three earlier segments.

In the same way, Andy Rooney's essays, which usually precede the letters, perform this function of closure by bearing witness to individualism, common sense, and rumpled tradition in the face of class pretension, institutional jargon, and modern contraptions. In 1990 Rooney used the powerful public persona of his own individualism to ward off threats from his own corporate employer, CBS News. Rooney was initially suspended for three months for homophobic comments he made during a television interview and for a racist remark that he allegedly made in an untaped telephone interview (a remark he denied making). Treading on thin ice here in places where competing commonsense attitudes—about gays and race—often break through to yield their fragile and contested nature, Rooney nevertheless managed to bring a three-month suspension to closure after only four weeks. Many viewers perceived Rooney as the wronged individual battling his own insensitive corporation; in the more than five thousand letters CBS received, 90 percent supported Rooney. It also did not hurt his cause that *60 Minutes*'s viewership dropped nearly 20 percent during Rooney's absence, and ratings jumped dramatically when he returned on March 4, 1990.[3]

Ultimately, Rooney (a kind of nonfiction Columbo), the letters that supported him, and the regular "Letters" on *60 Minutes*—those critical of *60 Minutes* and those opposed—celebrate the spirit of the individual (the right to our own opinions) and make us feel a part of our world and the narrative process that interprets that world.

But celebrating the spirit of individual reality often deludes us regarding individualism's limits in clarifying larger social realities. For example, these limits have been acknowledged by Michael Delli Carpini and Bruce Williams in their study of environmental news specials: "while institutions are portrayed as flawed and inadequate, the solution [to environmental problems] is never political organization aimed at institutional reform or change. Rather, individuals, acting on their own as individuals, are seen as the solution to the problem."[4] Once again, saluting the supremacy of the individual over the social often effectively blocks *60 Minutes* and the news from exploring collective rather than individual responses to communal problems and social change.

Beyond Narrative Conflict and Common Sense

While the reporters of *60 Minutes* provide us with synthetic knowledge about things we cannot experience for ourselves, their cultural meaning as mediators of narrative tension extends to other levels. At the level of discourse, their storytelling presents and mediates the following sets of implicit oppositions deeply embedded in the narrative process: (1) real and narrative time, (2) place and space, (3) observed and lived experience, (4) referent and reality, (5) product and process, and, finally, (6) the familiar and the novel. By resolving these broader cultural tensions, *60 Minutes* provides a center and firmly restores us to its version of common ground.

Narrative Time-Real Time

An apparently seamless union exists between real and represented time in the narratives of *60 Minutes*.[5] The experiences portrayed in any one segment may have taken years to unfold and may take a *60 Minutes* producer five to eight weeks to research and prepare. The segment we finally see, however, has collapsed time so that a narrative of thirteen or fourteen minutes becomes an undetermined amount of actual experience. *60 Minutes* does not portray the opposition of real and narrative time as problematic; indeed the program mediates the gap through the appearance of seamless edits stitched together through the continuity of the reporter's narration. In so doing, the program carves out a place in time and locates us in this fused state between past and present. As we watch in the present, the past is incorporated, and the two merge in the familiarity and comfort of the narrative.

In the fusion of real and narrative time, it is not unusual for a *60 Minutes* producer to film or tape a ninety-minute interview and then use a two-minute slice. A 1976 Mike Wallace interview with Daniel Schorr, former CBS reporter who leaked secret government reports on the CIA to a newspaper, illustrates part of the problem. While the final broadcast narrative ran thirteen minutes, the actual interview lasted more than an hour and generated seventy-five pages of manuscript. Critic Harry Stein contended at the time, "But what had been edited . . . was material that cast Schorr in a more favorable light, material that filled out his thought processes, lending the impression of a man under stress who had been trying hard to do the right thing. The elimination of that material also reinforced the impression of Wallace as the relentless interrogator."[6] Schorr later said, "My big mistake was in not insisting that the interview be done live or taped to time. I know the way to maintain control is to do it unedited."[7] This example illustrates how *60 Minutes* casts an interview into a particular narrative formula, a story that clearly one critic and the interview subject did not think rendered an accurate representation of what happened. Schorr wanted to collapse the gap between real and narrative time, but because news is in the business of transforming experience into narratives, Schorr's desire for control is one few interview subjects ever attain.

In fairness to *60 Minutes* and television news, the problematic gap between real and narrative time is not endemic to broadcast news. Print reporters too cover three-hour meetings and reduce time to a ten-inch story in a six-column format (indeed, this book contains only small sections from extensive interviews with Don Hewitt and Mike Wallace). Writers and reporters interview subjects for hours and may use only five to ten quotes. What they generally select are the most dramatic, most intriguing quotes from the interview or bits of action from the meeting, or a viewpoint which supports the reporter's particular narrative interpretation (one he or she is prevented from making directly because of the constraints of neutrality). Print reporters too are guided by the narrative impulse which freezes an idiosyncratic event into the time and space of the news report. Here the gap between the real and the represented is seldom construed as problematic, masked by "natural" narrative conventions.

Place-Space

In addition, and as I suggested in chapter 5, the formulas of *60 Minutes* mediate tensions between space and place.[8] In the narrative the reporter often takes us to unfamiliar terrain—a space. Through voice-overs and visual referents, the insecurity of space is transformed into place, a now-familiar, concrete setting that we come to know through our knowledgeable *60 Minutes* reporters. The insecurity and unfamiliarity of space ranges across a broad spectrum from xenophobia, to distrust of changing values, to general suspicion regarding other ways of being. Narrative news formulas, however, operating as metaphors, transform unfamiliar experience into a concrete, known place, resolving tension between the two and mediating between here and there, near and far, us and them. Viewers are presented with this reconstructed site where the ragged gaps between space and place, between the connected and unconnected, between the accessible and inaccessible have been repaired.

At other levels of meaning, *60 Minutes* reporters lay claim to the distinctive place they are afforded in the program's narratives. First, through both on-screen and voice-over narration, these well-informed reporters manage the narrative and any alien or new space the narrative may introduce. Second, visually located within the comfortable zone of the medium shot and its greater detachment and control, they claim the middle (or medium) ground. And third, situated outside direct contradiction, they stake out that preferred place between both sides of a borderline spectacle where competing viewpoints vie. Within the purview of this privileged narrative place, then, *60 Minutes* reporters tend the borders of common sense.

Observing-Living

Early in the 1980s, the Janet Cooke Pulitzer Prize hoax demonstrated the difference between personal responsibility to journalistic conventions—the reporter merely observing experience and telling stories—and social responsibility for the actual experience.[9] The major criticism against the Washington *Post* reporter focused on her fabrication of a report about an eight-year-old heroin addict and her responsibility to tell *true* stories. At the time, however, columnist Mike Royko criticized conventional journalism for permitting narrative conventions—"getting the good story"—to supersede journalism's responsibility to the experiences it reconstructs: "There's something more important than a story here. This 8-year-old kid is being murdered. The editors should have said forget the story, find the kid. . . . People in any other profession would have gone right to the police."[10]

Noting the lack of "existential responsibility" by conventional journalists toward experiences that are reconstructed in news, David Eason contends that conventions support the separation of observed experience—the reporter as detached onlooker—from lived or actual experience: "To become an observer is to see social reality as composed of active participants, who must take responsibility for their acts, and passive spectators, who bear no responsibility for what they watch."[11] In *60 Minutes* the reporters—despite their character portrayals—draw a boundary between observing and living. The reporters reconstruct experience—"tell the story"—but only the other characters in the narratives bear the responsibility for actual experience. Commonsense journalism and the cloak of objectivity, as Michael Schudson argues, operate as "concrete conventions which persist because they reduce the extent to which reporters themselves can be held responsible for the words they write" (or the pictures they broadcast).[12]

The explicit portrayal of reporters as characters—rather than as institutional representatives of the giant CBS conglomerate—provides an illusory resolution to the observed/lived dilemma. They appear as lone characters living out the story. However, we are given no clues about the reporters' relationship to CBS, no ongoing revelations concerning changes in the reporters' values or personal lives. Nor do the reporters' words typically convey personal responsibility and lived experience. Thus a mixed message: the presentation of reporters as individual characters, not merely as observers, is undercut by their actual roles as agents for an institutional observer (CBS). Journalism typically forecloses discussion on these matters because such discourse would explicitly violate journalistic codes of neutrality. The reporters, in other words, are observers; their appearance as central narrative figures smooths the seams, mediates tensions between observing and living. The reporters live as narrative characters—returning to the scene of the crime, riding in jeeps with politicians, crouching in the hills of Afghanistan, playing tennis with celebrities, walking the streets of Cairo—but without an acknowledged accountability for their role in constructing narrative simulation of experience. Once again *60 Minutes* centers the audience in that comfort zone between observed and lived realities.

Referent-Reality

In the practice of conventional journalism, a mirror metaphor has often been used as part of the professional mythology to demonstrate how reporters mediate between the world and their constructed reports about that world.[13] Reporters, so the myth goes, simply hold a mirror up to the world enabling readers and viewers to see "what's going on here." Of course, the process of constructing news stories and making sense of experience is far more complex than the mirror metaphor suggests. After all, the mirror metaphor excludes references to the symbolic process underlying news and to what gets left outside the frame of the mirror. The metaphor, through its routine, common-sense use, draws attention away from the constructed news story, which, although similar, *is* a different entity from the realities it claims to represent. Both reporters and audiences come to take such construction of news stories for granted. Once again, distinctions between referent and reality are seldom viewed as problematic; the mirror metaphor mediates their opposition.

In critiquing the common sense of news, Mary Mander focuses on the referent-reality problem: "The narrative(s) of news, whether print or the broadcast . . . pretend to reflect social reality, but in fact offer selected interpretations of discrete events and in so doing reinforce modern man's empirical prejudice that reality is knowable and coherent."[14] This empirical prejudice, an implicit tenet of traditional science, supports the mirror metaphor for journalism—one that values descriptions of a real, transparent outer world over attention to slippery reportorial conventions, to the practical and economic constraints of the report, or to the narrative structure that organizes and underlies news. Every news story is an interpretation of the world, not a mirror image.

In the case of *60 Minutes*, there is a more subtle metaphor on duty: the reporter, not as mirror, but as mediator. The strategy of characterizing the *60 Minutes* reporter is really the process by which the metaphorical role of the reporter is fleshed out. At one level, a mediator metaphor functions to resolve complexity within single segments, while at another level, it elides the *referents*—the narratives of *60 Minutes*—and their *realities,* culled from the multiplicity of idiosyncratic events and experiences. Eason argues that cultural referents such as television news reports function like language; they are made into common sense by individuals, "providing a means for the transformation of knowledge vital to existence into routine. Because their function is to 'naturalize' reality, they do not raise questions about their own appropriateness for revealing 'truth.' Like words which through convention come to be considered inseparable from their referents, cultural forms appear neutral and transparent, natural ways to know the world."[15] News and *60 Minutes* naturalize and convert social phenomena into the common sense of the news narrative. The narrative, also a taken-for-granted metaphor, gives pattern, formula, concreteness, and meaning—a center—to those phenomena.

Product-Process

The January 1988 on-air confrontation between CBS news anchor Dan Rather and then-presidential candidate George Bush suggests what can happen when viewers are let in on the usually camouflaged process of the news. Although reporters confront politicians daily as part of the political process, these confrontations are typically constructed and presented as finished products—as news packages to use the broadcast term. The rough edges are honed in the packaging—although those edges are often a part of the backstage give and take between journalists and politicians. We do not usually see a reporter being asked to account for his behavior (i.e., Bush calling attention to CBS going to black when Rather failed to appear for six minutes during a mysterious 1987 evening news broadcast). One explanation for the initial deluge of viewer animosity toward Rather (columnist Mike Royko called him a pit bull attacking an aristocratic poodle) is that he let viewers see, in part, the raw unedited process—

a process usually concealed. Journalistic convention was violated, and many viewers missed the comfort typically afforded by narrative packaging.

As a result of the convention of presenting news as finished performances, we are also not privy to reporters' relationships with the *process* of constructing stories and with their story subjects. How do their private values speak to or against the values produced and maintained in the narratives themselves? On *60 Minutes* we view only the product—the finished narrative. The performing of public, objectified dual roles as narrator-characters disguises the complexities of the reporters' private stock of knowledge and values. Both reporters and audiences routinely assume that there is little distance between the narrative product and the inchoate experience that the product represents. We accept one for the other, seldom questioning the process of transformation.

At another level of meaning, the narrative news product conceals the process of its economic constraints and connections. As John Fiske reminds us, "News is also a commodity. It is expensive to gather and distribute, and must produce an audience that is of the right size and composition to be sold to advertisers. . . . News has to be popular, it has to produce an audience."[16] A central contradiction in *60 Minutes* resides in its position against the impersonal institutional frameworks of government and big business; yet its narratives conceal the program's own role in a large-scale, commodity enterprise. While individual narratives cast reporters as heroes battling corrupt bureaucracies, the segments seldom contest the reporters' other identities as members of a business corporation whose function is to sell audiences to advertisers. Don Hewitt is proud of the nearly $1 billion the program has generated for CBS over the years, and he better than anyone knows the connection in American enterprise journalism between good stories and good business.[17] *60 Minutes* generates large audiences who once again are sustained by the finished narrative product which by its very structure masks the commodity process necessary to maintain the program.

Familiar-Novel

Cultural products—including television news—perform two important and contradictory functions. On one hand, they provide us with shared values and maps for meaning; they offer a sense of routine and unity through their familiar and accessible structures. On the other hand, they help us deal with the new and different; they provide us with contexts for confronting ambiguity and idiosyncracy. *60 Minutes* ultimately performs both functions, in part through its formulaic structures, and offers us a central site between these two poles.

A significant role that *60 Minutes* plays in American culture is its ability to balance the dialogic dimensions of the familiar and the novel, or to use the terminology of M. M. Bakhtin, the centripetal and centrifugal forces of language itself: "the centralizing and decentralizing (or decentering) forces in any language or culture."[18] Jimmie Reeves, who has adapted Bakhtin's literary analysis to the study of television, argues that "Bakhtin saw the meaning-making process as animated by a dialectical clash of two opposing forces: the centrifugal forces of social stratification and diversification; and the centripetal forces that tend toward social unification and systemization."[19] Thus, within the human condition, mirrored and mired in our everyday language, are these competing tensions of the familiar, pulling us back to a comforting center, to recognizable places and formulas, to the security of repetition; and the novel, pushing us outward from the center toward the new and different, toward the unknown and intrigue.

60 Minutes, at the level of intrigue, each week confronts sets of shifting social attitudes and rival commonsense views regarding poverty, disease, inequity, race, men and women, war, the economy, and foreign powers, among other phenomena. *60 Minutes*, however, manages rival and novel experiences by adapting them to familiar formulas. The mystery, for example, can accommodate raw experience as diverse as waterfront crime, a Vietnam colonel, spy satellites, government cover-ups, racial discrimination, child pornography, valium, diamond scams, the Teamsters, Brazilian machismo, Mormons, horse doping, art theft, cocaine, and the Nazis, all within repetitive and comforting story forms. Other *60 Minutes* formulas provide similar flexibility in assimilating novel events and issues into a handful of familiar, commonsensical representations.

Don Hewitt tells this compelling story about the connection between cultural familiarity and *60 Minutes*:

> I believe that very few things in America look the same way they did when you were a kid. The stores look different, the gas stations look

different, the toll booths look different, everything looks different. *60 Minutes* looks the same. There was some talk . . . about we ought to change it. . . . I said, "No!" It's almost like that comforting feeling when you go visit grandpa in the summer and you say, "Oh my God, that screen door still sticks. He never fixed it." And you love it. And if you went back and the screen door opened and it didn't squeak, you'd be disappointed. Well, I like the screen door to squeak a little and I like it to be familiar.[20]

While Hewitt illustrates here part of the reason for his program's appeal, we would not watch each week if we thought the programs were exactly the same. What *60 Minutes* manages instead is the intricate balance of the constant flow of novel experiences repacked each Sunday in the program's familiar and comforting formulas. My use of novel here is not merely confined to impulses relating to the new and unfamiliar. I also mean it in its generic sense. After all, *60 Minutes*, classifiable as language, fundamentally literary, dramatic, and narrative in pattern and form, "novelizes" the news.[21]

As a journalistic hybrid of the novel, *60 Minutes* resonates with certain aspects of Bakhtin's novel characteristics. For Bakhtin, unlike the static epic tale with its larger-than-life heroes, and its location in an ossified past, the novel is bound up with rich connections to everyday life. Experience in the novel comes "into contact with the spontaneity of the inconclusive present."[22] The novel breaks down "boundaries between fiction and nonfiction"; it engages in "isolated border violations" through its use of resources outside the borders of traditional literary genres: "[T]he novel often crosses the boundary of what we strictly call fictional literature—making use first of a moral confession, then of a philosophical tract, then of manifestos that are openly political, then degenerating into the raw spirituality of a confession, a 'cry of the soul' that has not yet found its formal contours."[23]

60 Minutes then is the flip side of Bakhtin's fictional novel. The program routinely re-presents these "extraliterary" resources and documents which journalists have always sought out. They are the resources and tracings of everyday life: letters, confessions, court testimony, tape recordings, and secret documents. At the same time, however, the program has pushed journalistic contours out in the explicit direction of the dramatic and the novel.

News Narrative at the Periphery

Despite its breakthroughs in pushing the ways we think about journalism toward the direction of storytelling, *60 Minutes* remains strapped by some of the familiar baggage of conventional journalism. At the outset of the 1960s, journalism remained entrenched in the implicit orthodox doctrine of neutrality. Much reportorial practice since the mid-nineteenth century had sought to contain and conceal the artifice and interpretive dimensions of the news process within that doctrine. And, a versatile stock of conventions masks the interpretive and narrative labor in news reports: the "inverted pyramid" news lead; the limitations on descriptive adjectives; the separation of hard news from soft features and from opinions; the use of quotation marks or broadcast actualities to highlight expert evidence; and the presentation of both sides of conflicting issues, among others. Eason contends that these "conventions ban discussion of the procedures necessary to transform an event into news, such as the relationship between reporter and form of discourse. Belief that such taboos produce objective accounts allows journalists to defend their reports in statements such as the 'facts speak for themselves.' "[24]

Facts-speaking-for-themselves remains a commonsensical metaphor (personification would actually be the more accurate literary term) underpinning how journalists and audiences think about reportorial process as neutral. *60 Minutes* most often typifies Bakhtin's notion of the centripetal force in its search for common ground. On occasion, though, the program flies out from its centering and stabilizing formulas to experiment. When the program breaks from its own formulas, re-invents and re-presents them in dramatic ways, *60 Minutes* most closely approximates the novel's centrifugal power to explore the unknown, "to reveal the limits, the artificial constraints" of its own formulas.[25]

One example from *60 Minutes* that pushes the program toward the novelization of news and the centrifugal forces that mark human experience is called "Homeless" (1/10/82). Produced by Joel Bernstein, it represents one of the first reports by Ed Bradley, who had joined the program the previous fall. Perhaps not yet indoctrinated into program's more familiar narratives, Bradley's character performance here provides a striking contrast to the mainstream formulas employed by *60 Minutes*. Even the abstract title, more rooted in a

171

social than an individual dimension, is far removed from another homeless segment, "Brown vs. Koch." The Bradley–Bernstein segment does contain elements of the mystery, adventure, and arbitration formulas. For example, Bradley searches for clues about the homeless, tours city streets and the Oregon backwoods, and arbitrates an argument about who should bear responsibility for America's growing homeless population. What distinguishes this narrative, however, is Bradley's role as involved-observer. He performs not as the aloof, superior detective hero, but as one of the street people he tries to understand. Criss-crossing America, he takes to the New York streets at night and talks to a "bum" sleeping in a cardboard box. He visits a shelter for the homeless in the Bowery district. He attends a hearing on homelessness in Brooklyn and tries to sort competing commonsense perspectives. He travels to Oregon, where he backpacks with a "hobo," Richard Huntley, whom he joins over a campfire in the back country. *60 Minutes* names this homeless man who so often goes nameless in conventional news. Together Bradley and Huntley discuss the have–have not discrepancies in American society. In all of the scenes, Bradley, in beard and out of the more common reporter suit-uniform, appears as a witness for the social conditions of the homeless.

This is also one of the few segments in which the individual–institution tension appears genuinely mysterious and complex. As referee, Bradley asks a social worker if it isn't the individual's responsibility to take care of his or her own needs. Then he turns around and asks the mayor of Portland, the institutional representative in the narrative, if it isn't the city's responsibility to shelter and care for the homeless. Both institutional figures articulate the problems institutions have in dealing with complex social problems. These kinds of insights into the internal workings of social organizations are featured occasionally on *60 Minutes* but are not the norm. The segment ends ambiguously with a shot of a city worker shutting the door of an overcrowded shelter in the faces of men who must return to the streets for the night.

Unlike most *60 Minutes* narratives, "Homeless" represents the program pushing journalism toward "cultural phenomenology," that form of literary journalism trying to make sense of the centrifugal forces of human experience. On the other hand, the "Brown vs. Koch" homeless story (chapter 7) presents an example of ethnographic realism, that is, a story that finally believes in its ability to sort reality from artifice and discover the hidden logic underneath. The literary journalism of ethnographic realism, as language, represents the centripetal as it seeks a center, a middle ground, finally elevating and celebrating individual over social "reality."

Bradley's homeless story, however, makes no claims about the logic of reality, symbolically leaving us at the end of the narrative outside in the cold with the homeless men. This segment offers us a narrative which cannot contain the scope of the human condition that it seeks to represent. Bradley offers no comforting resolution. The graphic and gripping image of the door closing in our faces is startling in its failure to make this particular reality cohere. Safe in our living rooms, we are only protected by the distance and insulation the television medium provides. But still we must acknowledge the unknown forces that these men, located insecurely outside the boundaries of Middle America, have to confront.

In "Homeless," *60 Minutes* has broken down the more typical distinction news makes between us and them. The us–them metaphor employed in "Brown vs. Koch," for instance, severely limits the potential meanings of Joyce Brown's experiences and those of the homeless in general. In this segment, middle-class viewers become the us, and the urban "underclass" becomes them. To restrict meaning to a two-dimensional battle between us and them, as Fiske suggests, denies "any sense that society is composed of a series of legitimate and necessary conflicts of interest that cannot be properly understood from one point of view only. These conflicts occur within society, and not between us and an alien."[26]

The *60 Minutes* "Homeless" report presents these conflicts of interest and the struggle of institutional representatives, more commonly made into villains on the program, as they work unsuccessfully within a messy social structure. News narratives, however, that turn social experience into cleaner us–them confrontations usually commend, rather than condemn, the social order. Such an order identifies those who progress economically as portraits in the triumph of ingenuity and those who regress as sketches in personal failure. Rather than focus on the generative mechanisms that contribute to social problems, which is what "Homeless" attempts in part, conventional news and "Brown vs. Koch" emphasize intellectual, mental, and moral deficiencies of individual members of the marginalized.

In the "Homeless" segment, *60 Minutes*, however briefly, explores a rich variety of techniques more commonly associated with the novel. There is a sense of Bakhtin's "spontaneity of the inclusive present" about the plight of homelessness and our responsibility for it. There is a feel for both rural and urban landscapes and the concerns of Middle Americans, the marginalized, and our institutional leaders. There is acknowledgment of our failure to come to terms with the human condition in spite of heroic efforts. This narrative illustrates one of the most powerful features of the novel for Bakhtin, that is, the inability of any single formula or genre to contain its own multiple dimensions and representations. To use a Bakhtinian metaphor, this segment "splashes over the brim" of its narrative borders revealing an "unrealized surplus of humanness" and the possibility of multiple realities that sometimes fail to cohere. If we acknowledge this centrifugal impulse as part of the human condition, it indeed makes the quest for center that much more difficult—and, contradictorily, even more imperative.

Conclusions and Contradictions

In many ways this book is about contradictions—its own as well as those found in *60 Minutes*. Making sense of contradiction—and spotting it at the heart of apparent resolution—is often what the analytical process is about. Still, I am at odds not only with the comfortable bounds of the narrative, but also with the comfortable bounds of my own analysis and retellings. At least two contradictions remain which I cannot contain.

First, I have often made reference to "us," to viewers, to a *60 Minutes* audience that is both everywhere and nowhere. That audience is a construct of this book in much the same way that *60 Minutes* constructs an audience "out there" to respond to particular narratives each week and to deliver to its advertisers. I have largely assumed that implied audience to represent some amorphous Middle America—even though a part of that audience may feel no affinity for the middle. Yet at the same time I cannot be sure who those Middle Americans are, or what their individual responses to the program are. The great variety of so-called Middle Americans whom

I have talked to about *60 Minutes* generally admire the program, but their specific responses span a broad range—from devotion to the program's admired reporters for their never-ending battle against injustice to outright contempt for these irreverent reporters who would attack our most sacred leaders, institutions, and traditions.

In fact, to solve this bind I have chosen to concentrate on interpreting the "texts" of *60 Minutes*—what I see—largely because I value the varied and contradictory responses to the program, responses that often fly out from the center where I would like to contain them. In addition, because I am critiquing journalism's obsession with the virtues of individualism, I want to resist ascribing meaning solely to viewers and their individual responses. I am interested in the public maps for meaning that *60 Minutes* provides and how those maps help us navigate our murky national character.

Although I criticize *60 Minutes* for its too frequent celebration of the individual at the expense of misinterpreting our institutions, in fairness, the often blind allegiance to this public virtue is central to much of everyday life—including academia. In spite of sophisticated neutral posturing (and the too frequent use of third-person point of view), the academy too is locked in its own celebration of individualism in which universities, like *60 Minutes*, honor and promote their own star researchers. Junior faculty members, especially if they do historical or interpretive analyses, are too often discouraged from pursuing collective or co-authored projects in order that their work be evaluated as the appropriate kind of individual private property that leads to landing tenure. And my own project is indeed the work of an individual interpreting the stories of *60 Minutes*. I too benefit from the mythology of individualism.

As a liberal-populist, however, I believe in other viewers' capacities to "read" *60 Minutes* in a rich variety of ways—to read against the program, to read against my own interpretations. In constructing a centrist, Middle-American viewer, I am guilty of the same bind that constrains *60 Minutes:* aiming at a middle ground that attempts to enclose meaning. I cannot fully come to terms with this bind because I believe in the importance and the mythologies of political, spiritual, and cultural centers. They are symbolic places that appear to hold us together even as we would explore different directions and move out to the periphery. Some call the center dominant ideology, but as James Carey has pointed out, to name culture *ideology* encloses its richness and mysteries around questions and discussions of power and class.[27] Although these are the most significant aspects of culture and should command our attention, culture finally is fluid and moves in more directions than the verticality of class and power would allow.

Often studies of television news have overlooked or discredited the diversity and fluidity among audiences, arguing that news is merely a hegemonic device, an extension of the existing power structure that uses news to maintain the hierarchy of social control. This reading is too narrow. In a society as multilayered as our own, such institutions as government, business, religion, education, and journalism create centers and provide frameworks for meaning. The key questions in a democracy become how much marginal activity will that center permit, how many disparate voices will it hear, how will it translate or misrepresent those voices, or allow them to speak at all.

While news and *60 Minutes* structure centered readings through its formulas, they cannot ultimately control our multiple responses to that centering. And the program itself, in part, celebrates viewer diversity through its semiregular "Letters" segment that offers commonsense viewpoints often in opposition to the program. It is perhaps the only program in the history of prime-time American television that, within its limited and carefully edited forum, explicitly encourages diverse and alternative readings of its own narrative interpretations.[28]

The second contradiction I acknowledge here involves my own ambiguous relationship with the stories of *60 Minutes* and television news in general. On one hand, individual reports transform experience and often create an uncommon common sense helping us come to terms with our world; on the other hand, other stories often distort experience and limit meanings within the boundary of formula. If the bottom line in news is "the story"—the reconstructed drama—then journalism runs the risk of sacrificing a traditional role as institutional watchdog for the thrill of the chase and the commodity appeal of the news product. Since late 1985, for example, network and local news operations have developed a taken-for-granted generic visual shot in their coverage of crack cocaine in inner city America.[29] In highly dramatic footage, a hand-held, shaky camera leaps from the back of police vans following gunwielding authorities as they break down the door of yet another crack house (see, for example, the CBS *48 Hours* special, "Return to Crack Street"). In forging this uneasy alliance with police, journalism too often abandons its own surveillance role in the social order to serve as an agent of the police—or at least to tell the story from the police point of view. When cocaine stories in the early 1980s focused on use and abuse by urban professionals and suburban high schools students, the camera did not so dramatically favor the side of the police. Because news so often serves Middle-American interests, we may assume that the camera would not be in the police vans if the focus of the current drug war was middle- or upper-class America rather than marginalized inner cities. In 1990 Ron Harris of the Los Angeles *Times* argued that, even among politicians, public officials, police officers, and judges, there is increasing awareness that "the war on drugs has in effect become a war on black people":

> While it is clear that whites sell most of the nation's cocaine and account for 80 percent of its consumers, it is blacks and other minorities who continue to fill the courts and jails. Law officers say that is largely because they are the easiest people to arrest.
>
> . . . police, judges, and attorneys say, under the current approach, black America is being criminalized at an astonishing rate. According to an analysis by the Sentencing Project in Washington, D.C. one in four black men in their 20s in America is either in jail, in prison, on parole, or on probation.[30]

With television's help, through the latter half of the 1980s and into the Bush administration, we convinced ourselves that the cocaine crisis is a black problem, marginalized in the inner cities. From Middle America's point of view, maybe the police and television news can contain it there.

To put it in my own commonsense terms, I believe that *60 Minutes* should be wary of serving drama at the expense of democracy; broaden the scope of their formulas; pay more attention to historical, social, and institutional context; follow up more systematically on particular characters and issues; do more programs that analyze both reportorial conventions and social issues raised in the news; and encourage each of us to take more responsibility for those human experiences converted to narratives.

For those who worry about the call here for more blatant, less balanced interpretive journalism, I can only respond again that every act of journalism is an act of interpretation. Those who demand that the news media achieve "balance"—if not objectivity—must acknowledge that *balance* is a code word for *middle*—Middle-American values. These values are encoded into mainstream journalism—how it selects the news, where it places its beat reporters, whom and how it promotes, how it uncritically reports and thereby naively supports government positions (in the Persian Gulf, for example). Journalism's safe, balanced, and often bulging middle needs to be challenged more frequently from within its own ranks, not just by conservatives on the right but by the radical left—if there are any of these types left who have not been shaken into the middle or run off by the dictates of "balanced" journalism.

On the other hand, however, I am also comforted by the familiarity and companionship of *60 Minutes* each Sunday. In our culture, *60 Minutes* plays a central role in the creation and maintenance of common sense. At its best, such sense prods those of us engaged in specialized realms of knowledge to "come clean," to be honest, to make our language more accessible, to seek common ground. At its worst, however, common sense refuses to see itself analytically, to acknowledge fully the unknown and the mysterious, and the margins where our uncommonness and differences reside.

For all of its formulas and conventions, *60 Minutes* remains unconventional dramatic journalism. Often criticized for being theatrical, for blurring the commonsense boundaries between fact and fiction, between information and entertainment, *60 Minutes* and television news remain under the commonsense scrutiny of print journalists. Only on rare occasions and usually in retrospect (John Kennedy's assassination, the civil rights struggle, space travel, Vietnam War coverage, and Tiananmen Square, for example) do critics acknowledge the power of television's visual language to describe and reveal, sometimes to explain and change the world. Former *60 Minutes* reporter Dan Rather offers this insight into the important role of television in personalizing the 1989 student uprising in China: "Television brought Beijing's battle for democracy to Main Street. It made students who live on the other side of the planet just as human, just as vulnerable as the boy on the next block. The miracle of television is that the triumph and tragedy of Tiananmen Square would not have been any more vivid had it been Times Square."[31]

Rather clearly believes in the centering power of television, in McLuhan's global village, in common ground.

More often than celebrated, however, television news is blamed for not being print journalism—as if newspapers had some kind of superior territorial claim on explanation and common sense. The print bias against television rises, first, from the television reporter's more central role as visible, active character in news dramas, often overwhelming the detached anonymity of institutional print voices. Second, and more important, there is blatant disregard of edited visual images as a "language" every bit as complex as—and often more powerful than—the printed word. (From a purely esthetic point of view, we need only look at the written transcripts of *60 Minutes* in Appendixes B-E to appreciate the prowess of the program's storytelling and the ability of its producers, reporters, editors, and writers to mesh both verbal and visual languages.)

The press resentment of television stems from our cultural obsession with a romanticized past, with nostalgia for the patriarchal tradition and supremacy of printed texts. W. J. T. Mitchell has noted the tendency in Western culture to elevate the printed word over the visual image.[32] Not unlike the journalistic and gendered celebration of hard over soft news, the superior claims of print have ties to masculine ways of thinking about the world; on the other hand, the inferiority of image often stems from its associations with disenfranchised feminine representations of experience. In addition, in terms of class distinctions, printed texts in modern culture have come to mark literate middle to upper classes, while visual images too often are aligned with the illiteracy of marginalized classes who have bypassed (*and* were passed by in terms of) traditional print literacy.[33] The taken-for-granted dualism that separates the printed from the visual too often provides a convenient ploy in the attack on the popularity of television. Because of its middle-ground standing, television's ability to cut across class, racial, and gender borders threatens both liberal and conservative elites and intellectuals and their hierarchical hold on what constitutes knowledge and virtue. By monolithically—and often uncritically—marking the television image as violent, illiterate, superficial, and profane, the privileged protect the status and dominance of their turf.

Whether it is the alleged supremacy of poetry over painting, or the printed report over televised newscast, visual language has too often been treated as an inferior by-product of mass culture. Instead of chasing the usual instinct to separate and categorize differences, we should focus, as Mitchell argues, on common ground and what printed texts and visual images can learn from one another.

This is a difficult task. From the commonsense point of view of conventional journalism, for example, television has not been around long enough to suit most reporters, editors—and much of the educated public. And in its naive arrogance, television has shifted the parameters of the way we are supposed to think about news; it has shifted the metaphor from the quasi-science of the printed word to dramatic, televisual stories of *60 Minutes, 20/20,* and *A Current Affair.* The newer metaphor makes print journalists and many of us uncomfortable. Instead of seeing news-as-drama as a way of enriching journalistic performance and the impoverished neutral model, however, we often condemn the metaphor as outside the boundaries of what constitutes news—as if print news is somehow natural and not manufactured by reporters working for business enterprises which in turn sell that news for profit.

But print journalists have no special language for interpreting the world; they also use the designs and devices of storytelling. After all, we call their products news *stories*. Print and its practitioners, however, often hide the narrative impulse in the inverted pyramid, hard-news style of conventional reporting. They prefer talking about news using "harder" science rather than "softer" literary metaphors. Secure in the trappings of science, they celebrate their neutrality and disclaim responsibility for the actual experiences they have appropriated for their stories. But with all the talk of facts, information, impartiality, and inverted pyramids, conventional print journalism is still storytelling—only too often with the passion and heart ripped out.

60 Minutes at its best restores the passion and heart. It extols rather than disguises the dramatic in news and in experience. It gives reporters a stronger personal voice rather than the detached voice of a corporation. The lesson the program offers for all journalism is that storytelling—with all its limitations—is the common ground from where we start. But news should not remain captive to the personal at the expense of the social. *60 Minutes* and the news need to develop formulas and narratives that reveal how individuals create, inhabit, and maintain our institutions.

As prime-time drama, *60 Minutes* is caught in a bind between its power to both distort and enrich, to deform and inform. Fiske notes that television news is always "caught in the tension between the need to convey information deemed to be in the public interest and the need to be popular. It attempts to meet these contradictory needs by being socially responsible in content, but popular in form and presentation, and thus runs the risk of being judged boring and irrelevant from one side, and superficial and rushed from the other."[34] Instead of the predictable call of the elite for television journalism to adhere to some "informational criteria" or model whereby news is judged "objective, true, educational, and important," Fiske demands, and I agree, that television news "make the events of the world" more *popular:* "The more valid criticism of television news is that it is not popular enough. Far from wishing to improve its objectivity, its depth, or its authority, I would wish to increase its openness, its contradictions, and multiplicity of its voices and points of view."[35]

The sin of *60 Minutes*, however, is that the multiple experiences and contradictions it reconstructs in its weekly segments are not fictional dramas imagined in the minds of creative artists. Instead, events of actual suffering, joy, and human complexity are appropriated and reconceived by a news organization, often as melodramatic tales and always as profitable commodities. The intricate relationships between everyday life and our social institutions are not always reducible to intriguing tales about individual heroes and bureaucratic villains.

Melodrama, myth, and *60 Minutes* render the world transparent, soluble, and commonsensical. In part, the mythic dimension of television news offers reassurance and order in a world where experiences sometimes refuse to cohere. However, in seducing us with compelling narratives which display a reconstituted moral order, television news—like its print counterpart—does not draw us or the institutions of journalism actively into bearing any responsibility for the reconstitution. And former NBC news president Lawrence Grossman says that this is exactly what television news must do— take responsibility: "We need a press that speaks with many voices and many views, a vigorous, lively, crusading, responsive, and independent press, a press that is not viewed as just another product line in some vast corporate bureaucracy."[36]

At its best *60 Minutes* appears to be Grossman's model for journalism. The grace of the program rests in its crusading reporters, who enhance each story through their lively character performances and who reinstate sense amid contradiction from week to week. This, again, is the function of the "open eye" of common sense. *60 Minutes* has the ability to help us see, to show us complexity and contradiction, to unmask pretense and villainy, and still reclaim individual integrity and the sense of a moral social order.

News, then, can be both a way of seeing and not seeing. Its conventions often limit what kinds of issues, people, and places get covered and transformed into narratives. In this regard, news represents the "closed eye" of common sense and its inability to see that taken-for-granted conventions and formulas require periodic maintenance. News is not natural and given. In its construction, news conventions and formulas serve not merely to meet the professional demands of time and space constraints but also to distance the reporter—and us—from actual experience.[37]

Constructing interpretations about the interpretations of *60 Minutes* is a contradictory business. I argue finally, however, that *60 Minutes* offers a centered reading, a map, from which we may take up a position either near that center or radiating out. This metaphor recalls the maps that covered our elementary school chalk boards. They flattened the world into two dimensions and located the United States squarely at the center. And while our gazes were drawn to that middle region because of its privileged and central placement, we could and did explore other mysterious regions of the map. In the same way, *60 Minutes* flattens the world within the television frame and offers a map through its formulaic narratives. The program gives us a place each Sunday from where to start out—but we do not have to stay there.

The stories of *60 Minutes* penetrate deeply into America's consciousness. The detective taps into our desires for truth, honesty, and intrigue. The analyst helps us come to terms with our inner self, with moral order, and with knowledge about experience. The tourist cherishes adventure, tradition, and authenticity. The referee honors fairness, balance, and compromise. Through these metaphors and the commonsense frame of the narrative, the reporters of *60 Minutes* help us interpret our world. In this way the program extends the possibilities of enriching rather than merely limiting experience.

Although one function of metaphor, Walker Percy has argued, is to mediate and "to diminish tension," more importantly metaphor is "a discoverer of being."[38] Through metaphor we discover who we are. What *60 Minutes* offers us through its formulas, through the metaphor of news as drama, is the comfort of a touchstone to go back to (or start out from) each week. David Eason notes, "We long for the new, that story that seems just beyond us, but we also long for the comfort of the predictable, the story that pulls us along in familiar ways."[39] In this place each Sunday, the familiar incorporates the novel.

James Carey has written of the crises in both self- and social representations in mass communication and contemporary society. The former suggests the contradictory need for individuals to both "construct and escape authoritative institutions." The latter dimension turns as well on another contradictory impulse: "to give democratic coherence to a large nation with a diverse population without allowing it to decline into factionalism...."[40] In its own way, *60 Minutes* attempts to mediate both crises through its community of viewers. *60 Minutes*—able to conceal within individual dramas its own construction as an authoritative institution—portrays the sinister aspects of other authoritative institutions. In terms of the *self,* each week the program arms us as individuals in our resolve to escape those institutions. In terms of the *social,* the program's staunch narrative affirmations of a Middle-American mythology mediate between cultural and political factions that would de-center that middle ground. The power of *60 Minutes* rests in its ability to both disclose and enclose social experience, and secure a common sense of place, where we map out meanings and try to discover once again who we are.

Appendix A

Key to Audio and Video Abbreviations
and Definition of Terms

B or BF	Objects or characters appear in bottom one-third of frame.
B/G	Objects and characters appear in background (tend not to dominate frame).
B & W	Black and white—still photos and film footage not in color.
CF	Objects or characters appear in center of frame.
CG	Character-generated titles and other text information appearing in the frame.
CU	Close-up shot (generally refers to shots of objects or part of a subject or character other than the face, e.g., hands, feet, a pocket—compare ECU and HS).
cut	An edit or break point in the film.
dissolve	One image of shots "melts" away as another image appears; for a brief moment, both shots share the frame as one is superimposed over the other; used to mark longer passage of time or change in space.
ECU	Extreme close-up of a subject's face featuring the top of the head cut off by the top of the frame.
EECU	Extreme, extreme close-up of a subject's face featuring both the top of the head and the bottom of the chin cut from the frame.
ELS	Extreme long shot from a distance usually revealing two or more subjects in the frame along with B/G and F/G objects (usually refers to *indoor* shots where most of a particular setting is revealed in the frame).
ES	Establishing shot (refers to an *outdoor* shot which reveals a setting from a long distance).
F or frame	The television screen in which action takes place; subjects and objects are revealed within the boundaries of the television frame.
F/G	Objects or characters appear in foreground (tend to dominate frame).

freeze frame Action frozen or paused in the frame (this is a special effect added during editing).

HA High-angle shot (camera appears to "look down" on subjects or objects—most shots on *60 Minutes* are shown at eye level).

HS Head shot revealing a subject from the shoulders up with space appearing between top of head and top of frame.

LA Low-angle shot (camera appears to "look up" at subjects or objects).

L or LF Objects or characters appear on left side of frame.

LS Long shot revealing two or more characters in frame, one or more of whom appear from knee or waist up (LS does not reveal as much of setting as ELS).

LT Long take (a single shot—lasting more than fifteen seconds—uninterrupted by an edit point).

M/G or MF Objects or characters appear in middle one-third area of frame (compare BF, B/G and UF).

MLS Medium long shot revealing the entire body of *one* subject in the frame along with B/G and F/G objects.

MS Medium shot revealing a character from mid-chest or waist up, allowing space between top of head and top of frame.

OffS Off-screen narration or dialogue (voice of narrator or character which appears to come from outside the frame; voice is addressing an on-screen character, see VO).

OnS On-screen narration or dialogue (voice of narrator or character who is actually appearing on screen, see VO).

OS Over-the-shoulder shot revealing the back of one character (positioned in F/G in LF or RF) and the front of a second character in MS or LS (positioned in CF).

QT Quick take (a single shot—lasting less than three seconds—usually juxtaposed with other shots of short duration).

R or RF Objects or characters appear on right side of frame.

scene Part of a segment; a series of shots in which all the action takes place in the same location within continuous time.

segment A self-contained narrative (on *60 Minutes* there are generally three segments per program).

sequence A series of shots and scenes generally related by time, space, and/or thematic unity (on *60 Minutes* there are generally six to seven sequences per narrative).

shot | The smallest unit of analysis; what the camera actually reveals to viewers on screen *between* each edit point or "cut"; shots may last from one or two seconds to nearly a minute (the average *60 Minutes* shot runs six to eight seconds).

VO | Voice-over narration (generally the reporter's) which is added to the segment during post-production editing (VO is distinguished from OnS or OffS narration or dialogue which is recorded as the camera films the visuals).

WS | Wild sound (ambient background noises or sound effects).

ZI | Zoom-in shot (camera perspective moves gradually from long-range to closer-range shot, all within an unedited take).

ZO | Zoom-out shot (camera perspective moves gradually from close-range to longer-range shot, all within an unedited take).

Appendix B

"The Death of Edward Nevin"

© Copyright by CBS News 1980
(For key to audio and video abbreviations, see Appendix A.)

Shot Number	Video	Audio

Sequence 1

| 1 | MS Rather in LF; dressed in blue suit coat, vest, tie. In B/G storybook frame with title "The Death of Edward Nevin" and producer's name. Also in B/G are test tubes marked "E. Nevin"—LT. | *OnS Rather:* Occasionally we run across a story that is so unusual it seems it should be fiction. The death of Edward Nevin is such a tale. He was an immigrant whose life could be the story of every Irishman who came to these shores. Edward Nevin was a patriot, a man who worshipped freedom, and yet a man whose death, so his family says, came at the hands of the country he loved. Until recently, the death of Edward Nevin was a mystery. It involved a secret government experiment so closely guarded it would be a quarter of a century before it could be told. |

Sequence 2

| 2 | LA of cross/grave marker set against overcast sky; camera pans/tilts down to Rather in RF, MS at grave of Edward Nevin in LF. Rather in F/G walks across grave in CF as | *OffS Rather* (becomes OnS after camera picks up Rather): That same autumn, a man named Edward Nevin, a seventy-five-year-old Irish immigrant who had come to San Francisco in 1905 and fathered |

camera follows him R to L in MS. He wears a trench coat, and his hands are in his pockets. He stops and faces the camera — LT.

3   ECU of Dr. Richard Wheat looking L to R — he wears glasses and a white medical coat.

4   Dissolve to a still photo of eight to nine medical students in white laboratory coats; camera pans R to L across picture and zooms in on a younger 1950 version of Wheat.

5   Dissolve to present; LS of Wheat walking in R B/G to L F/G in hospital hallway.

6   Cut to LS of Wheat in RF at nurses' station in hospital; nurse or secretary on telephone sits in LF lower F/G and another in RF; Wheat moves to CF in MS to LS where he looks through round file unit, pulls out a file, and opens it.

7   HS Wheat — slow ZI to ECU; Wheat looks R to L.

seven children, died. Mr. Nevin had just been through successful surgery and had been released from the hospital. Then, suddenly and without explanation, he became ill and was forced to return.

OnS Wheat: I became acquainted with Mr. Nevin when his illness was obviously severe, and he came to the medical service where I was a resident and we cared for him until his death.

VO Rather: In 1950, Dr. Wheat was a 28-year-old resident at Stanford University Hospital in San Francisco when he noticed that certain patients were coming down with a mysterious illness.

VO Rather: By the time the infection had run its course, eleven men had been stricken by a strange bacteria called *Serratia marcescens.*

VO Rather: What puzzled Dr. Wheat was that this particular bacteria had never before been seen in his hospital, or anywhere else in the San Francisco area.

OnS Wheat: Well, at first it was a curiosity and then it became a concern that perhaps we had something going that we didn't understand or didn't know about. So, with that in mind, we tried to find out where it was coming from and what had caused it, with absolutely no luck at all.

8   Cut to cover of a periodical—ZI to date: "October 1951 Volume 88 Number 4"

VO Rather: So puzzled was Dr. Wheat by the appearance of *Serratia marcescens* and the illness of the eleven patients that he published an account of the experience in a medical journal.

9   CU on type from Wheat's article—slow ZI to specific passage circled in red marker: "CASE 2—E.N."

VO Rather: Ten of the men eventually recovered from the infection, but one man did not, a man whose initials were E.N.

10   MS Rather back in cemetery as in shot 2—hands in trench coat pockets, framed by grave markers in R and LF: camera pans from Rather across to HA shot of small grave stone with cross and word *Nevin* on it.

OnS Rather (goes OffS as camera pans to marker): In November of 1950, Edward Nevin died. It would be twenty-six years before all the circumstances surrounding his death would be known.

11   Cut to old home movies showing Edward Nevin in MS, LF; he is a large man, nodding and laughing.

VO Rather: These old home movies of Edward Nevin, taken a few years before his death are the only remaining record of him.

12   Cut to another home movie shot—Nevin dances in MS, RF—room is crowded with people.

13   Jump cut—same footage as shot 12.

VO Rather: They reveal a vigorous, vital individual who looked younger than his age . . .

14   Another cut—same footage then camera pans crowd.

15   Another cut to Nevin in old movie holding a young girl in a pink dress

VO Rather: . . . a man who, by all rights, should have been able to resist the bacteria that

with blue ribbon in her hair; camera holds in FREEZE FRAME on Nevin and girl and begins slow ZI to MS of Nevin.

appeared from nowhere to kill him. And where it came from was a mystery.

Sequence 3

16 Dissolve to Harvard University building—ELS, HA man walking briskly from building, hands in pockets of overcoat; man continues to walk along sidewalk in LS; camera follows him.

VO Rather: We pick up the story three thousand miles across the country, at Harvard University, where this man, Dr. Matthew Messelson, is professor of biochemistry.

17 LA as camera follows Messelson in MS to LS; his head is framed by overcast winter sky and bare tree branches.

VO Rather: In 1965, Dr. Messelson's assistant had told him a story she had heard and kept secret since 1950.

18 Cut to HA of Messelson in ELS through fork in tree; he is still walking, turns away from camera, and begins to walk out RF; slow ZO—LT.

VO Rather: It concerned a U.S. Army biological-warfare experiment in San Francisco which, according to the woman's informant, had resulted in the death of a man. The experiment involved the use of live bacteria called *Serratia marcescens.*

19 ECU Messelson R to L framed by blackboard in B/G with numbers written on it—LT.

VO Rather: The woman was very nervous about telling this to Dr. Messelson.
OnS Messelson: She was frightened. She knew that I was then, as I have been for many years, very interested in chemical and biological arms defense and chemical and biological arms control, chemical and biological weapons. That's why she told

		me, and also because we were good friends. But she was afraid and asked me not to tell anybody.
20	MS Rather in dark suit coat, tie, framed by bookcase in B/G; he takes notes.	*OffS Messelson:* I then made a search of the medical . . .
21	ECU Messelson (same as shot 19).	*OnS Messelson:* . . . literature to see if I could find any articles about this because that would be rather unusual. I knew that it — deaths from *Serratia marcescens* — would be considered unusual. And I found an article . . .
22	Cut to CU of article co-authored by Wheat; slow ZI to CU of word, "Richard P. Wheat, M.D." which is highlighted as rest of frame dissolves to gray.	*VO Messelson:* . . . and I called one of the authors, Dr. Wheat.
23	ECU Messelson (same as shots 19, 21) — LT.	*OffS Rather:* And what did he tell you about the death? Did he tell you that he was pretty sure that it was caused by this? Or caused — *OnS Messelson:* The death itself was certainly caused by bacterial endocarditis and — due to *Serratia marcescens.* But as to the puzzle of where the bacteria came from in that and the other cases, which all occurred within a short interval of time, he was still as mystified as before, though he still, as I recall, believed, as he had written in his paper, that there had been a common source. But what that common source might be, he

		had no guess at the time. *OffS Rather:* But you had a guess? *OnS Messelson:* If he did, he didn't tell me. I had a guess. *OffS Rather:* You knew about . . .
24	HS Rather (same as shot 20).	*OnS Rather:* . . . the test. *OffS Messelson:* I knew about the test. And I told people in the government . . .
25	ECU Messleson (same as shots 19, 21, and 23).	*OnS Messelson:* . . . that this sort of thing was foolish and that it ought to be stopped. But I didn't know who the right people were to talk to. I don't think.

Sequence 4

26	Dissolve to MS and HS of crowded city street scene; people walk toward and around camera.	*VO Rather:* What Dr. Messelson also didn't know was that millions of Americans had already been used by the government as unwitting guinea pigs . . .
27	MS young woman carrying bag walking down street; camera pans and follows her; heads pass between her and camera while camera picks up MS of old man walking in crowd chewing gum; he moves toward camera to HS; taxi passes in front of him.	*VO Rather:* . . . in more than two hundred biological warfare experiments that took place between 1949 and 1968, when they were finally stopped.
28	Another city crowd shot; people on sidewalk walk to and away from camera, which is located among the pedestrians.	*VO Rather:* What was the army trying to learn from exposing millions of Americans to what they thought was completely harmless bacteria?

29	Another crowd/street shot; traffic cop moves into CF wearing white hat, dark bill—blows whistle, motions to crowd to move forward; little girl in BF seen beneath policeman.	*VO Rather:* They say it was the only way they could find out how to cope with a real germ-warfare attack should the Russians ever launch one.
30	Crowd moves off curb into street; MS little girl eating something; two other little girls in F/G; older man in B/G.	*VO Rather:* So, nineteen civilian targets were chosen to practice on.
31	CU of NY subway train moving L to RF; waiting riders seen at extreme LF.	(*WS:* loud subway train noises) *VO Rather:* One of them was the New York City subway system.
32	MS to LS of back of Harry Moses carrying paper bag, walking—wearing overcoat, floppy hat, gloves; camera follows him down the street; he turns to LF and descends dark subway; taxis, crowds, department store visible across street. Viewers never see his face.	*VO Rather:* As *60 Minutes*'s producer Harry Moses did the other day, the army's man in New York entered the subway carrying a light bulb . . .
33	CU gloved hand of Moses removing a light bulb from paper bag; puts it in overcoat pocket; camera ZI to pocket.	*VO Rather:* . . . only his light bulb contained live bacteria to be used in the experiment.
34	CU of subway door opening; graffiti sprayed on doors which slides open; Moses steps from shadows, pushes open door, and reaches down with light bulb.	*VO Rather:* As the train sped through the tunnel, the man opened the door separating two of the cars, stepped into the opening, and . . .

35	CU hands releasing light bulb onto subway tracks.	*VO Rather:* . . . dropped the light bulb on the . . .
36	ELS of subway track; camera in subway car shoots people waiting; car turns into dark tunnel.	*VO Rather:* . . . tracks, releasing the bacteria. Monitoring stations set up by the army showed that the experiment was a success. (*WS:* subway train roaring into tunnel.)
37	CU of "14th ST." sign, pan to subway car pulling into station; subway car passes camera; passengers visible inside.	*VO Rather:* The bacteria had traveled from 14th Street all the way up to 59th Street, a distance of more than two miles.
38	LS through airport window at airport; camera pans plane as it takes off down runway.	*VO Rather:* Similar tests were conducted at Washington's National Airport . . . (*WS:* airport noises, air planes taking off, announcer over loudspeaker.)
39	CU of Greyhound bus sign; bus passes camera; ZO to reveal bus moving by and out into street.	*VO Rather:* . . . at Greyhound bus terminals in Alaska and Hawaii, and in two tunnels on the Pennsylvania Turnpike.
40	CU of San Francisco cable car, passes by camera; young woman sitting and reading aboard; cable car pulls away and goes down hill; cars, traffic, street crowd in B/G.	*VO Rather:* But the biggest and the most bizarre biological-warfare test took place in September of 1950 in San Francisco, California.
41	Dissolve to ES of Golden Gate Bridge and ocean; camera in boat; begin to see wake of boat as it moves into range of panning camera; HA shot of boat as it passes from L and out of RF; camera tilts back up to bridge.	*VO Rather:* The object of the test, according to recently declassified army documents, was—quote—"to study the offensive possibilities of attacking a seaport city with a biological-warfare aerosol generated from a ship located some distance offshore."

42 LS Rather aboard boat (dressed as he was in cemetery—tie, red scarf, trench coat); Rather walks from M/G to F/G motioning with his hands and into MS range; he moves to RF and out of frame.

OnS Rather: And so, on a navy ship, about the size and length of this one, the U.S. Army's secret testing team steamed out into the middle of San Francisco Bay.

43 ES of San Francisco skyline in B/G with bay in M/G, boat's railing in F/G; Rather moves into frame from L, pauses in MS and uses hands to demonstrate; he stops in CF, MS framed by skyline and water in B/G; he turns toward RF.

OnS Rather: Attached to the railing of the fantail of the ship were three huge metal canisters containing the biological agent to be used in the experiment, a bacteria named *Serratia marcescens,* selected because of its supposedly benign characteristics and the bright red color it produced under laboratory analysis.

44 MS to HS Rather; bridge, skyline in B/G, hand visible in extreme BF; he turns toward RF again.

OnS Rather: At precisely 1700 hours, the testing team pointed the hoses attached to the canisters skyward, opened the valves of the nozzles and set forth an aerosol cloud of bacteria towards its intended destination, the city of...

45 Cut to ELS Rather with back to camera aboard boat in MF, HA; camera pans, tilts over and up, leaving him pointing in BRF; camera moves up boat's mast to ES of city's skyline.

VO Rather: ... San Francisco. As the cloud made its way across the bay, three aircraft hovered overhead...

46 White, cloudy dissolve to HA air shot looking down over tall buildings as camera fades in and pans city from above.

VO Rather: ... collecting meteorological data, and the twenty ground stations were obtaining figures on wind direction and velocity. While all this was happening, the army had established forty-three sampling stations at various locations throughout the Bay area to determine how great the bacteria's penetration had been. Volunteers stood by the windows of their homes, . . .

47 Another white dissolve to ELS of Rather CF, HA on top of building; aerial shot ZI Rather in trench coat holding something white in his hand.

VO Rather: . . . of government office buildings, even on their rooftops.

48 MS Rather on roof top holding "sievelike collector"; holds it up, points to it, pats it; sieve drops from frame as slight ZI to HS of Rather—LT.

OnS Rather: All were holding sievelike collectors, similar to this one, which would trap airborne bacteria released from the ship. After these collectors had been analyzed by the lab, the army learned that thirty square miles, or nearly all of San Francisco, had been exposed to the bacteria. Almost eight hundred thousand persons had breathed particles of *Serratia marcescens* that September day in 1950.

49 Cut again to ELS, HA of Rather on rooftop—aerial camera ZO and "flies" away as Rather grows smaller in CF; camera moves around and over him, and he passes out of frame at BRF; camera reveals city and hospital below.

VO Rather: Why, then, did only eleven people, one of whom died, feel the effects of the *Serratia marcescens*? The winds that day blew it directly over the hospital where those eleven patients were undergoing treatment that made them particularly susceptible to the infection.

50 Cut to another aerial shot HA of city harbor; camera flies over and along harbor area, revealing buildings along the dock and harbor area.

VO Rather: A common source for that infection was always suspected by Dr. Wheat, but as Dr. Messelson told us, there was no way of knowing what it was at the time.

Sequence 5

51	Out of focus shot of lights focuses to reveal a BART train (the San Francisco subway) in CU moving R to L in front of camera; pans BART as it whizzes by and follows it out of frame to reveal man waiting.	*VO Rather:* The spraying of San Francisco would remain a closely guarded secret until 1976, when an enterprising reporter found out about it, linked it to Dr. Wheat's article and filed his story.
52	CU of San Francisco *Chronicle* front-page story; slow ZI to headline: "Army Tested Biological War in S.F."	*VO Rather:* On December 22, 1976, the story hit page one of the San Francisco *Chronicle*. No one would feel its impact more greatly than . . .
53	BART subway station with man (Edward Nevin III) emerging from top of escalator reading newspaper in LS, CF; he wears a light suit, carries an umbrella; he walks out of LF.	*VO Rather:* . . . a young trial attorney who had been specializing in medical malpractice cases. He remembers it this way.
54	Cut to man coming into RF carrying newspaper, stands on subway platform in MS waiting for train; he turns as camera looks over his shoulder down the track; he looks down track, unfolds paper, and reads.	*VO Edward Nevin III:* I take BART from my home in Berkeley to work, and I was waiting for the BART train and I was reading the paper and . . .
55	ECU of Nevin looking down reading; camera ZI to EECU.	*VO Nevin III:* . . . I came upon a front-page article which was—the headline read "Bacteriological Warfare Experiment in 1950, San Francisco."

56	Cut to Nevin on subway, standing holding handle in MS, still reading paper; Nevin in RF, subway window in LF; see movement out of window as train moves.	*VO Nevin III:* As a trial lawyer, as someone who deals with these kind of cases, I looked at it without surprise . . .
57	LA Nevin in MS, RF still holding on and reading; another passenger sits in LF.	*VO Nevin III:* . . . but with a detached sort of objective view, a professional looking at something within his field.
58	OS shot as camera "reads" newspaper along with Nevin, who turns page.	*VO Nevin III:* I then discovered that the one person who died as a result of these experiments was Edward J. Nevin, . . .
59	HS of Nevin, appears to be reading.	*VO Nevin III:* . . . a retired San Francisco pipe fitter who died in Stanford Hospital on November 1, 1950.
60	LA, HS of Nevin framed by roof of subway train.	*VO Nevin III:* That was my grandfather.
61	LS camera now outside subway, pans to Nevin inside CF, still reading; train speeds by and out of frame.	(*WS:* subway noises.)

Sequence 6

62	ECU of Nevin R to L; law books behind him.	*OnS Nevin III:* I was stunned. I was angry. I was hurt.
63	MS of Nevin reveals more of red, black law books and office in B/G—LT.	*OnS Nevin III:* The government made a decision with extremely limited thought and preparation and investigation, made a decision to expose eight hundred thousand San Francisco citizens to bacterium, live bacterium, did not investigate the potentials for that bacterium causing disease to an ade-

quate degree, and proceeded, nevertheless, to, in effect, reverse the whole process of the purpose of our military and our defense system — that is, to protect the people of the United States of America. And instead, that very branch of our government attacked the people of the United States of America.

64	Old film footage of Pentagon building from the air; camera ZO then holds shot in freeze frame.	*VO Rather:* What does the Pentagon say about that? It refused our request for an interview, but maintains that any association between the bacteria that was sprayed on San Francisco with the bacteria that killed Edward Nevin is coincidence.
65	ECU Wheat (same shot as 3).	*OnS Wheat:* Of course, it was a fascinating coincidence, if that, since the time of their experiments was on the 26th and 27th of September, and our first case came in on the 29th of September. And Mr. Nevin, our gentleman who died of the disease, first became ill with this organism on the 2nd of October. The timing of those things is awfully interesting. *VO Rather:* "Awfully interesting"...
66	Dissolve to ELS of Edward Nevin III and his father Edward Nevin II in CF walking through woods; B/G features pile of leaves, farm buildings, woods as camera begins slow ZI on pair walking.	*VO Rather:* ... is not how the Nevin family would describe the relationship between the army experiment and the death of Edward Nevin. His son is far more vehement.

67	Dissolve to HS Edward Nevin II (Nevin's son); ZI to ECU; outdoor interview at farm.	(*WS:* birds in B/G.) *OnS Nevin II:* Well, I can't help remembering that the enemy did not do this to those eleven people in Stanford Hospital; that it was this government that did it, and it resulted in my father's death.
68	ECU Mrs. Bray (Nevin's daughter); she wears glasses, looks R to L in frame—LT.	*OnS Bray:* It's—it's—it just happened to the wrong person. *VO Rather:* Mr. Nevin's daughter. *OnS Bray:* You know, if it was somebody that wasn't a likeable person or didn't do good in the world. I feel that he did good . . .
69	Cutaway CU of Bray; hands holding black and white photo in gold frame; hands rest on table and lace doily.	*OffS Bray:* . . . in the world. He was . . .
70	HS Bray R to L with vase in extreme RF in B/G; white teapot in LF.	*OnS Bray:* . . . real proud of being an American. And, you know, my mother was too.
71	Cutaway to shot 69; tight CU of upper half of old photo showing Nevin and family; Bray's hands switch photo back and forth in frame.	*OffS Bray:* They never had any desire to go back. They wouldn't leave America. They loved it. He . . .
72	ECU Bray who begins to rub her eyes under her glasses.	*OnS Bray:* . . . left a wonderful heritage to all of us. I think we're a remarkable family. (She begins to cry.)

Sequence 7

73	MS to LS of Nevin family Christmas celebration; man giving out gifts to children; Christmas tree in RF; camera pans to child receiving gift as other children gather around him.	(*WS:* Christmas celebration; party noises.) *OnS Man:* Timmy, open it up, Tim! (*WS:* Christmas song comes on in B/G.)
74	CU record turntable.	(*WS:* Christmas music.)
75	HS baby in red smiling.	(*WS:* Christmas music, talking, laughing.)
76	HS older woman smiling.	*VO Rather* (with WS continuing): Each Christmas ...
77	HS, LA young boy.	... is a time of ...
78	HS young woman smiling.	... reunion for the Nevin clan.
79	MS older woman on couch; boy moves between her and camera.	*VO Rather:* And each Christmas all four ...
80	HS older woman smiling	... generations of the family ...
81	MS young man smiling.	... gather to celebrate ...
82	ECU older woman looking into camera.	... the season.
83	MS Edward Nevin II on couch, smiling.	*VO Rather:* The Nevins are there, of course, ...
84	MS older woman talking to young woman, drinking.	... and the Careys, too ...
85	EECU Mrs. Bray smiling.	... the Brays and ...
86	ECU man with moustache.	... the Gallaghers, ...
87	MS couple kissing.	... the Donahoes and the Mc-Faddens.
88	MS man passing child to older woman; tree in B/G.	*VO Rather:* And from the oldest to the youngest, there is a bond ...
89	MS two men stand at mantle framed by mirror behind them.	... and a resolve ...
90	ECU young girl, smiling.	... a purpose ...
91	ECU young man.	... that joins everyone.

92	MS, HA back of young girl; profile of another; tree in LF.	*VO Rather:* For all of these people—
93	HS young woman.	all sixty-five . . .
94	HS young man in profile.	. . . descendents of Edward J. Nevin—
95	MS to LS large group, singing, laughing, talking.	have united to file suit . . .
96	MS, HA young girl reads to baby.	. . . against the army, the navy . . .
97	LS three older women on couch, laughing.	. . . the Department of Defense, and the United States of America . . .
98	MS back of young man holding baby.	. . . for the wrongful death of the founder of this extended . . .
99	LS of party again (see shot 95).	. . . Irish-American family. And who will be arguing the case?
100	HS of Edward Nevin III (see shot 63).	*OnS Nevin III:* I'm Edward J. Nevin III. And thirty years later, I have an opportunity to present to the American people my grandfather's story for a very, very important purpose.
101	Jump cut to Nevin but a slightly more distant HS; slow ZI to ECU.	*OnS Nevin III:* You do not test people without them knowing it. You do not test in secrecy. You do not risk, no matter what limited risk you think you have—that you're taking, without having people knowingly submit to that risk.
102	Jump cut again to HS of Nevin; ZI to ECU.	*OnS Nevin III:* This is a question for all of us in a democratic society. We have to know.

Appendix C

"What Became of Eldridge Cleaver?"

© Copyright by CBS News 1975

(For key to audio and video abbreviations, see Appendix A.)

Shot Number	Video	Audio

Sequence 1

1	HS Wallace against black B/G—LT.	*OnS Wallace:* "Violence is as American as cherry pie." A black revolutionary said it in the sixties as black violence hit our major cities and law and order sometimes became police brutality. It was the Black Panthers who were the most militant of all blacks then, a gun-toting cadre self-appointed to protect the black ghetto, they said from the white pigs. And Eldridge Cleaver was then the most vocal of the Panthers.
2	MS Wallace in RF, gray suit, striped tie; story-book frame behind him features large, tightly cropped photo of Cleaver in LF, the title and the producer.	*OnS Wallace:* Whatever became of Eldridge Cleaver? *60 Minutes* talked to him five years ago in exile in Algiers. He is now in Paris, where we visited him to see what those five years had done to confirm his notions, or to change them.

Sequence 2

3	MS Wallace in RF outdoors in trench coat; he looks into gutted building; camera tilts up the house to reveal burn marks and bullet holes—LT.	*VO Wallace* (in flashback to five years earlier): Our report in 1970 began at this house in Oakland, California. Cleaver had survived a police shootout here. The walls were scarred by

bullets, charred by smoke and fire and tear gas. Another Panther had been killed by police guns when he ran from this house.

4   HS Cleaver; camera ZO to reveal shot as b & w photo still; Cleaver now in LS in handcuffs with policemen in RF, F/G.

VO Wallace: Cleaver stripped off his clothes, walked out stark naked to show he was unarmed. He was charged with assault with intent to kill, jumped bail, fled to exile, first in Cuba, . . .

5   LS street scene in Algiers; stark white mosque in B/G; camera shows people and traffic.

VO Wallace: . . . then to Algeria rather than go to prison.

6   LS street scene in Algiers; women with veiled faces walk up stairs.

VO Wallace: Then from safe haven in Algiers, Cleaver called for physical attack against . . .

7   MS Cleaver, wife, and child sitting on couch; Cleaver raises baby's fist in air.

VO Wallace: . . . the leaders of the U.S. government.

8   HS Cleaver.

VO Wallace: Five years ago we asked this question:
OffS Wallace: What purpose is served by talking of shooting your way into the Senate of . . .

9   EECU Cleaver, slight LA—LT.

OffS Wallace: . . . the United States, taking off the head of Senator McClelland, and shooting your way back out? What purpose is really served by that kind of talk, and what would be accomplished—?
OnS Cleaver: The goal—the goal is to take Senator McClelland's head. Now, the process of getting his head has to rely on a strategic technique. I mean, I can't just walk in and take his head and walk out, you see.

10	MS Wallace; LF hands folded posed on chin.	*OffS Cleaver:* I have to get past the guards and get past those . . .
11	EECU Cleaver (same as shot 9).	*OnS Cleaver:* . . . who might try to protect his pig head. So, to me I think that would mean shooting my way in and shooting my way out, because I wouldn't want to go in, take his head, and just sit there.
12	OS Wallace in LF; MS Cleaver in RF; portraits of black faces on wall in B/G; slow ZI on Cleaver.	*VO Wallace:* But when the American people hear that you want to shoot your way into the United States Senate, take off the head of a senator—
13	EECU Cleaver (same as shots 9, 11); hands move in front of face to emphasize point; eyes sometimes move out of frame—LT.	*OnS Cleaver* (talks over Wallace): Or into the White House and take off the head of Richard Nixon, you see.

Sequence 3

14	LS outdoor building; "Black Panther Party" sign visible; ZI to slogan: "We serve the people."	*VO Wallace:* Bravado from Eldridge Cleaver overseas . . .
15	MS of posters on wall showing black leaders who are in jail.	*VO Wallace:* . . . while his fellow Panthers here at home remained . . .
16	MS another poster of Panther party leader.	*VO Wallace:* . . . a small, demoralized, . . .
17	CU poster: "Free the N.Y. 21."	*VO Wallace:* . . . beleaguered group: never more than . . .
18	CU "Black Panther Party" sign; surrounded by posters, pictures, cartoons.	*VO Wallace:* . . . a thousand Black Panthers in the entire country, . . .
19	MS classroom session; teacher in MS, RF; children in MS, LF.	*VO Wallace:* . . . and they had been thoroughly infiltrated by police informers.

20	MS, LA "Black Panther Party: Serving the People" sign; ZO reveals child, mother, man in front of building.	*VO Wallace:* Panther leaders were being jailed or killed in shootouts with police, but still the party was teaching the next . . .
21	CU drawing of black man in beard wearing African headdress; camera tilts to poster: "Huey Must Be Set Free."	*VO Wallace:* . . . generation to take up the gun.
22	LS classroom scene; young black woman teaching; stands over thirteen to fifteen black children seated around table; ZI to MS teacher as she raises clenched fist; she and children appear in BF.	(*WS:* teacher leads singing: "Revolution has come/time to pick up the gun/off the pigs.") *VO Wallace* (as singing continues): This was a "liberation school," they called it, in Brooklyn.
23	HS young black girl; blue ribbon in hair, raising clenched fist.	*VO Wallace:* Brainwash indoctrination about the pigs . . .
24	MS to LS teacher reads to class; holds up poster; teacher, poster looms over children in BF. MS to LS of class — LT.	*VO Wallace:* . . . and about their own Panther heroes.
		OnS Teacher: Okay, who is this?

OnS Children (several answer separately): Huey P. Newton.
OnS Teacher: Who is it?
OnS Children (separately again): Huey P. Newton.
OffS Teacher (another teacher's voice): You say it loud.
OnS Children: Huey P. Newton!
OnS Teacher: And where is Huey?
OnS Children: In jail!
OnS Teacher (with VO Wallace covering answer): Who put him there?

25   MS two young girls fight-
      ing, slapping at each
      other.

VO Wallace: Newton had been
jailed for shooting a policeman.
On a retrial, he was acquitted,
went free.
VO Wallace: But now he has
jumped bail again, charged with
killing a seventeen-year-old
black girl in California.

26   Teacher stands behind
      large poster of Bobby
      Seale; Seale in HS in RF
      as teacher moves out into
      LF—LT.

OnS Teacher: Now, who took
Bobby away?

OffS Children: The pigs.

OffS Another Teacher's Voice:
Who took Bobby away?
OffS Children (louder): The
pigs!
VO Wallace: Bobby was Bobby
Seale, who had been arrested
for murder; a hung jury freed
him. Later, he was convicted
for sparking riots during . . .

27   CU on "Join the Conspir-
      acy" poster.

VO Wallace: . . . the '68 Democratic Convention. Then Seale
turned moderate, ran . . .

28   HS Seale in still photo;
      part of poster from shot
      27.

VO Wallace: . . . for mayor of
Oakland . . .

29   HS Seale in gray suit at
      speaker's podium in LF;
      U.S. flag in RF.

VO Wallace: . . . and lost.

30   LS Seale; crowd listens to
      him in F/G.

VO Wallace: He's dropped out
of sight now, . . .

31   HS Seale at microphone.

VO Wallace: . . . is being sought
by the Los Angeles police on
child-support charges.

Sequence 4

32   MS Cleaver CF; wife RF;
      baby LF.

VO Wallace: Five years ago,
with Cleaver in exile, . . .

33	MS to LS b & w still photo; Newton supine on table, shirt off; policeman, nurse loom over him; he looks injured.	*VO Wallace:* . . . Huey Newton in jail, . . .
34	LS Panther headquarters in Oakland.	*VO Wallace:* . . . Panther headquarters in Oakland was run by David Hilliard, . . .
35	LS Hilliard; OS Wallace in LF points to sand bags and protection system.	*VO Wallace:* . . . surrounded by sandbags and barricaded windows, fearing a shootout . . . (*WS:* Wallace asking Hilliard about steel plates and sandbags.) *VO Wallace:* . . . with police. Hilliard was later convicted of assault, . . .
36	HS Hilliard in CF.	*VO Wallace:* . . . served his time; he is now a counselor at a school for juvenile delinquents in California.
37	OS Wallace in LF; LS Cleaver in CF; African-American artifacts on wall in B/G.	*VO Wallace:* Eldridge Cleaver in Algiers five years ago was the Panthers' philosopher in exile.
38	HS Cleaver in LF; picture of mother holding baby on wall in B/G.	*OnS Cleaver:* The way I view the situation, I don't think that the government and the ruling class in the United States is going to relent or allow black people to enjoy freedom and liberation. I think that it has to be taken, . . .
39	Jump cut, HS Cleaver.	*OnS Cleaver:* . . . and I fully believe that we have to fight a war of liberation from the fascist, imperialist social order in the United States.
40	ELS street scene in Algiers; buildings, people milling about on street;	*VO Wallace:* The Algerian government helped subsidize Cleaver until 1972, when some

	camera moving, focusing in LS on people on street.	Panthers landed in Algiers with a hijacked American plane and half a million dollars in ransom.
41	ECU Cleaver; slow ZI to EECU.	*VO Wallace:* Cleaver protested when Algeria gave back the money along with the plane. This incident and others gradually wore out his welcome in Algeria.

Sequence 5 (five years later)

42	ES Paris; Eiffel Tower in B/G, trees in RF, F/G.	*VO Wallace:* So France became Cleaver's refuge, and in his flat there . . .
43	OS Wallace in LF, dark gray suit; MS to LS Cleaver; in B/G large zebra-skin rug adorns wall, frames Cleaver's head in B/G.	*VO Wallace:* . . . a graying Eldridge Cleaver has been thinking a good deal.
44	ECU Cleaver.	*OffS Wallace:* You knew, when you told me five years ago that you were going to shoot your way into the United States Senate and . . .
45	HS to MS Wallace; points thumb at Cleaver, motions with arm.	*OnS Wallace:* . . . take off the head of Richard Nixon, and that J. Edgar Hoover had to be apprehended, and so on; . . .
46	ECU Cleaver—LT.	*OffS Wallace:* . . . and you said it was not rhetoric. You meant it. *OnS Cleaver:* Okay. Now, I would say this. You see, my feelings then and my feelings now is that Richard Nixon absolutely had to be taken out of the White House, you see. *OffS Wallace:* But the system did it.

OnS Cleaver: The system did it at long last. I'm very happy that the system did it; therefore, I don't feel any need to talk about going in there and taking him out myself. But I say this: That as long as that man was in the White House, I felt the need to go in there and take him out. I—I can't say that I don't feel that, you see. And I don't feel ashamed about that. I—See, I'm proud about that, you see.

47	HS to MS Wallace, motioning, scratching his head; pictures of pottery and blacks in African costume in B/G behind him.	*OnS Wallace:* You said it was going to be necessary to "fight a war of liberation against the fascist, imperialist United States." You no longer believe that?
48	EECU Cleaver.	*OnS Cleaver:* I think that we can solve our problems without fighting a war of liberation, simply because the system itself has reacted to the pressure that was brought upon it by that kind of organizing and that kind of mobilization and that kind of rhetoric.
49	MS Wallace in CF, scratches his right ear.	*OffS Cleaver:* Now, this doesn't mean that by doing that that solves all of our problems, . . .
50	ECU Cleaver.	*OnS Cleaver:* . . . but it does eliminate, I think, the kind of concentration camp solution to the black problem that we thought we were faced with.
51	HS Wallace, hand at eye; scratches above left eye.	*OnS Wallace:* Are you telling me, at bottom, that you wish you hadn't said "violence," "gun," "take off the head," "shoot your way into the Senate?"

52	HS Cleaver; wall zebra skin frames him in B/G— LT.	*OffS Wallace:* Are you telling me that political action would have been better? *OnS Cleaver:* Well, I'm saying this. Here's what I'm saying. I think it would have been possible, given—and this is all with hind-sight now, Mike. *OffS Wallace:* Sure. *OnS Cleaver:* Because at the time . . .
53	MS Wallace; OS Cleaver in RF	*OffS Cleaver:* . . . I didn't see any alternative. I can say now that . . .
54	HS Cleaver (same as shot 52).	*OnS Cleaver:* . . . I wished that I had had a better knowledge of how to deal with our political situation.
55	HS Wallace (same as shot 53); Cleaver's hand motions visible in bottom CF.	*OffS Cleaver:* I no longer am interested in going around talking about . . .
56	HS Cleaver (same as shots 52, 54); hand scratches chin.	*OnS Cleaver:* . . . guns or advocating just violence in the abstract or calling people pigs.

Sequence 6

57	ES cathedral in Paris; camera tilts down church to reveal Cleaver and wife as they stroll along river bank in LS; ZI to MS of couple (they look like middle-class tourists).	*VO Wallace:* These days the Cleavers, Eldridge and Kathleen, stroll the Left Bank in the Paris spring like many exiles before them. It's been a twisted route for him . . .
58	Cut to MS from back of couple as they walk away from camera; bridge and city in B/G—LT.	*VO Wallace:* . . . since the days when he was the acclaimed author of *Soul on Ice,* that brilliant and bitter story of his early years, and another assault conviction that sent him to San Quentin prison. That was the time he was the hero of many white radicals.

59	LA, MS of Cleaver in b & w still photo; wears dark glasses, stands at a podium; camera tilts down still to reveal "Cleaver for President" sign.	*VO Wallace:* He was even a candidate for the presidency in 1968 for the Peace and Freedom party.
60	MS Cleaver in profile at typewriter; puffs on a pipe and begins typing.	*VO Wallace:* But now he wants to come home, says he's ready to stand trial for that Oakland shootout, but insists that he not be locked up before the trial. (*WS:* typing noises).
61	CU typewriter keys.	*VO Wallace:* He supports himself . . .
62	MS Cleaver (same as shot 60).	*VO Wallace:* . . . with a publisher's advances, no longer a black symbol . . .
63	ECU Cleaver; smoke from pipe drifts in front of his face; intent on his typing.	*VO Wallace:* . . . of resistance to white capitalism, imperialism.
64	MS to LS Cleaver still works at typewriter and desk.	*VO Wallace:* He is no longer an invited guest in communist lands.
65	ECU Cleaver; zebra skin again visible on wall in B/G.	*OnS Cleaver:* The point is this—that in the communist countries they don't have any kind of machinery for the people to bring their will to bear on the decision-making process.
66	MS Wallace (same as shots 53, 55).	*OffS Cleaver:* I am forced to conclude—I'm happy to conclude—
67	HS Cleaver; camera has pulled back from shot 65; Wallace revealed in OS in LF—LT.	*OnS Cleaver:* I don't—I don't do it with any reluctance, you know—that we do have that in the United States, you see. And—
		OffS Wallace: We do have—?
		OnS Cleaver: We do have the political freedom, a certain amount of political freedom. I think that our institutions,

rather than be destroyed, they need to be perfected, they need to be . . .

68   HS Wallace; slow ZO to MS Wallace; he gestures with his hands and counts off ways Cleaver has changed —LT.

OffS Cleaver: . . . further developed.

OnS Wallace: Let me understand. Do I understand Eldridge Cleaver in 1975 correctly? You renounce violence, the gun, under present conditions in the United States? You're not as enamored of the communist states as you once were? The fact that a man has a black skin does not necessarily make him your brother? All this is fairly accurate, no?

69   HS Cleaver.

OnS Cleaver: I think it's accurate, yeah.

70   MS Wallace; see hands in BF.

OnS Wallace: And you want to go home?

71   HS Cleaver (same as shot 69)—LT.

OnS Cleaver: And I want to go home. And I think I will go home, too, you see. Like, people who don't want me to come back, or who don't have the same interests in me coming back as I do, they—they can look at it academically, but to me it's a very personal thing. I think I have a right to come back without going to prison before going to trial, and I'm working for that; and I'm going to do everything I can to be able to. I want to be back there no later than the Fourth of July on the 200th anniversary of our country. And if I'm not back there, then I don't know where I'll be.

Sequence 7

72	MS Wallace returns to magazine frame—LT.

OnS Wallace: Cleaver's father, Leroy Cleaver, died in Chicago a week ago at the age of seventy-two. His son could not come home for the funeral. The Panthers these days are a changed outfit, working in the black community for nonviolent social reform, backing their own political candidates, their rhetoric muted, their energies devoted to laboring inside the system.

Appendix D

"Rolls-Royce"

(For key to audio and video abbreviations, see Appendix A.)

Shot Number	Video	Audio

Sequence 1

1	MS Safer in RF with storybook frame in B/G showing old clocks and word "Yesterday"—LT. (Original 1971 title, "Rolls-Royce," and producer's name not displayed.)	*OnS Safer:* Now another of our so-called "golden oldies." When this story about Rolls-Royce cars was first broadcast nine years ago, we said the cheapest Rolls sold for $24,000, the most expensive for $50,000. Here's what inflation has done: the cheapest is now $85,000 and the most expensive $156,000. But enough talk of money. This story is about quality. And this is the way we began it back in November 1971.

Sequence 2

2	CU of hands painting hood of black R-R car.	*VO Safer:* Rolls-Royce is the longest lasting and the last of the great handmade cars—
3	CU of hands rubbing car with cloth.	*VO Safer:* Hispano-Suiza, Duesenberg, Packard, Isotta . . .
4	MS older worker in LF, balding; sleeves of light-brown mechanic's suit rolled up; he touches up paint and rubs car's finish.	*VO Safer:* . . . Fraschini, all of them dead. But Rolls survives, . . .

215

5	MS two men in dark suits and ties, scrutinizing back end of R-R; men in LF, car in RF; man lifts recessed gas panel.	*VO Safer:* . . . more old ones on the road than new ones—one of the few things in life not built for the junkyard.
6	HS to MS of another older worker in long, light-blue laboratory coat; carefully shuts black R-R door, checking fit.	*VO Safer:* The statistics bear this out in a remarkable way. In the sixty-seven years since Sir Henry Royce built his first motorcar, . . .
7	MS another worker in plaid work shirt; older worker in glasses, seems to be riveting; pieces of metal in LF.	*VO Safer:* . . . only sixty-five thousand have been built.
8	CU of hands of worker; takes notes, handles small parts of engine spread out on work table; camera pans R; hands leave frame; slow ZI to sign:	*VO Safer:* Of those, thirty thousand are still on the road in daily use. In its best week, the Rolls plants produce fifty-three cars; just over two thousand a year. GM makes twenty-one thousand cars in a single day.

CARS

TO

MARKETING DEPARTMENT

OR COACH BUILDERS

LAST WEEK

53

9	MS worker in brown mechanic's uniform in LF, beating tool on metal.	(*WS:* beating on metal.) *VO Safer:* It's a difference in philosophy. Henry Ford wanted to put the world on his wheels.
10	LS black R-R being driven; camera follows, keeping it in CF.	*VO Safer:* Henry Royce wanted to build the world's best car, one at a time.

Sequence 3

11	MS to HS Safer L profile driving a car; looks at camera; piles of junk in B/G out window; camera	*OnS Safer:* All of us know the frustration of Willy Loman, the tragic hero of Arthur Miller's play *Death of a Salesman*.

follows him as he stops
and gets out—LT.

"Once in my life," he said, "I
would like to own something
outright before it's broken. I'm
always in a race with the junkyard. I just finish paying for the
car and it's on its last legs.
They time them so when you
finally pay for them they're
used up."
(*WS:* Safer pulls brake on,
stops car.)

12 LS of old nondescript
two-tone blue European
compact car; Safer in LS
in back of it; walks R to
LF around front of car
and begins talking as he
walks toward camera; in
LS he stops, turns back to
look at a car; from TF
machine drops and
crushes in top of car as
Safer looks on in extreme
LF; Safer walks into CF,
MS hands in pockets, as
machine continues to
crush car; Safer addresses
camera—LT.

(*WS:* Safer slams car door, machine noises in B/G.)

OnS Safer: Willy was right, you
know, and this will soon be the
fate of the car you're driving
today.

(*WS:* loud banging as machine
crushes car, window pops out
and shatters.)

OnS Safer: The trouble really is
that nothing these days is built
to last, and the motorcar best
represents the fact that we live
most of our lives in a junk so-
cicty. Our durables are not very
durable.

13 MS to quick ZI to CU of
machine destroying car;
picks it up, lifts it off
ground; ZO reveals car
held in the air.

OffS Safer: But when something is built by hand out of
materials given by nature, . . .

14 MS white R-R moving R
to L across frame and out
of LF.

VO Safer: . . . old-fashioned
pride is maintained, a throw-
back to the principle of "The
One-Horse Shay"—

15 LS blue R-R moving diag-
onally across frame out of
RF.

VO Safer: . . . the schoolboy
poem by Oliver Wendell
Holmes.

16	LS cluttered workshop full of wood, metal, hand tools; worker in LS in RF, back to camera.	*VO Safer* (he reads poem):
17	MS worker picks up oak slab, moves out of frame.	"So the Deacon inquired of the village folk.
18	MS to CU buzz saw ripping wood.	Where he could find the strongest oak,
19	CU flying wood chips.	That couldn't be split nor bent nor broke—
		That was for spokes and floors and sills.
		He sent for lancewood to make the thills;
20	MS worker in white apron, glasses; works with large wrench and metal strips.	The crossbars were ash from the straightest trees;
		The panels of white-wood, that cuts like cheese,
21	CU stacks of dripping metal plates (looks like melting cheese).	But lasts like iron for things like these;
22	CU of hands moving plane diagonally across wood.	Step and prop iron, bolt and screw,
23	CU of bolt threaded by hand.	Spring, tire axle, and linchpin too.
24	CU of hand using screwdriver.	
25	MS roller rides over large sheet of metal.	Steel of the finest, bright and blue;
26	MS metal tools used for cutting and smoothing leather; ZI to hands smoothing leather with tool.	Thoroughbrace bison-skin, thick and wide;
		Boot, top, dasher, from tough old hide
27	CU hands cutting leather, using template as guide.	Found in the pit when the tanner died.
28	LA, MS young worker; ZI to door frame being fitted onto car body.	That was the way he 'put her through.'

29	MS to HS of Safer's reflection from chrome on car hood; ZO to reveal Safer in MS, LF with car hood in RF outdoors.	'There!' said the Deacon, 'Naow she'll dew!' (Safer reads the last line OnS; during poem *WS* of work heard in B/G.)
30	MS hand reaches through hole to smooth metal joints with small hand tool.	*VO Safer:* At the Rolls-Royce factories in London and Crewe, the same philosophy is maintained.
31	CU gloved hands at work with hot silver metal; hands weld and smooth malleable metal.	*VO Safer:* The car division of Rolls was saved from the bankruptcy...
32	CU and ZI to tool applied to hot metal to join welds.	*VO Safer:* ... that faced the Rolls-Royce airplane engine complex.
33	CU washer shoved on metal extension.	*VO Safer:* So it's built today in the same painstaking way, engineering always taking place...
34	CU worker's hands; turns small tool that tightens nut onto bolt.	*VO Safer:* ... over styling. The car seems almost too well made.
35	MS front end of blue R-R in factory; hands in extreme RF painting; ZI to hands carefully painting thin line of finish trim on front side of R-R.	*VO Safer:* The cheapest car they make costs $24,000, and you can pay as much as $50,000 for one. And you wonder, is it all really necessary, all that care?
36	MS testing device; worker places device onto tube.	
37	EECU of stethoscope-like device placed in ears of worker.	*VO Safer:* The testbeds look more like an incubator ward...
38	CU of hands; ZO to reveal testing engineer working with stethoscope in MS.	*VO Safer:* ... than a production line. Every 100th engine is pulled to pieces. A piece of every crankshaft is snipped off and filed away with the number and pedigree...
39	MS engineer; hand reaches into RF to probe car part.	*VO Safer:* ... of the car it was built for. (*WS:* saw, workshop noises.)

40	LA, MS worker at table in RF; cat in LF on table watches man work; he scratches cat's ear.	*VO Safer:* It is the atmosphere of a cottage industry — local craftsman . . .
41	CU flame, smoke, bottles, and jar; hands in RF pick up tool.	*VO Safer:* . . . doing what they know best. The salaries at Rolls are slightly lower than those in the big automotive plants, . . .
42	MS of two workers from waist to neck working with hot metal.	*VO Safer:* . . . but the tyranny of machines . . .
43	CU of hands welding small, delicate pieces.	*VO Safer:* . . . does not exist here. They say that the car has a personality, and the men who build it have managed to keep their own.
44	ECU profile of older worker, wears glasses — LT.	*OffS Safer:* Is this a perfect car?
		OnS Worker: Well, I would say it is, yes. Why I say that is I've been at it all my life — forty-eight years. Naturally it's — varied slightly in those period of years. I mean, it used to be all timber at one time and now we're getting bits of timber and metal.
45	MS Safer in LF, LA; hand leans on R-R frame; factory seen in B/G; Safer pounds door frame with hand for emphasis.	*OnS Safer:* Well, what's the difference between this and a stamped-out car?
		OffS Worker: Well, a stamped-out car is just a stamped-out . . .
46	ECU worker (same as shot 44).	*OnS Worker:* . . . car, isn't it? I mean, anybody can build them.
47	MS Safer (same as shot 45).	*OnS Safer:* How long does a door like this take to make?
48	ECU worker (shots 44 and 46); slow ZO to reveal car on which he is working, and Safer is in extreme	*OnS Worker:* Well, it comes to me assembled like that, and I have to hang it and lock it and put the frames in — it takes me

LF, OS; man now in HS with car frame between him and Safer—LT.

49 MS Safer (same as shots 45 and 47).

50 MS worker in RF; car frame in LF; Safer's hand visible.

51 MS to LS two workers in factory polishing, rubbing metal and car frame.

52 HS of Managing Director David Plastow CF; indoors at factory in B/G; slow ZO reveals Safer's head in OS shot; more of factory and workers revealed; by end of shot Plastow in MS gesturing to Safer in bottom LF—LT.

five days. That's each side. So that's ten days for each—for the complete job, you see.

OnS Safer: And then once it's done and you see it drive out the back—

OnS Worker: Well, I feel rather proud at times, naturally.

OnS Safer: How would you like to work in one of the big auto plants and run a machine . . .

OffS Safer: . . . that simply punched out one of those every ten seconds?

OnS Worker: Well, I think it would bore me in two or three hours, I think. I'd sooner use my hands and make it myself.

VO Safer: The youngest of the craftsmen at Rolls is the managing director.

VO Safer: David Plastow was only thirty-eight when Rolls-Royce Engines went bankrupt. He has managed to keep the car division out of the hands of the receiver.

OnS Safer: What about this car costs $24,000? What makes it cost that much money?

OnS Plastow: The amount of time that we spend making the pieces, after we've selected the very best materials. And in that context, you know, we make a lot of our own nuts and bolts because, in that way, we can check the material before we make the nuts and bolts, probably a very good example. And then we take a lot of time inspecting at the various stages of assembly, and eventually when the car is put together we test it extensively as well. And the whole gestation period is something like three or four months from the time that we issue an instruction to our workshops to build a car. And that's a very expensive process. And to get our cars quite significantly better than these very good American cars costs a great deal of money.

Sequence 4

53	CU on little red book titled *The Rolls-Royce Chauffeur;* ZO reveals Safer in MS, RF holding book; in LF is white R-R with well-dressed man leaning on it in B/G.	*OnS Safer:* Rolls-Royce produced their little red book long before Chairman Mao thought of his, but there is something about the language and the tone of the voice that give the two a great deal in common.
54	MS black R-R drives through L to RF.	*VO Safer:* The book is the *Rolls-Royce Chauffeur's Guide.* Just listen to some of this.
55	MS silver R-R moving L to RF; man driving rests arm out window.	*VO Safer* (quotes from book): Under deportment—"Never drive with your arm on the windowsill even when alone. You will not have . . .
56	CU front end of moving silver R-R; car drives diagonally through and out of frame.	*VO Safer:* . . . full control of the car in an emergency and it looks untidy."
57	HS chauffeur in black cap looking L to R; ZO to MS.	*VO Safer:* Under personal appearance—"A chauffeur must always present a smart appearance in full uniform and should wear a white shirt and collar, a black tie and black shoes.

58	CU hands on steering wheel of R-R; hands pull on white gloves.	*VO Safer:* Leather gloves must be worn when driving . . .
59	HS man in cap driving car; head in profile.	*VO Safer:* . . . and your cap at all times.
60	MS to LS guardsmen on horses moving away from camera, seen through front window of R-R.	*VO Safer:* When driving members of the royal family, see 'Royalty.' "
61	LS black R-R driving; camera follows as it turns corner, moves away.	*VO Safer:* Passenger comfort— "It is your duty to ensure your passengers arrive safely and ready to conduct . . .
62	CU of front grill of black R-R featuring winged chrome hood ornament and R-R symbol; car moves across camera L to RF.	*VO Safer:* . . . business in a pleasant state of mind. Let there be no doubt in their opinion that this is the best car in the world."
63	MS of black R-R; camera follows along focusing on front of car only.	*VO Safer:* After completing the course and after a three-year trial period of driving, . . .
64	ECU chauffeur in cap; hat in CF; ZI to pin on cap.	*VO Safer:* . . . the chauffeur receives the most coveted prize in Rolls-Roycery—the sterling silver cap badge.
65	MS front of R-R grill; car parked; man passes in front; car takes off and camera follows.	*VO Safer:* There is something about a Rolls-Royce that is indisputably British. The style of the car changes every ten years, . . .
66	LS blue R-R passes across camera which follows R-R around corner.	*VO Safer:* . . . and all these cars are at least twelve—some of them fifteen—years old.
67	MS black R-R driving R to L diagonally across frame.	*VO Safer:* But there is nothing dated about them.

68	MS black R-R moving L to R diagonally across frame.	*VO Safer:* It's said that owning a Rolls changes . . .
69	MS grill work of older R-R moving R to L.	*VO Safer:* . . . the attitude of the owner. He begins to care about how he drives and how the car is looked after, . . .
70	CU hood ornament atop moving blue R-R; car moves away from camera and turns corner.	*VO Safer:* . . . one reason why the Rolls lasts so long. Letting the car down . . .
71	LS gray R-R coming down street straight at camera.	*VO Safer:* . . . is somehow un-patriotic, and the familiar complaint about depreciation . . .
72	LS silver R-R moving L to R; Mercedes also in RF.	*VO Safer:* . . . by new car owners can hardly be applied to the Rolls.
73	LS silver R-R moving L to R down street.	*VO Safer:* John Gordon, a London used-car dealer—
74	MS Gordon in brown suit; Safer in extreme LF, OS.	*OnS Gordon:* A very strong possibility with certain cars, already of the postwar era, that
75	MS silver R-R front end driving into camera, stops.	they have appreciated—certainly, yeah. We would say that a Silver Cloud, one today we are selling for more or less the same sort of price as we were three years ago.
76	LS convertible R-R, silver; camera follows it through intersection.	*VO Safer:* How long do you think a Rolls is meant to last when it's built?
77	MS Gordon.	*OnS Gordon:* (laughs): Well, this one's 1934—so this has lasted for, you know, thirty-six, thirty-seven years, and it's going to last another thirty-six or thirty-seven years, one—
78	CU hood ornament; ZO reveals older blue R-R; car dominates RF, F/G; Safer in LS in front of Gordon extreme LF—LT.	well, you know, one can say without any fear of contradiction.

Sequence 5

79	R-R sign on outside of brick factory; ZO to LS of factory with pan across to exit where workers leave.	*VO Safer:* One reason why Mr. Gordon's thirty-seven-year-old car will last so long is that Rolls-Royce is a British institution with an almost mythical tradition. In the bowels of the factory, . . .
80	OS Safer in RF; two men (Quigley, Trimming) MS in L and CF; office window behind them.	*VO Safer:* . . . two men who are the very pillars of the institution—
81	HS, LA Quigley.	*VO Safer:* . . . Quigley, spare parts; Trimming, records.
82	HS Trimming.	
83	ZO from HS to MS of Quigley, Trimming; Quigley smokes; Safer's shoulder in extreme RF.	*VO Safer:* From Quigley you can get a connecting rod for a 1910 Silver Ghost, and from Trimming the complete engineering history of every car ever built.
84	LS, CF Safer as he sits on desk framed by MS of Trimming's back in RF; Safer holds up document and reads; Trimming moves out of frame—LT.	*OnS Safer:* Mr. Trimming, we've done a little bit of research of our own and we found that the longest continuous owner of the same Rolls-Royce is a Miss Overend of Dublin, who bought the car in 1926 and the chassis number is GNJ 52. *VO Safer* (lips not synced even though he is on-screen): Do you think you could find that for us?
85	MS to LS Trimming moves down aisle of files to look up record; searches through filc which looks like a library card catalogue; ZI on card and ZO as he finds cards, walks back toward camera—LT.	*VO Trimming:* I have a record of that. (*WS:* Trimming looks through drawers that squeak.) *OnS Trimming:* Miss L. Overend, and it—delivered on the 9th of June, 1927.

Sequence 6

86	MS on older woman (Lutitia Overend) as she drives her 1927 R-R convertible; she can barely see over steering wheel.	*VO Safer:* We went to Dublin and found her. She is named Lutitia Overend. She is ninety-one and has been driving the car steadily since the day she bought it in 1927.
87	LS Overend in car; seen through pine tree as camera follows car.	*VO Safer:* Miss Overend and her mother ventured from Dublin to London to make the purchase. At first they looked at a Bentley, but decided on a Rolls because . . .
88	Camera now in car's back seat; shot over top of Overend's head as it pulls to a stop; Safer approaches in RF, LS; in MS he leans into car as it rolls forward a bit; Safer in MS walks alongside car; HS of Overend in profile in F/G—LT.	*VO Safer:* . . . a Rolls could be started with a crank. Miss Overend would not have a car that could not be started by hand. She stopped cranking this one every day when she was eighty-seven, on doctor's orders. *OnS Safer:* Miss Overend, you've had this car for forty-five years now. *OnS Overend:* Yes, forty-four. Yes. *OnS Safer:* Are you a satisfied customer? *OnS Overend:* Absolutely, I wouldn't change it for anything.
89	MS Overend in profile; she sits in car facing L to R; Safer at beginning of shot visible in B/G; ZI to EECU of of Overend.	*OnS Safer:* Did you ever feel like trading it in on a new one? *OnS Overend:* I never did, indeed. I wouldn't lose it for anything.
90	MS Safer leaning on car in CF; Overend in RF, F/G.	*OnS Safer:* What do you think of the new Rolls-Royce or the new Silver Shadow?

91	HS Overend looking L to R.	*OffS Safer:* You're disappointed in the new — *OnS Overend:* Oh, I — very much.
92	MS head-on of new R-R; sun glistens off hood.	*VO Overend:* And they — they've lowered the bonnets; it's not half as dignified. And they have . . .
93	CU engine of new R-R; ZO to MS of engine.	*VO Overend:* . . . the engine, it looks to me as if someone without much knowledge had taken a lot of components and just thrown them together. And you could not . . .
94	MS camera pans a speeding new black R-R.	*VO Overend:* . . . maintain it yourself — too complicated.
95	LS pan of new black R-R as it drives out onto road.	*VO Safer:* The new Rolls-Royce sent many old Rolls fanciers into shock. They said it looked like something out of Detroit in the fifties, with the fins cut off. They felt that Rolls had finally fallen victim to . . .
96	LS new silver R-R in city scene.	
97	LS old footage of black/ gray R-R.	*VO Safer:* . . . the fickle hands of modernity. Too many gimmicks, they cried.
98	CU to MS shot of driver shifting gears inside a R-R.	*VO Overend:* I think automatic is an excellent thing for people with some disability, . . .
99	EECU Overend L to R; appears still to be sitting at steering wheel.	*OnS Overend:* . . . but if you have the use of your arms and legs and hands, I don't see what you want.
100	MS Safer (same as shot 90).	*OffS Overend:* Because the interest of driving is doing these things. *OnS Safer:* Your car is almost forty-five years old now. How do you service it?
101	EECU Overend (same as shot 99).	*OnS Overend:* I service it myself — altogether myself.

102	Cut to MS Overend out of car pointing to engine; Safer behind her, barely visible; slight pan across hood as Overend and Safer raise hood to look inside.	*VO Overend:* There are about thirty greasers; each of them takes five actions of your hand. I do the greasing; . . .
103	CU on 1927 hood ornament of Overend's car— winged chrome figure; ZO reveals grill work and old head lamps.	*VO Overend:* . . . always started up till about four years ago when I got bad flu and the doctor wouldn't let me start it by hand after that, because it was quite bad. I'm all right now, . . .
104	ECU Overend L to R.	*OnS Overend:* . . . but I start it up by the starter. But there's this handle. *OffS Safer:* Crank handle. *OnS Overend:* For cranking it, yes.
105	CU her hands on wheel; she rubs steering wheel; slow ZO to reveal Safer in MS in B/G (head cut off).	*OffS Overend:* And I think it's a wonderful thing. I think you should treat it as you would an animal or a person. Have sympathy with it and understanding of it and help it along.
106	HS Overend R to L; ZO as she opens door to show Safer leather interior; Safer appears in RF, MS as he opens door for her.	*OnS Overend:* I couldn't imagine a Rolls owner neglecting their car. Now look at that leather. That's the original. It's real leather.
107	MS Safer examining inside of car door; peers over door from outside of car; Overend in RF, OS; Safer closes door.	*OffS Overend:* Now look at that, that's forty-four years there. Never renewed. Isn't that good?
108	EECU Overend R to L.	*OnS Overend:* You should be proud of being able to have the fruits of a man's brain that can produce a thing like this. That's the way I look at it (laughs).

109	MS from in front of car; Safer in LF with hand on car window; leans in to talk to her; Overend at wheel in MS, RF.	*VO Safer:* You've been driving now?
110	EECU Overend—LT.	*OnS Overend:* Since 1919. Count that (laughs). *OffS Safer:* Fifty— *OnS Overend:* Two years. *OffS Safer:* —two years. *OnS Overend:* The first was a Ford, a secondhand Ford, very good. The second was a Hillman, a two-seater, very good. The third was a Talbot. *OffS Safer:* A Talbot. *OnS Overend:* And then the— this one. And this will see me out.
111	HS to MS Safer in front of black B/G.	*OnS Safer:* And, indeed, it did. Lutitia Overend died a few years ago. The car, however, is still going strong.

Appendix E

Shot Number	Video	Audio

Sequence 1

1	MS Safer in LF; dark suit, tie; storybook frame behind him features title of segment and name of producer—LT.	*OnS Safer:* When it comes to a job, seniority is a sacred word. Seniority means the longer you've held a job, the more security you have, especially if you have a strong union to protect you. Last-hired, first-fired. And last-hired, first-fired usually means blacks, women, and other minorities are the first to go. With the Civil Rights Law of 1964, the government told all of its private contractors and business in general: Put minorities on the job and keep them there. But civil rights leaders are complaining that only a few employers are doing that; and where they are doing it, white workers are complaining it's discrimination in reverse. They're asking: Why me? Why a white with seniority is being laid off, and a black with little seniority is being kept on? That issue is now before the Supreme Court. Well, tonight we look into discrimination, and reverse discrimination, in an unlikely place.

230

Sequence 2

2	ELS, HA Safer in a large computerized operating control center at Nevada test site; wears dark suit, tie.	*OnS Safer:* This is the last place in the world you want to have a labor-relations problem or a racial problem. This is the Operations Control Center of the Nevada test site.
3	HS, HA Safer; slow ZO as Safer begins to walk away.	*OnS Safer:* It used to be called the Atomic Energy Commission.
4	LS (same as shot 2) Safer; he walks around control center—LT.	*OnS Safer:* Today it's known as ERDA, the Energy Research and Development Administration. Anyway, it's where we monitor all of our atomic tests. The problem they're facing here is being faced in hundreds of other factories and establishments across the country. Quite frankly, we chose this site because of its exotic background . . .
5	MS Safer in CF; sits on table—LT.	*OnS Safer:* . . . right here where our genius for harnessing nature and our genius for destroying this planet live side by side. Here is where you have two very basic, very simple, very human aspirations set on a collision course: the right of a man to get a job, and the right of another man to protect his job.
6	Cut to CU of hands loading a gun.	(*WS:* Bullet chamber clicks.)
7	HS white guard in black hat; wears ID tag.	*VO Safer:* This man's job is to . . .
8	CU of gun placed in holster.	*VO Safer:* . . . protect whatever needs protecting . . .
9	HS guard moves out of frame.	*VO Safer:* . . . at our nuclear test site.

10	LS guards coming outside building from large door.	*VO Safer:* They are men from Wackenhut, . . .
11	LS guards in parking lot; mountains in B/G.	*VO Safer:* . . . private security guards.
12	ES from air, HA; road cuts through mountain; camera follows lone car.	(*WS:* sounds of wind, car driving.)
13	MS, OS white guard in car driving; camera follows him.	*VO Safer:* Their word is law . . .
14	LS on car driving (see shot 12); ZO to reveal guard patrol car; camera moves off car into ES of desert, mountains.	*VO Safer:* . . . throughout the land they survey. The territory they cover is almost as big as the state of Connecticut.
15	MS, OS guard in car (like shot 13, but car moving in opposite direction).	*VO Safer:* Their job is to clear . . .
16	ES, HA desert shot from air again; camera moves slowly over terrain.	*VO Safer:* . . . this desert of everyone who doesn't belong here, a tedious but vital job. And because of that, discipline is as strict as the army.
17	LS guard house gate; MS guard in LF/G; car in LS in CF; guard house in RF; camera pans left to watch guard as he directs car's driver into ERDA.	*VO Safer:* The Wackenhut guards are everywhere—at the gates and in the random search areas. Anybody working at a government bomb site can be searched.
18	CU on sign: VEHICLE SEARCH AREA AUTHORIZED PARKING ONLY	*OffS Guard:* Step up, please.
19	MS guard in dark glasses, hat; he searches trunk, walks out of frame.	*VO Safer:* If any employee has anything that doesn't belong to him, . . .
20	LS pick-up truck with camper top being searched by guard; four men look on from outside car.	*VO Safer:* . . . he can be fired.

21	ELS entrance to cavelike work area; one guard seen at cave's entrance; another at guard house; ZI to LS of guard watching machinery being driven out from tunnel/cave entrance.	(*WS:* Siren blares.) *VO Safer:* This tunnel leads to ground zero. Today, all atomic tests are carried out underground.
22	MS as machinery rig rolls by; camera follows rig; guard in MS in F/G.	(*WS:* Siren again.) *VO Safer:* Guard pay is good, . . .
23	MS guard in hard hat; standing in LF next to tunnel opening.	*VO Safer:* . . . and there's built-in overtime.
24	MS another rig rolls by; worker aboard rig as camera pans L to R; guard's back in BF.	*VO Safer:* And a man can average $14,000 a year.
25	CU hands hold papers; scene shifts back indoors.	*VO Safer:* But there's a recession in . . .
26	HS guard captain taking roll.	*VO Safer:* . . . the bomb business, too. (*WS:* Captain takes roll call.) (*WS:* Roll call continues.)
27	MS to LS two rows of guards at attention; camera pans across rows (almost all guards are white in this shot)—LT.	*VO Safer:* And more and more guards are being laid off. Ten years ago, when Wackenhut bid for the government contract, almost all the guards were white.
28	HS guards in profile; camera looks down row.	*VO Safer:* In order to win the bidding . . .
29	MS captain of guards; LF talking to men in RF; ZO to reveal row of guards.	*VO Safer:* . . . they had to stipulate they would give . . .
30	MS three guards (two black, one white); slow ZO to LS of guard with HS of captain in RF; pan left to guards again.	*VO Safer:* . . . equal opportunity to minorities. Wackenhut increased its minority hiring— but barely. Then, three years ago,

31	CU on contract title page showing two criss-crossed guns; tilt down page to contract wording: "Agreement between Wackenhut Services and Independent Guard Association of Nevada Local No. 1, Las Vegas, Nevada."	*VO Safer:* . . . under severe government pressure, the company pushed through a new union contract . . .
32	CU of contract's minority provision.	*VO Safer:* . . . that raised minorities up to . . .
33	White on black CG letters; "10% by 1973 12% by 1974 14% by July 1975."	*VO Safer* (reading statistics): Ten percent by 1973, 12 percent by '74, and 14 percent by July 1975.
34	CU on contract again; ZI on white employee provision—clause 6.4.	*VO Safer:* But one clause stuck in the craw of the white employees, and that was clause 6.4: . . .
35	White on black CG letter in CU (Safer reads this).	*VO Safer:* "The non-minority male with the least amount of seniority will be laid off first."
36	Dissolve to next part of contract in CU (Safer paraphrases this part).	*VO Safer:* In other words, white guards with seniority would be laid off before black guards with less seniority.
37	MS three guard/captains—QT.	
		VO Safer: So, last-hired not necessarily first-fired. And indeed, white guards . . .
38	Row of guards—QT.	
39	HS guard; profile L to R—QT.	
40	HS guard; profile R to L—QT.	
41	HS guard; side profile L to R.	*VO Safer:* . . . with years of seniority have been laid off.
42	HS two black guards in CF; ZO to MS of group of guards milling around.	*VO Safer:* But black guards with very little experience—as little as three months—have been kept on.

43	LS outdoor of gate, stop sign at entrance site.	*VO Safer:* The white guards claim they are victims of blatant racial prejudice.
44	MS white guard in L to R profile; truck in CF; camera pans as guard checks ID of man in truck.	*VO Safer:* So, all the racial good will that so many people worked for . . .
45	MS as guard steps back from truck.	*VO Safer:* . . . and so many others, perhaps reluctantly, accepted . . .
46	MS black man in white truck; camera pans R to L as he drives away; camera rests on white guard in CF as truck leaves frame.	*VO Safer:* . . . seems to go right out the window when a man's job is at stake.

Sequence 3

47	ECU white guard—LT.	*OnS White Guard Number 1* (Cleghorn): The intent was to try to unite the country. Instead of that, it's splitting it and causing even more dissention and more racial problems than it had before. *OffS Safer:* So there is . . .
48	LS Safer with back to camera in L F/G and eight guards in M/G and B/G in CF and RF (four are black; four are white).	*OnS Safer:* . . . at the very center of your complaint, is racism, right?
49	ECU white guard (same as shot 47).	*OnS White Guard Number 1* (Cleghorn): We are being discriminated against solely because you're white.
50	MS Safer sitting at desk; Safer points to guard OS in R F/G.	*OnS Safer:* Mr. Jones, you— you, being . . .
51	HS black guard.	*OffS Safer:* . . . the newest man here, right?

52	MS four guards (two black, two white); all look R to L.	*OffS Safer:* What do you say to that?
53	HS Safer L to R.	*OffS Black Guard Number 1* (Jones): I say that . . .
54	HS black guard (same as shot 51).	*OnS Black Guard Number 1* (Jones): . . . in order to get seniority, you have to be hired in the first place, and this seems to be the whole problem. If they had been hiring way back, . . .
55	HS another black guard nods agreement.	*OffS Black Guard Number 1* (Jones): . . . this situation probably wouldn't exist.
56	ECU black guard (the one in shots 51 and 54).	*OnS Black Guard Number 1* (Jones): It's like this outfit, and most of the others—they wasn't hiring blacks. So how do you get seniority?
57	MS Safer on desk (as in shot 50); slow ZI to HS.	*OnS Safer:* He makes a good point. How on earth do blacks ever get seniority if they don't get hired and are able to hold onto their jobs for awhile?
58	MS one white guard standing; one black guard sitting; pan, ZI another white guard in MS to HS to ECU—LT.	*OnS White Guard Number 2* (Singer): Since I have been here, we have had well over the 15 percent blacks hired. The blacks have went, as Bill told you, to other jobs, and— *OffS Safer:* Yeah, but that's the right of any employee, regardless of his color. *OnS White Guard Number 2* (Singer): It's the right of them to leave, but they have not been—they have not been discriminated against in any way since I have been here. Not that I know of.

59	MS white guard—QT.	*OffS Safer:* You feel, obviously, that you've got the law, justice, tradition on your side, right?
60	ECU another white	
61	guard—QT.	
62	ECU another white guard (Cleghorn)—QT.	*OnS White Guard Number 1* (Cleghorn): That's right.
63	LS Safer with back to camera (same as shot 48); camera to ZI to MS black guard (Stewart)—LT.	*OnS Safer:* Last-fired—last-hired, first-fired. What do you have on your side?

OffS Safer: You feel, obviously, that you've got the law, justice, tradition on your side, right?

OnS White Guard Number 1 (Cleghorn): That's right.
OnS Safer: Last-fired—last-hired, first-fired. What do you have on your side?

OnS Black Guards (two of them answer): Nothing.
OnS Safer: Nothing?
OnS Black Guard Number 2 (Stewart): Yeah, what—who set the laws? The laws were made by whites. Blacks haven't made no laws, set no laws since the day of the history of this country.

64	MS white guard (Cleghorn).	*OffS Black Guard Number 2* (Stewart): How many blacks were hired before you, Bill?
65	HS black guard (Stewart).	*OnS Black Guard* (Stewart): Not a one, not a one. There was not a black man on this job before you came here, and there's a big gap between you and I.
66	HS black guard (Matlock).	*OnS Black Guard Number 3* (Matlock): This is good for them. I mean, what they got to suffer, if it pertains to me, I've got to suffer it also.
67	HS Safer.	*OnS Safer:* Is it possible, do you think, that this whole fight, this last-hired, first-fired, is a red herring, a cover-up for old-fashioned racial discrimination?

68	LS on seven of the guards; slow ZI on white guard who answers questions in MS.	*OnS White Guard Number 2* (Singer): No sir. There is racial discrimination taking place here. It is discrimination due to color. The whites are being . . .
69	MS Safer, listens to answer.	*OffS White Guard Number 2:* . . . discriminated against in order for the blacks to maintain their quotas.
70	MS white guard listens to Safer's question; ZI to ECU as he answers; shot held as he again listens to Safer's responses/questions — LT.	*OffS Safer:* But isn't the very fact of a quota discrimination? *OnS White Guard Number 2* (Singer): The very fact of a quota is discrimination— *OffS Safer:* Against the blacks? (*WS:* Two guards answer "That's correct" and "Right.") *OnS White Guard Number 2:* No. This is attempting to maintain—what am I trying—this is attempting to right a wrong that was perpetrated possibly two hundred years ago, which none of us had anything to do with. This don't— *OffS Safer:* But don't you have a responsibility? *OnS White Guard Number 2:* I don't believe I owe them a responsibility. I didn't do them any wrong.
71	ECU another white guard.	*OnS White Guard Number 3* (Howard): I don't—I don't believe that we owe the black people any more than you owe white people, or anything else. Everything should be equal under our laws in this land, and they are I think now. In fact, they're getting to where they're reversed. (*WS:* Mumbling heard in B/G.)

72	ECU black guard.	*OnS Black Guard Number 3* (Matlock): I'm not asking anybody to bend over backwards, but I'm looking for what is right for me and my people, and everything. Now, if this is what we're due, then this is what we're supposed to get.
73	MS to LS (as shot 48) Safer's back in F/G; four guards present in shot.	*OffS Safer:* Do you feel that it's fair and just—if they had some layoffs here—and they would keep . . .
74	HS black guard listens to Safer.	
75	MS two black guards— man and woman sitting.	*OffS Safer:* . . . you with your sixty days'—
76	ECU black guard listens.	*OffS Safer:* or even five years' tenure?
77	MS Safer, arms folded; white guard in MS and black guard in EECU in RF.	*OnS Safer:* That you have greater protection than, say, . . .
78	MS white guard listens.	*OffS Safer:* . . . Mr. Cleghorn here who has fourteen years on the job?
79	MS Safer listens; white guard in R F/G.	*OffS Black Guard Number 3* (Matlock): Yes, this is just.
80	LS six guards (two black, four white) listening.	*OffS Black Guard Number 3* (Matlock): Well, like I said—it should have been a long time . . .
81	HS Safer listening.	*OffS Black Guard Number 3:* . . . ago, though. We . . .
82	LS seven guards (four black, three white); black guard in far RF speaks.	*OnS Black Guard Number 3:* . . . wouldn't have had this problem right now.
83	MS Safer (same as shot 77).	*OnS Safer:* Mr. Stewart, do you think that this contract, this blue book here, does amount to reverse discrimination?

84	HS black guard; ZI to ECU as he talks—LT.	*OnS Black Guard Number 2* (Stewart): No, I don't feel there's reverse discrimination, you see, I feel like we're just trying to catch up. You know what Ralph Waldo Emerson say: "If you start off behind in a race, you have to run twice as fast as the man in front of you to catch up, or you'll forever remain behind." So, we are trying to make up some of the gap that was left by my father, my forefather, all these people's fathers and grandfathers.
85	MS two black guards listen (same as shot 75).	*OffS Black Guard Number 2:* They was kicked, pushed down for years; . . .
86	ECU black guard talks.	*OnS Black Guard Number 2:* . . . never got a chance, like you say, in these hiring halls. Those hiring halls back East, everywhere, you know, in the Midwest and the West, they was lily-white, and blacks never got a chance . . .
87	MS Safer listens (same as shot 77).	*OffS Black Guard Number 2:* . . . to get in those unions. This place was like this . . .
88	ECU black guard talks.	*OnS Black Guard Number 2:* . . . when I came here in 1961. Blacks was—was out here, but they was digging ditches, washing dishes, making beds, or mopping floors or serving in the chow line.
89	ECU black guard listens.	*OffS White Guard Number 1* (Cleghorn): They feel that they are the only ones that have ever come up . . .

90	EECU white guard talks — LT.	*Ons White Guard Number 1:* . . . through the hard knocks. The white people have come up through the hard knocks just as much as they have. Nobody handed it to us on a silver platter, this job. We all applied, we all waited, we all had to be cleared, we all had to work our way up through seniority. I've been laid off when I was new hired. Nobody offered to say, "Hey, let's all work a three-day week so that we can keep Bill Cleghorn on and keep him on the job." When the layoff come, Bill Cleghorn went down the road. Now I've got fourteen years' seniority. I don't think it's fair that I give up my job just to keep somebody on because he's black.
91	ECU black guard listens.	*OffS White Guard Number 1:* The town I was born and raised in didn't have a black in it.
92	ECU white guard talks.	*OnS White Guard Number 1:* There wasn't none. I had no racial discrimination or prejudice at all, but I'm certainly developing it over this kind of a situation here.
93	LS five guards listen and begin to talk among themselves.	*OnS Black Guard Number 2* (Stewart): Since when? (*WS:* B/G argument among rest of guards.)
94	ECU white guard turns to hear responses of others.	*OffS voice:* You know, like you — *OffS Black Guard Number 2:* Since when? You've been . . .

95	ECU black guard listens.	*OffS Black Guard Number 2:* . . . like that ever since I knew you. *OffS Safer:* Does it come down to this? You're saying, "Look fellas, give a little."
96	ECU white guard listens.	*OffS voice:* That's what I'm saying. *OffS another voice:* Right. *OffS Safer:* And you're saying "No."
97	LS Safer, back to camera; all eight guards in B/G (same as shot 48).	(*WS:* Guards argue indistinctly among themselves.)

Sequence 4

98	HS Wallace Hawkins.	*VO Safer:* Wackenhut's manager of operations, Wallace Hawkins, . . .
99	OS Safer; MS Hawkins.	*VO Safer:* . . . has to tread neutral ground in the dispute; . . .
100	ECU Hawkins.	*VO Safer:* . . . but is there neutral ground; . . .
101	OS Safer; MS Hawkins	*VO Safer:* . . . at "ground zero"?
102	ECU Hawkins.	*OnS Hawkins:* I think both sides have good points. I prefer, considering my position as manager, not to take sides. My job here—and I'm oriented—job-oriented—is to try to retain this contract with the government.
103	HS Safer.	*OnS Safer:* In other words, to keep your contract with the government, you've got to waive that business . . .
104	HS Hawkins listens to Safer, then answers question—LT.	*OffS Safer:* . . . of last-hired, first-fired? *OnS Hawkins:* That's substantially correct, yes.

OffS Safer: Would you be doing that if your government contract didn't depend on that?
OnS Hawkins: I don't wish to comment on that, Morley. I have tried to refrain from taking sides in this problem in view of my position here, and I do what I think I must. I do what I think our client, ERDA, desires. You see, we're in business.

Sequence 5

105	CU on shoulder patch of guard; ZO to reveal white guard in LS at desk; he speaks into microphone.	*(WS:* Guard talks over loud-speaker.) *VO Safer:* And in order to stay in business, Wackenhut . . .
106	EECU, OS of guard working at monitor panels; ZO to reveal two white guards seated at panel in profile.	*VO Safer:* . . . had to comply with federal laws . . .
107	MS black guard looking at log entry book; pan from black guard to two white guards.	*VO Safer:* . . . demanding more minorities on the job. And the only way to do that was to get rid of the hard-won seniority clause.
108	CU on ID badge; ZO to MS of Bernard Menke.	*VO Safer:* Bernard Menke, a federal labor relations expert, speaks for the government.
109	ECU Menke, who wears beard—LT.	*OnS Menke:* You're right, it was a hard-won benefit over the years in collective bargaining, and many regard it as an inalienable right. However, one should not forget, I think, that it is, in fact, a creature of the collective bargaining process. And you know, unions can win it, and they can lose it, or they

can bargain it away, or, as happened in this case, a compromise was reached.

110   MS Safer on desk in RF
       talks; OS Menke in RF.

OnS Safer: Some compromise for a man with ten, twelve years of seniority! How is that a compromise?

111   MS Menke; OS Safer in
       LF.

OffS Safer: It's a sellout.
OnS Menke: Bear in mind that in any collective bargaining process, no party perhaps achieves all of the objectives that they would like to achieve.

Sequence 6

112   ES desert with cactus,
       mountains in B/G; ZO to
       reveal atomic test site
       fence in L F/G.

(WS: Wind blowing.)
VO Safer: As we said, the atomic test site near Las Vegas is an exotic place.

113   CU Nevada test site sign.

VO Safer: The sheer background gives you the shivers: . . .

114   ES desert, mountains, sky
       in B/G; dirt road cuts
       through F/G; camera pans
       slowly R to L across land-
       scape.

VO Safer: . . . aspirations and discrimination and reverse discrimination and nuclear fusion all mixed up together. But just an hour's drive . . .

115   ELS of modern suburban
       neighborhood; camera re-
       veals black family going to
       work; ZI as they get into
       car.

VO Safer: . . . and you have this, and this is what we're really talking about. Black workers who've come up . . .

116   MS black man climbs
       aboard motorcycle; two
       other black men look on.

VO Safer: . . . through a lifetime of racism, perpetual victims of last-hired, first-fired, who've managed . . .

117   LS black boy riding bike
       in neighborhood; camera
       pans as he rides L to R
       past more children in B/G
       playing on a front porch.

VO Safer: . . . to build families and homes and a life like this one in North Las Vegas.

118	LS two kites flying against sky; camera tilts from kite to white people playing softball.	*VO Safer:* And we're talking about white people . . .
119	LS batter hits ball; camera pans to follow him to first base; other white players in B/G.	*VO Safer:* . . . who live in communities like this in Las Vegas, . . .
120	LS white adults help children fly kites.	*VO Safer:* . . . who have children and playgrounds and . . .
121	ELS middle-class suburb features Las Vegas home; two white male adults doing yard work.	*VO Safer:* . . . homes like these . . .
122	LS kite being dragged along ground; flips over and comes to stop.	*VO Safer:* . . . and who can lose them if they lose their jobs.
123	ECU Menke.	*VO Safer:* What does Bernard Menke tell these men? *OnS Menke:* With anybody who's facing a loss of their job, I have a great deal of sympathy for them.
124	MS Menke; OS Safer in LF (same as shot 111, end of sequence 5).	*OffS Safer:* Something more than sympathy, no?
125	ECU Menke.	*OnS Menke:* No. (Nods head.)

Sequence 7

| 126 | LS Safer back in control room at atomic test site (similar to shots 2 and 3); camera begins slow ZI to reveal Safer in MS at desk, then in HS—LT. | *OnS Safer:* The problem is as ancient as the question "Why me?"—a question no collection of judges or philosophers or gurus will ever be able to answer. Stalin or Molotov or one of those infamous old Reds talking about revolution said, "You can't have an omelet without breaking some eggs." Well, you can't have orderly change, either, without someone paying the price, making a sacrifice. |

But all that high-falutin' logic means nothing to a fellow out there who's worked hard all of his life, never discriminated against anyone, has a family to support and a job to protect. When he asks the question, "Why me?" he wants a job, not an answer.

Notes

Introduction

1. Harry Reasoner, *Before the Colors Fade* (New York: Alfred A. Knopf, 1981), p. 170.

2. James W. Carey, ed., "Editor's Introduction: Taking Culture Seriously," *Media, Myths, and Narratives: Television and the Press* (Newbury Park, Calif.: Sage, 1988), p. 15.

3. For key examples over the years, see Michael Arlen, "The Prosecutor," *The New Yorker,* November 23, 1977, pp. 44-46; Donovan Moore, "60 Minutes," *Rolling Stone,* January 12, 1978, pp. 43-46; Harry Stein, "How '60 Minutes' Makes News," *New York Times Magazine,* May 6, 1979, pp. 28-90; E. J. Kahn, Jr., "Profiles: The Candy Factory, Part I," *The New Yorker,* July 19, 1982, pp. 39-61, and Part II, July 26, 1982, pp. 37-55; John Weisman, " '60 Minutes'—How Good Is It?" *TV Guide,* April 16, 1983, pp. 5-14; William A. Henry III, "Don Hewitt: Man of the Hour," *Washington Journalism Review* (May 1986): 25-29; Peter Boyer, " '60 Minutes': A Hit Confronts the Odds," *New York Times,* September 13, 1987, sec. 2, p. 1.

4. See, for example, Stein, "How '60 Minutes' Makes News," pp. 29, 74, 89; Jonathan Black, "The Stung," *Channels* 1 (April-May 1981): 46; and Paul Good, "Investigating the Investigators: Why You Can't Always Trust *60 Minutes*' Reporting," *Panorama* (September 1980): 40. On libel issues, also see Don Hewitt, *Minute by Minute . . .* (New York: Random House, 1985), pp. 216-20; and Mike Wallace and Gary Paul Gates, *Close Encounters: Mike Wallace's Own Story* (New York: Berkeley Books, 1984), p. 493.

5. See, for example, Stein, "How '60 Minutes' Makes News," pp. 78, 80; and Peter Funt, "Television News: Seeing Isn't Believing," *Saturday Review* 7 (November 1980): 30-32.

6. See Kahn, "The Candy Factory, Part II," p. 46.

7. Wallace and Gates, *Close Encounters,* pp. 489-92.

8. See Kahn, "The Candy Factory," Part II, pp. 46, 50. The program did not have an on-screen female reporter until Diane Sawyer in 1984, sixteen years after *60 Minutes* had been on the air. Given the prominent display in news of male authorities and sources, the dominance of males

is not surprising. Between 1968 and 1985, for example, in more than fifty selected segments I viewed which focused on a single character or interview subject, fewer than 20 percent featured a woman in this role. In fairness to *60 Minutes,* similar percentages hold up when counting quoted male sources in articles and news photos in issues of *Time* and *Newsweek.* For a television news study on myth and the role of women, see Robert R. Smith, "Mythic Elements in Television News," *Journal of Communication* 29 (Winter 1979): 76-80.

9. John Fiske, *Television Culture* (London: Methuen, 1987), p. 308.

10. See especially, Robert C. Allen, "Reader-Oriented Criticism and Television," in *Channels of Discourse: Television and Contemporary Criticism,* ed. Robert C. Allen (Chapel Hill: University of North Carolina Press, 1987); Martin Allor, "Relocating the Site of the Audience," *Critical Studies in Mass Communication* 5 (September 1988): 217-33; John Fiske, "Television: Polysemy and Popularity," *Critical Studies in Mass Communication* 3 (December 1986): 391-408; Stuart Hall, "Encoding/decoding," in *Culture, Media, Language,* ed. Stuart Hall, Dorothy Hobson, Andrew Lowe, and Paul Willis (London: Hutchinson, 1980); Elihu Katz and Tamar Liebes, "Once upon a Time, in Dallas," *Intermedia* 12 (May 1984): 28-32; David Morley, *The "Nationwide" Audience* (London: British Film Institute, 1980); David Morley, *Family Television: Cultural Power and Domestic Leisure* (London: Comedia, 1986); and Janice Radway, *Reading the Romance: Women, Patriarchy, and Popular Literature* (Chapel Hill: University of North Carolina Press, 1984).

11. Fiske, "Television: Polysemy and Popularity," p. 404.

12. Horace Newcomb and Paul Hirsch, "Television as a Cultural Forum," *Quarterly Review of Film Studies* 8 (Summer 1983): 53.

13. At the Library of Congress (Motion Picture, Broadcasting and Recorded Sound Division) in Washington, D.C., *60 Minutes* programs are available for viewing on 16mm film (1968-75) or ¾-inch videotape (since 1975). The library is one to two years behind in cataloguing more recent episodes.

14. CBS News, *60 Minutes Verbatim* (New York: Arno Press, 1980).

15. Tom Wicker, quoted in Hewitt, *Minute by Minute . . . ,* p. 217.

16. Clifford Geertz, *The Interpretation of Cultures* (New York: Basic Books, 1973), p. 25.

17. Geertz, *Interpretation of Cultures,* p. 20.

18. James Carey, "Mass Communication Research and Cultural Studies: An American View," in *Mass Communication and Society,* ed. James Curren et al. (London: Edward Arnold, 1977), p. 418.

19. Geertz, *Interpretation of Cultures,* p. 5.

20. Gaye Tuchman, *Making News: A Study in the Construction of Reality* (New York: Free Press, 1978), p. 217.

21. Carey, "Mass Communication Research and Cultural Studies," p. 421. For another discussion of qualitative methodology, see Todd Gitlin, *The Whole World Is Watching* (Berkeley: University of California Press, 1980), pp. 303-5.

22. Carey, "Editor's Introduction," p. 15.

23. John Cawelti, *Adventure, Mystery, and Romance: Formula Stories as Art and Popular Culture* (Chicago: University of Chicago Press, 1976), p. 6.

24. David Thorburn, "Television as an Aesthetic Medium," *Critical Studies in Mass Communication* 4 (June 1987): 167-71.

Chapter 1

1. This information is based on ratings figures through the 1989-90 television season. In February 1990, there was some evidence that *60 Minutes* was dropping in the ratings. One week that month the CBS program lost its time slot to another network's regularly scheduled program (ABC's *America's Funniest Home Videos*) for the first time since the mid-1970s. By early 1991 the program had bounced back, vying with NBC's *Cheers* as the most-watched program in America.

2. See Tim Brooks and Earle Marsh, *The Complete Directory to Prime Time Network TV Shows: 1946-Present,* 4th ed. (New York: Ballantine, 1988), pp. 973-75.

3. Don Hewitt, interview conducted at *60 Minutes*, CBS News, New York (February 21, 1989).

4. Axel Madsen, *60 Minutes: The Power and the Politics of America's Most Popular News Show* (New York: Dodd, Mead, 1984), p. 17.

5. Don Hewitt, *Minute by Minute . . .* (New York: Random House, 1985), p. 129.

6. The figures for 1990 national advertising rates were verified in a telephone call to the Detroit network sales division of CBS.

7. Hewitt interview.

8. For example, in February 1990, *60 Minutes* ratings hovered around 20, which means that 20 percent of the more the ninety million U.S. television households were tuned in on any given Sunday. In contrast, during the same time period a single issue of the *Wall Street Journal,* the mostly widely circulated daily newspaper in the United States, was selling just under two million copies per issue.

9. For a fuller discussion of this opening program, see Mike Wallace

and Gary Paul Gates, *Close Encounters: Mike Wallace's Own Story* (New York: Berkley Books, 1984), pp. 123-25.

10. See Madsen, *60 Minutes*, p. 13.

11. Hewitt, quoted in "Father of *60 Minutes*: Taking the Heat as No. 1," *Chicago Tribune,* April 3, 1981, sec. 2, p. 15. See also Robert Slater, *This . . . Is CBS: A Chronicle of 60 Years* (Englewood Cliffs: Prentice-Hall, 1988), pp. 244-49.

12. Hewitt, *Minute by Minute . . .* , p. 29.

13. Hewitt interview.

14. Rooney joined *60 Minutes* as an essayist in 1978. In February 1990, CBS News briefly suspended Rooney from *60 Minutes* (pp. 161-62).

15. See Madsen, *60 Minutes*, p. 21; also Duff Wilson, "*60 Minutes* Gets Story Tips by the Ton," Columbia News Service, reprinted in *The Milwaukee Sentinel,* March 29, 1982, sec. 3, p. 2; and Burton Benjamin, from interview conducted at the Department of Communication, University of Michigan, Ann Arbor (October 29, 1987). Benjamin was a former CBS news producer who was part of the initial meeting at which *60 Minutes* was proposed.

16. Wallace and Gates, *Close Encounters,* p. 124.

17. Safer, quoted in E. J. Kahn, Jr., "Profiles: The Candy Factory, Part II," *The New Yorker,* July 26, 1982, pp. 54-55.

18. For an analysis of this speech, see Edward J. Epstein, *News from Nowhere: Television and the News* (New York: Vintage Books, 1973), pp. 6-8.

19. On a minor front, I should add to the mix critics and academics who in the late 1960s and early 1970s began focusing on the impact of television violence. Although the major critique involved fictional television fare, concern was extended to television news by the prolonged social and political effects of graphically visualizing the Vietnam War in American living rooms night after night. For examples, see Michael Arlen, *Living-Room War* (New York: Viking Press, 1969), and George A. Comstock and E. A. Rubinstein, eds. *Television and Human Behavior,* vol. 1 (Washington, D.C.: U.S. Government Printing Office, 1972).

20. Michael Schudson, *Discovering the News: A Social History of the American Newspapers* (New York: Basic Books, 1978), p. 162.

21. Schudson, *Discovering the News,* pp. 163, 183. Written in 1974 as a detective story with roots deep in investigative, turn-of-the-century journalism, Robert Woodward and Carl Bernstein's *All the President's Men* would become a chief symbol of both the literary and muckraking traditions.

22. Hewitt interview.

23. Schudson, *Discovering the News,* pp. 88-120.

24. Hewitt interview. About seventy-five people at any given time work for *60 Minutes.* By 1990, the *60 Minutes* shop included six reporters and more than thirty producers (each reporter is generally assigned five producers).

25. Curtis D. MacDougall, *Interpretative Reporting,* 9th ed. (New York: Macmillan, 1987), p. 16.

26. Different kinds of common sense are claimed by different individuals and social groups across different times and cultures. For example, during the 1988 vice-presidential debate, Republican candidate Dan Quayle aligned his midwestern values, his grandmother's advice, and his party with common sense—a virtue, to Quayle, sadly lacking among liberals. On the other hand, Democrats and news columns for months criticized the youthful Quayle's placement on the GOP ticket as a decision also lacking common sense. The psychologist Roy Schafer reminds us that common sense is "not fixed": "The common sense presented in proverbs and maxims . . . is replete with internal tension and ambiguity. Most generalizations have countergeneralizations (A penny saved is a penny earned, but one may be penny-wise and pound-foolish; one should look before one leaps, but he who hesitates is lost, and so on), and just as common sense may be used to reaffirm traditional orientations and conservative values (Rome wasn't built in a day), it may also be used to sanction a challenge to tradition (A new broom sweeps clean) or endorse an ironic stance (The more things change, the more they remain the same)." See Roy Schafer, "Narration in the Psychoanalytic Dialogue," in *On Narrative,* ed. W. J. T. Mitchell (Chicago: University of Chicago Press), p. 27.

27. A number of disciplines and contexts ranging from the sociology of knowledge to cultural anthropology to ideological and cultural studies have attempted to define common sense. See Peter Berger and Thomas Luckmann, *The Social Construction of Reality: A Treatise in the Sociology of Knowledge* (Garden City: Anchor-Doubleday, 1966); Robert Park, "News as a Form of Knowledge: A Chapter in the Sociology of Knowledge," *American Journal of Sociology* 45 (1940): 669-86; Alfred Schutz and Thomas Luckmann, *The Structures of the Life-World,* trans. R. M. Zaner and T. Engelhardt (Evanston: Northwestern University Press, 1973); Clifford Geertz, "Common Sense as a Cultural System," in *Local Knowledge* (New York: Basic Books, 1983), pp. 73-93; Antonio Gramsci, *Selections from the Prison Notebooks,* trans. Q. Hoare and G. N. Smith (London: Lawrence and Wishart, 1971); and Stuart Hall et al., *Policing the Crisis: Mugging, the State, and Law and Order* (London: Macmillan, 1978).

28. Geertz, "Common Sense," p. 75.

29. Ibid., p. 76; see also Schafer, "Narration in the Psychoanalytic Dialogue," p. 27.

30. Geertz, "Common Sense," pp. 85-91.

31. Theodore L. Glasser and James S. Ettema, "Common Sense and the Education of Young Journalists," *Journalism Educator* 44 (Summer 1989): 20.

32. Glasser and Ettema, "Common Sense and the Education of Young Journalists," p. 20; see also Gaye Tuchman, *Making News: A Study in the Construction of Reality* (New York: Free Press, 1978).

33. Glasser and Ettema, "Common Sense and the Education of Young Journalists," p. 21.

34. Ibid., p. 20.

35. Ibid., p. 21.

36. In this way, the prevailing structures of news may accurately yet accidentally support an assumption that much of human experience is actually incoherent and disconnected.

37. Geertz, "Common Sense," p. 91.

38. Mike Wallace, from interview conducted at the Michigan Journalism Fellows Program, University of Michigan, Ann Arbor (April 18, 1989).

39. John Fiske, *Television Culture* (London: Methuen), p. 385.

40. See Epstein, *News from Nowhere,* pp. 25-26.

41. Hall et al., *Policing the Crisis,* p. 155.

42. Park adapted these distinctions between "acquaintance with" and "knowledge about" from William James.

43. Park, "News as a Form of Knowledge," pp. 669-672; Gramsci in *Selections from the Prison Notebooks* (pp. 323-25) has made a similar distinction between common sense (assumptions held in common by a society, characterized by incoherency and transparency) and good sense (systematic and empirical knowledge, characterized by the coherence of "intellectual order").

44. Hall et al., *Policing the Crisis,* pp. 152-55.

45. Schutz and Luckmann, *Structures of the Life-World,* p. 331. I thank Jimmie Reeves for his help with the conceptualization of the well informed; see Reeves, "Television Stardom: A Ritual of Social Typification and Individualization," in *Media, Myths and Narratives: Television and the Press,* ed. James W. Carey (Newbury Park, Calif.: Sage, 1988), pp. 146-60.

46. Schutz and Luckmann, *Structures of the Life-World,* p. 331.

47. See Alfred Schutz, "The Well-Informed Citizen," in *Collected*

Papers, vol. 2: *Studies in Social Theory* (The Hague: Martinus Nijhoff, 1964).

48. Gary Paul Gates, *Air Time: The Inside Story of CBS News* (New York: Harper and Row, 1978), p. 411.

49. Wallace interview; for a sociological persepctive on hard versus soft news, see Tuchman, *Making News,* pp. 47-48.

50. Schudson, *Discovering the News,* pp. 106-20.

51. Ibid., pp. 89, 3-11.

52. See Epstein's discussion of "The Professional Analogy," in *News from Nowhere,* pp. 25-28.

53. Maxwell McCombs, Donald L. Shaw, and David Grey, eds., *Handbook of Reporting Methods* (Boston: Houghton Mifflin, 1976), pp. 42-43.

54. Schudson, *Discovering the News,* p. 71.

55. Tuchman, *Making News,* pp. 82-103; see also Robert P. Snow, *Creating Media Culture* (Beverly Hills: Sage, 1983), pp. 47-53.

56. Jack Lule, "News as Drama: The Study of News Language," paper presented to the Qualitative Studies Division of the Association for Education in Journalism and Mass Communication (AEJMC), Washington, D.C., August 1989, p. 3.

57. Margaret Morse, "The Television News Personality and Credibility," in *Studies in Entertainment: Critical Approaches to Mass Culture,* ed. Tania Modleski (Bloomington: Indiana University Press, 1986), p. 56.

58. David Eason, "Telling Stories and Making Sense," *Journal of Popular Culture* 15 (Fall 1981): 125.

59. See Morris Dickstein, *Gates of Eden: American Culture in the Sixties* (New York: Basic Books, 1977); and Todd Gitlin, *The Sixties: Years of Hope, Days of Rage* (Toronto: Bantam Books, 1987).

60. Tom Wicker, *On Press* (New York: Viking Press, 1978), pp. 3-5.

61. Schudson, *Discovering the News,* p. 160.

62. See Everette E. Dennis and William L. Rivers, *Other Voices: The New Journalism in America* (San Francisco: Canfield Press, 1974), pp. 104-35.

63. See Dennis and Rivers, *Other Voices,* pp. 186-202, and Philip Meyer, *Precision Journalism: A Reporter's Introduction to Social Science Methods* (Bloomington: Indiana University Press, 1973).

64. Wolfe, quoted in Leonard W. Robinson, "The New Journalism: A Panel Discussion with Harold Hayes, Gay Talese, Tom Wolfe and Professor L. W. Robinson," in *The Reporter as Artist: A Look at the New Journalism Controversy,* ed. Ronald Weber (New York: Hastings House, 1974), p. 67.

65. Tom Wolfe and E. E. Johnson, eds., *The New Journalism* (New York: Harper and Row, 1973), see introduction.

66. See Norman Sims, ed., *The Literary Journalists* (New York: Ballantine Books, 1984), p. 16.

67. Some reporters, like Wolfe and Talese, left newspaper work in the 1960s because the limits of the conventional print model did not give them "room to go into a subject as deeply" as they wished. According to Talese, there was a realization that "the old journalism" could not tell "the whole story." What the new journalists wanted was freedom to do the kind of intensive reporting—or "saturation reporting"—that would get under the surface of an *objective* world. See Gay Talese, "The Book as a Medium for Journalism," in *Liberating the Media,* ed. Charles C. Flippen (Washington, D.C.: Acropolis Books, 1973), p. 42, and Robinson, "The New Journalism: A Panel Discussion," p. 68.

68. Hewitt, quoted in "Father of *60 Minutes* . . . ," p. 15.

69. Hewitt interview.

70. Kramer, quoted in Sims, *Literary Journalists,* pp. 7, 16-18.

71. A. William Bluem, *Documentary in American Television* (New York: Hastings House, 1965), p. 109.

72. David Eason, "The New Journalism and the Image-World: Two Modes of Organizing Experience," *Critical Studies in Mass Communication* 1 (March 1984): 51-65.

73. Eason, "The New Journalism," p. 52.

74. Ibid.

75. Ibid., pp. 53, 63. In a later version, Eason simplifies this conception as realist versus modernist writers.

76. Joan Didion, *The White Album* (New York: Pocket Books, 1979), p. 13.

77. Schafer, "Narration in the Psychoanalytic Dialogue," p. 27.

78. Glasser and Ettema, "Common Sense and the Education of Young Journalists," pp. 20-21.

Chapter 2

1. Mike Wallace and Gary Paul Gates, *Close Encounters: Mike Wallace's Own Story* (New York: Berkeley Books, 1984), pp. 352-53.

2. Walker Percy, *Lost in the Cosmos: The Last Self-Help Book* (New York: Farrar, Straus and Giroux, 1983), pp. 143-44.

3. Reasoner, quoted in Wallace and Gates, *Close Encounters,* pp. 124-25.

4. Don Hewitt served as studio director on *See It Now* and later as

a producer and executive producer for *CBS Reports;* Palmer Williams, a former senior producer and managing editor for *60 Minutes*, was an associate producer for *See It Now* and later a director and an executive producer for *CBS Reports;* Joseph Wershba, a *60 Minutes* producer, was a reporter for *See It Now* and later a producer for *CBS Reports;* William McClure, also a *60 Minutes* producer, worked as a cameraman on *See It Now* and later as a producer for *CBS Reports;* Al Wasserman, a *60 Minutes* producer, served as a writer-producer-director for *CBS Reports;* and Philip Scheffler, senior producer at *60 Minutes*, also worked as a producer for *CBS Reports.*

For more on these producers and television documentary, see Erik Barnouw, *Tube of Plenty: The Evolution of American Television,* rev. ed. (New York: Oxford University Press, 1982), p. 172; A. William Bluem, *Documentary in American Television* (New York: Hastings House, 1965), pp. 111, 282; CBS News, *60 Minutes Verbatim* (New York: Arno Press, 1980), p. xiii; Daniel Einstein, *Special Edition: A Guide to Network Television Documentary Series and Special News Reports, 1955-1979* (Metuchen: Scarecrow Press, 1987); Charles Hammond, *The Image Decade: Television Documentary, 1965-1975* (New York: Hastings House, 1981), pp. 40, 94-98; Don Hewitt, *Minute by Minute . . .* (New York: Random House, 1985); Hal Himmelstein, "Television News and the Television Documentary," in *Television Myth and the American Mind,* ed. Himmelstein (New York: Praeger, 1984), pp. 197-232; Axel Madsen, *60 Minutes: The Power and the Politics of America's Most Popular TV News Show* (New York: Dodd, Mead, 1984), pp. 44-77; Alex McNeil, *Total Television: A Comprehensive Guide to Programming from 1948 to 1980* (New York: Penguin Books, 1980), pp. 92-101; and Donovan Moore, "60 Minutes," *Rolling Stone,* January 12, 1978, pp. 43-46.

5. Hammond, in *The Image Decade,* notes that "What Murrow and Friendly were after . . . was the exposure of injustice. They were muckrakers. If there was a theme in their collective work, it was the belief that a set of rules exists for keeping society fair and equitable; when a person, such as Senator McCarthy, or an event, such as the Korean War, assaulted these rules, then proper attention must be paid, via public exposure to redressing or eliminating such acts" (p. 40).

6. Ibid., p. 12. For a complete listing and summary of *See It Now* programs, see Einstein, *Special Edition,* pp. 469-97. *See It Now* was the television version of the short-lived radio documentary *Hear It Now,* which ran in 1951 on CBS radio.

7. Don Hewitt holds Williams's work for the program in high regard: "Palmer understood right off the bat what we were trying to do

here. . . . Palmer had the sixth sense I've got and the smarts I don't have, and he was invaluable." From interview conducted at *60 Minutes,* CBS News, New York (February 21, 1989).

8. Bluem, *Documentary,* p. 94. Although *See It Now* drew upon a number of the models for journalistic practice, it did not feature reporters routinely as characters and heroes as *60 Minutes* later would. *See It Now,* however, did provide television journalism with interpretive and investigative models for journalistic practice, but it would not be until the late 1960s on *60 Minutes* that commercial television news documentary would more fully foreground narrative structure.

9. For an overview of *CBS Reports,* see ibid., pp. 100-111; and McNeil, *Total Television,* p. 122; for a listing of *CBS Reports* topics, titles, and air dates, see Einstein, *Special Edition,* pp. 112-56.

10. Hammond, *The Image Decade,* p. 70. The "decline" of *CBS Reports* began with the arrival of *60 Minutes* "where more and more investigative pieces ended up"; as a result, *CBS Reports,* redefined with less journalistic status than *60 Minutes,* turned to topics and themes which were considered "softer" than the reports *60 Minutes* began featuring. Like *See It Now* in its later years, *CBS Reports* featured hour-length stories on a single issue, event, or person, a basic difference between it and the magazine or multiple-story format of *60 Minutes.*

11. Friendly, quoted in Joseph Michalak, "*CBS Reports* Covers Assortment of Topics," *New York Times,* December 13, 1959, sec. 2, p. 21.

12. For example, cross-cut editing, the extensive use of the close-up shot in interview sequences, and the employment of field reporters are three devices that *60 Minutes* uses extensively. Drama was captured through "cross-cut" interview technique, which Murrow and Friendly developed: "[T]he technique involved . . . recording many interviews at great length and in considerable detail—a certain way to achieve the conviction Murrow and Friendly sought—and then fragmenting them into a series of shorter statements to be 'shotgunned' throughout a program." This "process permitted not only arresting and rapid flow of visual interest, but a bold juxtaposition of different points of view in short emphatic bursts." Such a technique, which became extremely important on *60 Minutes,* "served to heighten interest and drama in a clash of opinion between opposing forces. . . ."

Along with cross-cutting, another legacy of *See It Now* and *CBS Reports* includes the use of the close-up in interview sequences. This dramatic technique, also adopted by *CBS Reports,* featured "the recording of people's faces as they contributed their opinions" and told their own stories about current social topics and issues. *CBS Reports* perfected the *See It Now* technique of "presenting strings of direct quotations in intercut narrative sequences": "The dialogues conducted with an interviewer were normally trimmed to a smooth flowing exchange of pro and con monologues between the interviews—and the reporter was often edited out." *60 Minutes* intercuts close-ups of interview subjects but with one important variation: in order to foreground the narrative structure, the reporter—featured in reverse and reaction shots—is put back into the frame and into the flow of the interview as a character.

See It Now and other network documentaries also began the convention of visually inserting the television reporter in the story. *See It Now* placed field reporters at the scene of a news story in contrast to the earlier practice of anchors simply reading reports behind a desk and showing film footage bought from independent newsreel companies. Again, however, in many programs these reporters—in a gesture to journalistic neutrality—did not appear in their stories. In 1968 *60 Minutes*, however, began making distinctions between a "field producer," the reporter who does most of the research and some of the interviewing on any particular story, and the "correspondent," the principal reporter who appears on camera as narrator of a segment. See Bluem *Documentary*, pp. 96-104, and Hammond, *The Image Decade*, pp. 165-70, on CBS News and interview techniques.

13. Thomas Kuhn, *The Structure of Scientific Revolutions*, 2d ed. (Chicago: University of Chicago Press, 1970), p. 23; see also Linda Steiner, "The Uses of Science: On Rereading Thomas Kuhn," *Critical Studies in Mass Communication* 3 (March 1986): 106-11.

14. Stuart Hall, "Encoding/decoding," in *Culture, Media, Language,* ed. Stuart Hall et al. (London: Hutchinson, 1980), p. 129.

15. John Fiske, *Television Culture* (London: Methuen, 1987), p. 283.

16. Mary Mander, "Narrative Dimensions of the News: Omniscience, Prophecy, and Morality," *Communication* 10, no. 1 (1987): 63.

17. Mander, "Narrative Dimensions," p. 63.

18. Reuven Frank, "Memorandum from a Television Newsman," reprinted as Appendix 2 in Bluem, *Documentary,* p. 276.

19. See Hammond, *The Image Decade,* pp. 38-41.

20. In "The Nazi Connection" (5/16/82), Wallace appears in more than sixty shots.

21. See Richard Campbell and Jimmie L. Reeves, "Covering the Homeless: The Joyce Brown Story," *Critical Studies in Mass Communication* 6 (March 1989): 21-42.

22. Hewitt, quoted in William A. Henry, "Don Hewitt: Man of the Hour," *Washington Journalism Review* 8 (May 1986): 25.

23. Burton Benjamin, interview, the Department of Communication, University of Michigan, Ann Arbor (October 29, 1987).

24. John Fiske reminds us that "textually, there is not a lot of difference between television news and television series or serial drama" (*Television Culture*, p. 281).

25. Wallace, quoted in Madsen, *60 Minutes*, p. 33.

26. Hugh Downs and Mike Wallace, "The Craft of Interviewing," in *Television: The Creative Experience, a Survey of Anglo-American Progress*, ed. A. William Bluem and Roger Manvell (New York: Hastings House, 1967), p. 169.

27. Sarah Ruth Kozloff, "Narrative Theory and Television," in *Channels of Discourse: Television and Contemporary Criticism*, ed. Robert C. Allen (Chapel Hill: University of North Carolina Press, 1987), p. 45.

28. Mike Wallace, interview, the Michigan Journalism Fellows Program, University of Michigan, Ann Arbor (April 18, 1989).

29. See Claude Lévi-Strauss, "The Structural Study of Myth," in *Structural Anthropology*, trans. Claire Jacobson and Brooke Grundfest Schoef (Garden City: Anchor-Doubleday, 1967), pp. 202-28.

30. Graham Knight and Tony Dean, "Myth and the Structure of News," *Journal of Communication* 32 (Spring 1982): 144-61.

31. Knight and Dean, "Myth and the Structure," p. 156: "Both sides of the official response to the embassy seizure are presented to us as evidence of moral character and purpose: 'discipline.' On the one hand we see disciplined ruthlessness, swiftness, deadliness. But these two sides are never allowed by the text to develop the full force of a contradiction that would undermine myth and its power. Both sides are simply the obverse of the same discipline, a discipline that gave us an 'assault' that was 'brilliant' *and,* not but, 'ruthless.' "

32. Ibid., p. 160.

33. Peter Funt, "Television News: Seeing Isn't Believing," *Saturday Review* 7 (November 1980): 32.

34. Walters, quoted in Funt, "Television News," p. 32.

35. This strategy was explored in the film *Broadcast News;* after the actual interview, a reporter edited in a staged reaction shot which featured him crying in response to the emotion elicited from an interview subject.

36. Wallace interview.

37. Benjamin interview.

38. Hewitt interview. For a sociological discussion of the meanings of private versus public camera distances, see Gaye Tuchman, *Making News: A Study in the Construction of Reality* (New York: Free Press, 1978), pp. 109-24.

39. Todd Gitlin, "Wasted Images," *Channels* (February-March 1982): 15.

40. Hewitt interview.

41. Robert C. Allen, "Reader-Oriented Criticism and Television," in *Channels of Discourse,* argues also that "the characterized addressee is established not just to personalize and textualize the implied viewer but to make an interpersonal exchange out of a one-way, mass-communication phenomenon" (p. 92).

42. Robert Stam, "Television News and Its Spectator," in *Regarding Television: Critical Approaches, an Anthology,* ed. E. Ann Kaplan (Los Angeles: University Publications of America, 1983), p. 39.

43. Hewitt interview.

44. Jonathan Alter, "When Anchors Meet Actors," *Newsweek,* July 24, 1989, pp. 44-45.

45. James W. Carey, *Communication as Culture* (Boston: Unwin Hyman, 1989, p. 30.

Chapter 3

1. See William A. Bloodsworth Jr., *Upton Sinclair* (Boston: Twayne, 1977); Leonard Downie, Jr., *The New Muckrakers* (Washington, D.C.: New Republic, 1976); Alice Fleming, *Ida Tarbell: The First of the Muckrakers* (New York: Dell, 1971); Justin Kaplan, *Lincoln Steffens: A Biography* (New York: Simon and Schuster, 1974); C. C. Regier, *The Era of the Muckrakers* (Chapel Hill: University of North Carolina Press, 1932); Upton Sinclair, *The Jungle* (1905, repr. New York: Signet, 1960); Lincoln Steffens, *The Autobiography of Lincoln Steffens,* vol. 1 (New York: Harcourt, Brace, 1931), pp. 357-442; Lincoln Steffens, *The Shame of the Cities* (New York: Sagamore Press, 1957); Ida Tarbell, *All in the Day's Work: An Autobiography* (New York: Macmillan, 1937); Ida Tarbell, *The History of the Standard Oil Company,* 2 vols. (New York: McClure, Phillips, 1904); and Kathleen Turner, *Ida Tarbell: Portrait of a Muckraker* (New York: Seaview-Putnam, 1985).

2. See Kaplan, *Lincoln Steffens,* pp. 106-7; Tarbell, *Autobiography,* pp. 228-29, 231-53; and Steffens, *Autobiography,* vol. 1., pp. 357-442.

3. Regier, *Era of the Muckrakers,* p. 2; see also Steffens, *Autobiography,* vol. 1, pp. 357-67.

4. Steffens, quoted in Kaplan, *Lincoln Steffens,* p. 106.

5. Sinclair, *The Jungle;* see "Aftermath" by Robert B. Downs, p. 344.

6. See Kaplan, *Lincoln Steffens,* p. 116; Regier, *Era of the Muckrakers,* pp. 7-9.

7. Kaplan, *Lincoln Steffens,* pp. 117, 120.

8. Ibid., pp. 103-6, and Steffens, *Autobiography,* vol. 1, pp. 357-65.

9. Michael Schudson, *Discovering the News: A Social History of the American Newspapers* (New York: Basic Books, 1978), p. 189; see also Judith Bolch and Kay Miller, *Investigative and In-Depth Reporting* (New York: Hastings House, 1978), p. 2.

10. Edward J. Epstein, *Between Fact and Fiction: The Problem of Journalism* (New York: Vintage Books, 1975), p. 10.

11. See Melvin Mencher, *News Reporting and Writing,* 2d ed. (Dubuque: Wm. C. Brown, 1981), pp. 258-59.

12. See Carl Bernstein and Robert Woodward, *All the President's Men* (New York: Warner Paperback Library, 1974).

13. Hewitt, quoted in William A. Henry, "Don Hewitt: Man of the Hour," *Washington Journalism Review* 8 (May 1986): 26.

14. See Richard Campbell, "The Reporter as Detective: Journalism and Metaphor," M.A. thesis, University of Wisconsin–Milwaukee, 1980.

15. Maxwell McCombs, Donald L. Shaw, and David Grey, eds., *Handbook of Reporting Methods* (Boston: Houghton Mifflin, 1976), p. 174.

16. Daniel Schorr, "Unraveling Watergate," *The Progressive* 38 (July 1974): 41-42.

17. Here I follow John Cawelti, *Adventure, Mystery, and Romance: Formula Stories as Art and Popular Culture* (Chicago: University of Chicago Press, 1976). There is a distinction between classical detectives and the hard-boiled or American private-eye formula. In this latter model, detectives are portrayed as uncertain, speculative, and less detached.

18. Theodore L. Glasser and James S. Ettema, "Investigative Journalism and the Moral Order," *Critical Studies in Mass Communication* 6 (March 1989): 2.

19. See Cawelti, *Adventure, Mystery, and Romance,* pp. 80-138; William O. Aydelotte, "The Detective Story as Historical Source," in *The Mystery Writer's Art,* ed. Francis M. Nevins, Jr. (Bowling Green: Bowling Green University Popular Press, 1970), pp. 306-25; David I. Grossvogel, *Mystery and Its Fictions: From Oedipus to Agatha Christie* (Baltimore: Johns Hopkins University Press, 1979); Howard Haycraft, *Murder for Pleasure* (New York: D. Appleton-Century, 1941); and Julian Symons, *Mortal Consequences: A History—from the Detective Story to the Crime Novel* (New York: Harper and Row, 1972).

20. See Schudson, *Discovering the News,* pp. 121-22.

21. See Cawelti, *Adventure, Mystery, and Romance,* pp. 80-138; Jacques Barzun, "Detection and the Literary Art," Elliot Gilbert, "The Detective as Metaphor in the Nineteenth Century," and Ross Macdonald, "The

Writer as Detective Hero," all in *Mystery Writer's Art,* ed. Nevins, pp. 248-62, 285-93, and 295-305.

22. Schudson, *Discovering the News,* p. 121.

23. Cawelti, *Adventure, Mystery, and Romance,* pp. 80-98.

24. Hewitt, quoted in Henry, "Don Hewitt," p. 29.

25. Cawelti, *Adventure, Mystery, and Romance,* pp. 88-89.

26. James, quoted in an interview following "Cover Her Face," episode 4, *Mystery,* Public Broadcasting Service, WGBH, Boston, 1984.

27. See Cawelti, *Adventure, Mystery, and Romance,* pp. 139-91.

28. Ibid., p. 90.

29. See Appendix A for definitions of key audio-video terms.

30. Cawelti, *Adventure, Mystery, and Romance,* p. 84.

31. James Fernandez, "The Mission of Metaphor in Expressive Culture," *Current Anthropology* 15, no. 2 (1974): 124.

32. Mary Mander, "Narrative Dimensions of the News: Omniscience, Prophecy, and Morality," *Communication* 10, no. 1 (1987): 64.

33. Don Hewitt, from an interview conducted at *60 Minutes,* CBS News, New York (February 21, 1989).

34. Robert N. Bellah et al., *Habits of the Heart: Individualism and Commitment in American Life* (Berkeley: University of California Press, 1985), p. 149.

Chapter 4

1. Robert N. Bellah et al., *Habits of the Heart: Individualism and Commitment in American Life* (Berkeley: University of California Press, 1985), pp. 47-48, 121-22.

2. T. J. Jackson Lears, "From Salvation to Self-Realization: Advertising and the Therapeutic Roots of Consumer Culture, 1880-1930," in *The Culture of Consumption: Critical Essays in American History, 1880-1980,* ed. R. W. Wightman and T. J. Jackson Lears (New York: Pantheon, 1983), p. 15. See also Warren I. Susman, *Culture as History: The Transformation of American Society in the Twentieth Century* (New York: Pantheon, 1973, 1984), pp. 275-80.

3. Lears, "From Salvation," p. 15.

4. Susman, *Culture as History,* p. 271.

5. Joseph Veroff, Richard A. Kulka, and Elizabeth Douvan, *Mental Health in America: Patterns of Help-Seeking from 1957 to 1976* (New York: Basic Books, 1981), pp. 6-7.

6. Susman, *Culture as History,* p. 276.

7. Lears, "From Salvation," pp. 6-11.

8. Bellah et al., *Habits of the Heart,* p. 17.

9. Roy Schafer, "Narration in the Psychoanalytic Dialogue," in *On Narrative,* ed. W. J. T. Mitchell (Chicago: University of Chicago Press), p. 27.

10. Schafer, "Narration," p. 27.

11. Bellah et al., *Habits of the Heart,* p. 317.

12. See Walter Lippmann, *Liberty and the News* (New York: Harcourt, Brace and Howe, 1920) and *Public Opinion* (New York: Macmillan, 1922).

13. For detailed analysis and history of the press–radio war, see Sammy R. Danna, "The Rise of Radio News" and "The Press–Radio War," in *American Broadcasting,* ed. Lawrence W. Lichty and Malachi C. Topping (New York: Hastings House, 1975), pp. 338-50; Daniel L. Doeden, "The Press–Radio War: A Historical Analysis of Press–Radio Competition, 1920-1940," Ph.D. diss., Northwestern University, 1975; and Paul W. White, *News on the Air* (New York: Harcourt, Brace, 1947), pp. 30-42.

14. Curtis D. MacDougall, *Interpretative Reporting* (New York: Macmillan, 1938), p. v.

15. *Problems of Journalism* (American Society of Newspaper Editors, 1933), p. 74, see also pp. 66-67.

16. Lippmann, *Liberty and the News,* p. 92.

17. Curtis D. MacDougall, *The Press and Its Problems* (Dubuque: Wm. C. Brown, 1964), pp. 143, 188, 189.

18. Edwin Emery, *The Press and America: An Interpretative History of the Mass Media,* 3d ed. (Englewood Cliffs: Prentice-Hall, 1972), p. 562.

19. Frank Luther Mott, *American Journalism, a History: 1690-1960,* 3d ed. (New York: Macmillan, 1962), p. 688.

20. MacDougall, *The Press and Its Problems,* p. 143.

21. Mott, *American Journalism,* pp. 691-92; Michael Schudson, *Discovering the News: A Social History of the American Newspapers* (New York: Basic Books, 1978), p. 150; and Cabell Phillips, *Dateline Washington* (Garden City: Doubleday, 1949), p. 176.

22. Lowell Thomas, *History as You Heard It* (Garden City: Doubleday, 1957), p. 1. H. V. Kaltenborn, at the time a newspaper reporter in Brooklyn, is often credited with the first radio commentary dating from 1922 and broadcast on WVP in New York.

23. Danna, "The Rise of Radio News," p. 340.

24. Lawrence W. Lichty and Thomas W. Bohn, "Radio's *March of Time*: Dramatized News," *Journalism Quarterly* 51 (Autumn 1974): 458.

25. This is also the prototype for 1990s' wave of network reenactment

news shows used in such syndicated programs as *A Current Affair* and *Inside Edition* and in such network news programs as NBC's short-lived *Yesterday, Today and Tomorrow* and CBS's *Saturday Night with Connie Chung,* also defunct.

26. Luce, quoted in W. A. Swanberg, *Luce and His Empire* (New York: Charles Scribner's, 1972), pp. 142-43. Don Hewitt has said that *60 Minutes* owes a debt to news magazines such as *Time* and *Life,* started by Luce in 1936, because of the blend of words and pictures and the appeal to a large general audience. See Mike Wallace and Gary Paul Gates, *Close Encounters: Mike Wallace's Own Story* (New York: Berkeley Books, 1984), p. 381, and Hewitt, *Minute by Minute . . .* (New York: Random House, 1985).

27. Lippmann, *Liberty and the News,* p. 64.

28. Schudson, *Discovering the News,* p. 150.

29. See Quincy Howe, "The Rise and Fall of the Radio Commentator," *Saturday Review,* October 26, 1957, pp. 40-42.

30. Don Hewitt, from interview at *60 Minutes,* CBS News, New York (February 21, 1989).

31. See Wallace and Gates, *Close Encounters,* p. 381.

32. Schafer, "Narration," pp. 31-32.

33. Bellah et al., *Habits of the Heart,* p. 136.

34. Hayden White, "The Value of Narrativity in the Representation of Reality," in *On Narrative,* ed. Mitchell, p. 20.

35. White, "Value of Narrativity," p. 14.

36. Mary Mander, "Narrative Dimensions of the News: Omniscience, Prophecy, and Morality," *Communication* 10, no. 1 (1987): 64.

37. Ian Connell, "Monopoly Capitalism and the Media," in *Politics, Ideology and the State,* ed. Sally Hibbin (London: Lawrence and Wishart, 1978), p. 83.

38. Bellah et al., *Habits of the Heart,* p. 122.

39. John Cawelti, *Adventure, Mystery, and Romance: Formula Stories as Art and Popular Culture* (Chicago: University of Chicago Press, 1976), p. 35.

40. Bellah et al., *Habits of the Heart,* pp. 126-27.

41. Ibid., p. 136.

Chapter 5

1. John Cawelti, *Adventure, Mystery, and Romance: Formula Stories as Art and Popular Culture* (Chicago: University of Chicago Press, 1976), p. 40.

2. T. J. Jackson Lears, "From Salvation to Self-Realization: Adver-

tising and the Therapeutic Roots of Consumer Culture, 1880-1930," in *The Culture of Consumption: Critical Essays in American History, 1880-1980,* ed. R. W. Wightman and T. J. Jackson Lears (New York: Pantheon, 1983), p. 6-11.

3. See John Lukacs, *Outgrowing Democracy* (Garden City: Doubleday, 1984).

4. For additional views on the meaning of the term *middle* in middle class, see Robert N. Bellah et al., *Habits of the Heart: Individualism and Commitment in American Life* (Berkeley: University of California Press, 1985), pp. 119-20, and Stuart M. Blumin, *The Emergence of the Middle Class: Social Experience in the American City, 1760-1900* (Cambridge: Cambridge University Press, 1989).

5. Dean MacCannell, *The Tourist: A New Theory of the Leisure Class* (New York: Schocken Books, 1976), p. 3.

6. MacCannell, *The Tourist,* p. 3.

7. Daniel J. Boorstin, "From News Gathering to News Making: A Flood of Pseudo-Events," in Boorstin, *The Image: A Guide to Pseudo-Events in America* (New York: Atheneum, 1978), p. 9.

8. Daniel J. Boorstin, "From Traveler to Tourist: The Lost Art of Travel," in *The Image,* p. 78.

9. Dean O'Brien, "The News as Environment," *Journalism Monographs* 85 (September 1983): 9.

10. MacCannell, *The Tourist,* p. 159.

11. Ibid., p. 16.

12. Safer is lifting from a much longer poem, "The Deacon's Masterpiece; or, The Wonderful 'One Hoss-Shay' "; at the ellipsis, he deleted five lines from the original; see Oliver Wendell Holmes, *The Poetical Works,* vol. 1 (Boston: Houghton, Mifflin, 1982), pp. 417-21.

13. The depersonalization of the workers is not pejorative, but suggests rather that they are the stuff of legend and myth, not anonymous villains.

14. M. M. Bakhtin, *The Dialogic Imagination: Four Essays,* ed. Michael Holquist, trans. Caryl Emerson and Michael Holquist (Austin: University of Texas Press, 1981), p. 243.

15. Bakhtin, *The Dialogic Imagination,* p. 243.

16. Erik Cohen, "A Phenomenology of Tourist Experiences," *Sociology* 13 (May 1979): 183. Cohen's article sets up five modes of tourist experience: recreational, diversionary, experiential, experimental, and existential. He also provides a useful critique of the differences between Boorstin and MacCannell.

Chapter 6

1. James Carey, "Commentary: Communications and the Progressives," *Critical Studies in Mass Communication* 6 (September 1989): 271-72.

2. Carey, "Commentary," p. 272.

3. Walter Lippmann, *Liberty and the News* (New York: Harcourt, Brace and Howe, 1920), p. 67. See also Daniell Czitrom, *Media, and the American Mind* (Chapel Hill: University of North Carolina Press, 1982), p. 110.

4. Walter Lippmann, *Public Opinion* (New York: Macmillan, 1922), p. 256.

5. See Michael Schudson, *Discovering the News: A Social History of the American Newspapers* (New York: Basic Books, 1978), pp. 3-11.

6. Once again I am grateful to Jimmie Reeves for his help with this conceptualization. See Richard Campbell and Jimmie L. Reeves, "TV News Narration and Common Sense," *Journal of Film and Video* 41 (Summer 1989): 58-74.

7. See distinction between the well informed, the layman, and the expert in Alfred Schutz and Thomas Luckmann, *The Structures of the Life-World,* trans. R. M. Zaner and H. T. Engelhardt (Evanston: Northwestern University Press, 1973), p. 331.

8. Alfred Schutz, "The Well-Informed Citizen," in *Collected Papers,* vol 2: *Studies in Social Theory* (The Hague: Martinus Nijhoff, 1964), pp. 131-32.

9. Walker Percy, *Lost in the Cosmos: The Last Self-Help Book* (New York: Farrar, Straus and Giroux, 1983), p. 75.

10. Jonathan Alter, "News Media: Round up the Usual Suspects," *Newsweek,* March 25, 1985, p. 69.

11. Hannah Arendt, *The Human Condition* (Chicago: University of Chicago Press, 1958), p. 209; see also Roy Schafer, "Narration in the Psychoanalytic Dialogue," in *On Narrative,* ed. W. J. T. Mitchell (Chicago: University of Chicago Press, 1981), p. 27.

12. Jack Kroll, "Ka-boom, Ka-bam, Ka-Bond," *Newsweek,* July 17, 1989, p. 52. For a commonsense rendering of how academics regard television, see *"Love Boat* Goes to College," *Channels* 6 (October 1986): 67-69, and *60 Minutes,* CBS News, "All About Television" (3/5/89).

13. George Will, quoted in F. Stevens Redburn and Terry F. Buss, *Responding to America's Homeless: Public Policy Alternatives* (New York: Praeger Publishers, 1986), p. 127.

14. See Richard Campbell and Jimmie L. Reeves, "Covering the Homeless: The Joyce Brown Story," *Critical Studies in Mass Communication* 6 (March 1989): 27.

15. Edward J. Epstein, *News from Nowhere: Television and the News* (New York: Random House, 1973), pp. 168-69.

16. David Thorburn, "Television as an Aesthetic Medium," *Critical Studies in Mass Communication* 4 (June 1987): 167-71.

17. Thorburn, "Television as an Aesthetic Medium," p. 168.

18. Ibid.

19. For historical and contemporary discussions of the concept of Middle America, see Robert N. Bellah et al., *Habits of the Heart: Individualism and Commitment in American Life* (Berkeley: University of California Press, 1985), pp. 142-63; Stuart M. Blumin, *The Emergence of the Middle Class: Social Experience in the American City, 1760-1900* (Cambridge: Cambridge University Press, 1989); Herbert Gans, *Middle American Individualism: The Future of Liberal Democracy* (New York: Free Press, 1988); Hal Himmelstein, *Television Myth and the American Mind* (New York: Praeger, 1984), pp. 202-18; and Warren I. Susman, *Culture as History: The Transformation of American Society in the Twentieth Century* (New York: Pantheon, 1973, 1984), pp. 271-85.

Chapter 7

1. Claude Lévi-Strauss argues that myth provides a "logical model"—in the form of a narrative structure—that resolves abstract conflicts between nature and culture, life and death, good and evil, among others. He observes that within the metaphorical structure of myth "two opposite terms with no intermediary always tend to be replaced by two equivalent terms which admit of a third one as mediator." See Lévi-Strauss, "The Structural Study of Myth," in *Structural Anthropology,* trans. Claire Jacobson and Brooke Grundfest Schoef (Garden City: Anchor-Doubleday, 1967), pp. 206, 221.

2. See Public Broadcasting Service, *Moyers: Joseph Campbell and the Power of Myth,* a six-part series, 1987; see also *Joseph Campbell: The Power of Myth, with Bill Moyers,* ed. Betty Sue Flowers (New York: Doubleday, 1988).

3. Robert N. Bellah et al., *Habits of the Heart: Individualism and Commitment in American Life* (Berkeley: University of California Press, 1985), p. 334.

4. Bellah et al., *Habits of the Heart,* pp. 279-81.

5. As Knight and Dean point out in their study of British news, "Though it is a conceptual tool more commonly associated with the analysis of belief in primitive and ancient cultures, myth has also proven itself applicable to modern forms of culture." Graham Knight and Tony

Dean, "Myth and the Structure of News," *Journal of Communication* 32 (Spring 1982): 146.

6. John Hartley, *Understanding News* (London: Methuen, 1982), p. 30.

7. Roger Silverstone, *The Message of Television: Myth and Narrative in Contemporary Culture* (London: Heinemann, 1981), pp. 10, 181.

8. Edmund Leach, "Claude Lévi-Strauss: Anthropologist and Philosopher," in *Theory in Anthropology: A Source Book,* ed. Robert Manners and David Kaplan (Chicago: Aldine, 1968), p. 547.

9. Bellah et al., *Habits of the Heart,* pp. 142, 148.

10. John Fiske, *Understanding Popular Culture* (Boston: Unwin Hyman, 1989), p. 3.

11. See Richard Campbell and Jimmie L. Reeves, "Covering the Homeless: The Joyce Brown Story," *Critical Studies in Mass Communication* 6 (March 1989): 21-42.

12. Josh Barbanel, "Hospitalization of Homeless Challenged," *New York Times,* November 3, 1987, p. B2.

13. The network evening news also ran stories about Joyce Brown— CBS on November 5, ABC on November 6, and NBC on November 10, 1987; see Campbell and Reeves, "Covering the Homeless."

14. My interview with Don Hewitt provided a reading that I thought went against the visual and verbal evidence: "When that piece was all over, I thought we really sided with Koch and against her. Isn't that funny—because Morley came by and said, 'You won't believe the ACLU on this. You can't believe their position.'"

15. At a press conference held during the 1988 Moscow Summit, Reagan defended the nation's treatment of the homeless by citing the Brown case: "A young lady living on the sidewalks of New York, living out there on the sidewalk, winter and summer, and so for her own sake, the police picked her up to bring her to where she could be placed in a shelter and she took her case to court and won her case in court that she should be allowed to go back and sleep on the sidewalk, where she had been because that's what she preferred to do," *Detroit Free Press,* June 2, 1988. The same account reported that Brown, when asked to respond to Reagan's remarks, said, "Although I have my freedom, I still do not have adequate housing. Why doesn't the president assist me in getting permanent housing?"

16. See F. Stevens Redburn and Terry F. Buss, *Responding to America's Homeless: Public Policy Alternatives* (New York: Praeger Publishers, 1986); William Julius Wilson, *The Truly Disadvantaged: The Inner City, the Underclass and Public Policy* (Chicago: University of Chicago Press, 1987); and U.S. Department of Housing and Urban Development,

A Report to the Secretary on the Homeless and Emergency Shelters (Washington, D.C.: Office of Policy Development and Research, 1984).

17. Stuart Hall et al., *Policing the Crisis: Mugging, the State, and Law and Order* (London: Macmillan, 1978), p. 62.

18. See Joseph Campbell, *Hero with a Thousand Faces* (New York: Meridian, 1949, 1973).

19. John Fiske, *Television Culture* (London: Methuen, 1987), p. 294.

20. Fiske, *Television Culture,* p. 284. For an enlightened journalistic perspective on the use of expert sources, see Jonathan Alter, "Round up the Usual Suspects," *Newsweek,* March 25, 1985, p. 69.

21. Mike Wallace, interview at the Michigan Journalism Fellows Program, University of Michigan, Ann Arbor (April 19, 1989). More recent news updates on Joyce Brown report that in the spring of 1988 she was back on the street, although she was living in a city shelter at night. In September 1988, news stories reported that she had been arrested for drug possession.

22. Fiske, *Understanding Television Culture,* p. 284.

23. Ibid., pp. 294-95.

24. Wallace interview. For another reading of TV news tensions between individuals and institutions, see Hal Himmelstein, *Television Myth and the American Mind* (New York: Praeger, 1984), pp. 203-4.

25. Edward J. Epstein, "State and Press: Who Governs?" *Columbia Journalism Review* 18 (September/October 1979): 19.

26. Edward J. Epstein, *Between Fact and Fiction: The Problem of Journalism* (New York: Vintage Books, 1978), p. 32.

27. Michael Schudson, *Discovering the News: A Social History of the American Newspapers* (New York: Basic Books, 1978), p. 180.

28. The segment titled "The Reagans" (1/15/89) offers an interesting and contrasting point of view. In a separate interview with Nancy Reagan, Mike Wallace affirms a fundamental tenet of American individualism, the right to disagree. Nancy Reagan confesses that she does not regard Oliver North as "a national hero." Surprised, Wallace inquires, "You do disagree with your husband about that?" She nods in the positive and comments, "Oh, sometimes we disagree."

29. Don Hewitt, "I'm (Choose One): Conservative. Liberal," *New York Times,* March 12, 1989, sec. 4, p. 25.

30. Hewitt, quoted in William A. Henry, "Don Hewitt: Man of the Hour," *Washington Journalism Review* 8 (May 1986): 28. For a discussion of the relationship between TV news anchors and the middle class, see Himmelstein, *Television Myth,* pp. 209-11.

31. Don Hewitt, interview conducted at *60 Minutes,* CBS News, New York (February 21, 1989).

Chapter 8

1. Mike Wallace and Gary Paul Gates, *Close Encounters: Mike Wallace's Own Story* (New York: Berkley Books, 1984), p. 420.

2. Reasoner, quoted in Wallace and Gates, *Close Encounters,* p. 380.

3. For overviews of this story, see Jeremy Gerard, "CBS News Ends Rooney's Suspension," *New York Times,* March 2, 1990, p. B1; John Carmody, "Rooney Returns Sunday," *Washington Post,* March 2, 1990, p. D1; James Barron, "Rooney, Back on the Air, Has Some New Questions," *New York Times,* March 5, 1990, p. B3; and Marc Gunther, "Unmasking Homophobia Is Irony of Rooney Mess," *Detroit Free Press,* March 6, 1990, p. 5C.

4. Michael X. Delli Carpini and Bruce A. Williams, "Is Dan Rather More Real Than E.T.?: 'Fictional' and 'Non-fictional' Television Celebrates Earth Day," paper presented to the Popular Communication Division of the International Communication Association (ICA), Dublin, Ireland, June 1990, p. 36.

5. For a discussion of narrative time, see Gérard Genette, *Narrative Discourse: An Essay in Method,* trans. Jane E. Lewin (Ithaca: Cornell University Press, 1980); and Paul Ricoeur, "Narrative Time," in *On Narrative,* ed. W. J. T. Mitchell (Chicago: University of Chicago Press, 1980), pp. 165-86.

6. Harry Stein, "How '60 Minutes' Makes News," *New York Times Magazine,* May 6, 1979, p. 80.

7. Schorr, quoted in Stein, "How *60 Minutes* Makes News," p. 82.

8. See Dean O'Brien, "The News as Environment," *Journalism Monographs* 85 (September 1983): 3-9.

9. See David Eason, "On Journalistic Authority: The Janet Cooke Scandal," *Critical Studies in Mass Communications* 3 (December 1986): 429-47.

10. Royko, quoted in "News Media: A Searching of Conscience," *Newsweek,* May 4, 1981, p. 53.

11. David Eason, "The New Journalism and the Image-World: Two Modes of Organizing Experience," *Critical Studies in Mass Communication* 1 (March 1984): 57.

12. Michael Schudson, *Discovering the News: A Social History of the American Newspapers* (New York: Basic Books, 1978), p. 186. See also Gaye Tuchman, "Objectivity as Strategic Ritual: An Examination of Newsmen's Notions of Objectivity," *American Journal of Sociology* 77 (January 1972): 660-79.

13. For a critical discussion of this metaphor, see Edward J. Epstein, *News from Nowhere* (New York: Vintage Books, 1973), pp. 13-25.

14. Mary Mander, "Narrative Dimensions of the News: Omniscience, Prophecy, and Morality," *Communication* 10 (1987): 54-55.

15. David Eason, "New Journalism, Metaphor and Culture," *Journal of Popular Culture* 15 (Spring 1982): 143; see also Peter L. Berger and Thomas Luckmann, *The Social Construction of Reality* (Garden City: Anchor Books, 1967).

16. John Fiske, *Television Culture* (London: Methuen, 1987), p. 281.

17. Don Hewitt, interview conducted at *60 Minutes*, CBS News, New York (February 21, 1989).

18. M. M. Bakhtin, *The Dialogic Imagination: Four Essays,* ed. Michael Holquist, trans. Caryl Emerson and Michael Holquist (Austin: University of Texas Press, 1981), p. 425.

19. Jimmie L. Reeves, "Television Stardom: A Ritual of Social Typification and Individualization," in *Media, Myths, and Narratives: Television and the Press,* ed. James W. Carey (Newbury Park, Calif.: Sage, 1988), p. 151.

20. Hewitt interview.

21. I am grateful to Jimmie Reeves for suggesting this conceptualization.

22. Bakhtin, *Dialogic Imagination,* pp. 27, 33.

23. Ibid., p. 33.

24. Eason, "New Journalism, Metaphor and Culture," p. 145.

25. Bakhtin, *Dialogic Imagination,* p. xxxi.

26. Fiske, *Television Culture,* p. 292.

27. Carey, ed., *Media, Myths, and Narratives,* p. 13.

28. *60 Minutes,* however, does frequently try to recenter oppositional letters by providing a roughly equal number of letters that support the program each week.

29. Richard Campbell and Jimmie L. Reeves, "Representing the Sinister: TV News Coverage of the Drug 'Problem' during the Reagan Years," paper presented to the Popular Communication Division of the International Communication Association, Dublin, June 1990.

30. Ron Harris, "Victimized: War on Drugs Becomes Battle against Minorities, Experts Say," *Los Angeles Times,* repr. in *Ann Arbor News,* May 8, 1990, pp. C1, 3.

31. Dan Rather, "The Threat to Foreign News," *Newsweek,* July 17, 1989, p. 9.

32. See W. J. T. Mitchell, *Iconology: Image, Text, Ideology* (Chicago: University of Chicago Press, 1986), pp. 109-12, and Mitchell, "Going Too Far with the Sister Arts," in *Space, Time, Image, Sign: Essays on Literature and the Visual Arts,* ed. James A. W. Heffernan (New York: Peter Lang 1987), pp. 1-11.

33. Mitchell, "Going Too Far," p. 4.

34. John Fiske, *Reading the Popular* (Boston: Unwin Hyman, 1989), p. 7.

35. Fiske, *Reading the Popular,* pp. 185, 197.

36. Lawrence K. Grossman, "TV News: The Need for a New Spirit," *Columbia Journalism Review* (July-August 1990): 47-48.

37. The segment "Looking at *60 Minutes*" (9/27/81) is the closest the program has gotten to examining some of taken-for-granted practices underlying its own narrative construction. In its more-than-twenty-year history, *60 Minutes* has provided this introspection only once. Regarding this segment, see Wallace and Gates, *Close Encounters,* pp. 421-26.

38. Walker Percy, "Metaphor as Mistake," in *The Message in the Bottle* (New York: Farrar, Straus and Giroux, 1975), p. 70.

39. David Eason, "The New Journalism and the Image-World," in *Literary Journalism in the Twentieth Century,* ed. Norman Sims (New York: Oxford University Press, 1990), p. 203. This quote represents a slight revision of the ending of his 1984 article, which has been revised for this anthology on literary journalism.

40. James Carey, "Commentary: Communications and the Progressives," *Critical Studies in Mass Communication* 6 (September 1989): 269.

Index

ABC News, 4, 36, 39, 41, 119
advertising, 2, 4, 5, 6, 34, 94, 168, 174
  (*see also* news, as commodity)
advocacy journalism, 20
affirmative action, 39, 123-32
Agnew, Spiro, 8
AIDS, 4-5, 122
Alice, 2
Allen, Robert C., 40
All the President's Men, 45-47, 154
Alter, Jonathan, 117
American Society of Newspaper Editors,
  71
"Anderson of Illinois" (2/17/80), 76-77,
  80, 139
"Anne Lindbergh" (4/20/80), 139
"Another Elvis?" (8/12/79), 52
The Armies of the Night, 21-22
"Away from It All" (8/1/76), 98
"The Ayatollah" (11/18/79), 31, 139

Baker, Ray Stannard, 43
Bakhtin, M. M., 111, 169-71, 174
"Barry Goldwater" (3/9/80), 139
Bass, Saul, 3
Bellah, Robert, 67, 69-70, 74, 91-92, 138
Benjamin, Burton, 31, 37, 93
Bergman, Lowell, 5
Bernstein, Carl, 45-46, 154-55
Bernstein, Joel, xvii, 171-72
"Bette Davis" (1/20/79), 139
"Big John" (12/30/79), 139
"Birds, Bees and Ballots" (12/9/69), 134
"Black Jack" (5/17/81), 31
Black Panthers, 81-89, 91, 119
"Bobby Knight" (3/9/80), 139
Boorstin, Daniel, 95
Bradley, Ed, 4, 6, 31, 37, 65, 77, 122,
  171-74
Brokaw, Tom, 68
Brown, Joyce, 30, 145-53, 156, 267-
  68*n21*

"Brown vs. Koch" (1/14/88), 30, 145-53,
  159, 172-73
Buchwald, Art, 3
"Bugs Are a Negative Factor" (3/19/78),
  118
Bush, George, 151, 167, 177

Campbell, Joseph, xxiii, 138
Capote, Truman, 21-22
Carey, James, xi-ii, xvii, xxi-ii, 1, 41,
  113, 175, 183
"Castro" (9/30/79), 139
Cawelti, John, xxiii, 51-52, 91, 93
CBS, xiii, xix, 2, 7, 15, 25, 34, 37, 49,
  66-67, 72, 161, 165, 168, 177
CBS Evening News, 4, 31, 167
CBS Reports, 3, 26-27, 40
Chandler, Raymond, 51
"Charity Begins at Home" (2/4/79), 96
"Citizen Loeb" (2/24/80), 139
Clark, Ramsey, 3
Cleaver, Eldridge, 38, 81-89, 92
Close-Up (ABC), 3
close-up shot, 36-38, 54-56, 61-63, 79,
  82-84, 86, 256-257*n12,* defined, 184
Cohen, Erik, 112
Collins, Marva, 139, 160
Columbo, 48, 56, 91-92, 162
common sense, xxi, xxiii, 1, 6, 15-16,
  18-20, 23-24, 27-28, 31, 34-35, 41-42,
  44, 56, 88, 92, 98, 112, 117-18, 122-
  32, 135, 137, 145-47, 149-50, 153, 156-
  57, 161, 169, 178, 182, 251*n26-27;* defined as news, 9-13; characteristics, 10-
  13; therapy and, 69-70; in hierarchy of
  discourse, 114-16
community, 74, 142, 153
Connell, Ian, 81
consensus, xxiv, 1, 17, 18, 19, 23, 116,
  118, 135-36, 147, 151, 153, 156, 160
consensus narrative, xxiv, 135-36
Cooke, Greg, xvii

Cooke, Janet, 164-65
crack cocaine, 64, 176-77
Cronkite, Walter, 4, 10
cultural studies, xvi, xix, xxi
A Current Affair, 4, 180

Dallas, xv, 2, 31
Dean, Tony, 34-35
"The Death of Edward Nevin" (2/17/
    80), 52-63, 139; transcript of, 187-202
Death of a Salesman, 102
Delli Carpini, Michael, 162
Dewey, John, 113
dialectical model (of news), 120-21, 131,
    134
Didion, Joan, xv, 22, 23, 25
Diekhaus, Grace, xvii, 4
"Dirty Water" (12/16/84), 100
discourse, xix, 30, 37-40, 83, 102, 166;
    defined, 33; hierarchy of, 114-20, 146
"Distressed" (5/3/81), 65
docudramas, 72-73
documentary (television), 25, 27, 73, 93,
    156, 254-55*n4, 256-57n12;* demise of,
    3-4
Doyle, Arthur Conan, 47, 49
The Dukes of Hazzard, 2
Dunne, John Gregory, 22, 43

"Earn It!" (12/16/79), 120-22
Eason, David, 19, 22-23, 165, 167, 171,
    183
editing techniques, xviii, 163, 256*n12*
The Ed Sullivan Show, 2
"Edward Rubin, M.D." (10/21/79), 139
The Electric Kool-Aid Acid Test, 21
elitism (and news), xviii, 12, 16-17, 105,
    138, 152, 156-57, 179-81 (*see also* pop-
    ularity)
Emory, Edwin, 72
"The Empress" (5/18/75), 79
"The Enemy" (3/19/89), 90
Epstein, Edward, 131, 154
"Equal Justice" (8/24/80), 49
"The Establishment vs. Dr. Burton"
    (5/18/80), 139
Ettema, James, 10-11, 24, 47
experts, 6, 12-14, 19, 28, 53-56, 114,
    116-17, 119-20, 122, 128, 130, 133,
    145, 149-50, 154

"Extremism in Defense of Liberty"
    (7/20/75), 79

"Fake" (12/27/81), 31
"Fellini" (5/11/80), 139
Fernandez, James, 65
Fiske, John, xviii, xix, 12, 28, 142, 152-
    53, 168, 173, 180-81
Fitzgerald, F. Scott, 37
football, 33
formulas, 33-34, 41-42, 139, 154, 182;
    defined, xxiii-iv; detective, 43-67; ana-
    lyst, 68-92; adventure, 93-112; arbitra-
    tion, 113-36; combination, 132-35
48 Hours (CBS), 177
Frank, Reuven, 29
Friendly, Fred, 26-27, 256*n12*
"From Burgers to Bankruptcy" (12/3/
    78), 50
Funt, Peter, 36

Gans, Herbert, 137
Gates, Gary Paul, xvi, 15
Geertz, Clifford, xx, xxi, 10, 12
"General Ky and Big Minh" (10/21/71),
    80
"George Who?" (1/13/79), 139
Gitlin, Todd, 39, 249*n21*
Glasser, Ted, 10-11, 24, 47
Goldin, Marion, xvii
Goodman, Ellen, 9
Gorin, Norman, xvii
"The Gospel According to Whom?"
    (1/23/83), 96
Green, Bob, 66
Greenfield, Jeff, 66
Gregory, Dick, 3
Grossman, Lawrence, 181
"Guns" (part 1, 9/18/77; part 2, 9/25/
    77), 120, 131
Gunsmoke, 2

Habits of the Heart, 43, 67, 91, 138, 158
Hadden, Briton, 72
Hall, Stuart, 13, 27-28, 151
Hammett, Dashiell, 51
Hard Copy, 4
Harris, Ron, 177
Hart, Lee, 37
Hartley, John, 139

Hearst, William Randolph, 16
" 'Here's . . . Johnny' " (4/27/80), 139
Herr, Michael, 31
Hewitt, Don, xvi, xvii-iii, 15, 22, 25, 26, 31, 41, 48, 93, 163, 168-70, 254*n4;* on *60 Minutes* profits/ratings, 2, 3; on personal journalism, 3, 21; on documentaries, 3, 93; on storytelling, 8, 21, 41; on common sense, 9; on camera distance, 37; on importance of audio, 39; on reporters as characters, 45-46; on news and morality, 66; on truth, 113; on liberalism and conservatism, 155-56; on Middle America, 156-57, 169-70
Hill Street Blues, 126
Himmelstein, Hal, 137
"Hired Gun" (5/2/76), 120
Hirsch, Paul, xix
Holmes, Oliver Wendell, 103-4
Holmes, Sherlock, 46-47, 48, 65, 154
"Homeless" (1/10/82), 171-74
homelessness, 145-52, 160, 171-74, 267*n15-16*
Horne, Lena, 31
"How to Live to Be 100" (7/5/81), 98
Hussein, Saddam, 32

ideology, 135, 137, 175-76
individualism, 61-63, 66-67, 69, 75, 85, 99, 100, 131, 133, 137-57, 161, 175, 183; therapy and, 92; reality and, 144, 156, 162; limits of, 151-53, 162
"Inside Afghanistan" (4/6/80), 31
Inside Edition, 4
institution(s), 22, 44, 67, 75, 88, 92, 134-35, 153-57, 172, 176, 179, 181, 183; *60 Minutes* as an, 1-2, 24, 66, 130; as villain, 34, 53, 56, 58, 61, 64-65, 99, 102, 128, 130, 154, 160, 173
interpretive reporting, 70-73
interviewing, xviii, 36-38, 61, 91; strategies, 12, 32, 36, 80-81, 256-57*n12*
"In This Corner Weighing 2000 Pounds" (10/27/70), 133
"Invade Nicaragua" (10/27/85), 80
investigative reporting, 15, 43-47 (*see also* reporters, as detectives)

Jackson, Glenda, 35

Jackson, Jim, xvii
James, P. D., 51
The Jeffersons, 2
Jennings, Peter, 39, 68
"Jesse Jackson & Billy Graham" (9/16/79), 139
"Joe Clark" (3/6/88), 133
"John Singer's Coming Back" (3/12/89), 49

Kennedy, John, 68, 178
Kennedy, Robert, 23
Kennedy, Ted, 142
Kesey, Ken, 21
Knight, Graham, 34-35
knowledge: socially derived, 115; specialized, 116-18; hierarchy of, 146, 150 (*see also* discourse)
Koch, Ed, 30, 145-52
"The Kongsberg Connection" (4/10/88), 115-16
Koppel, Ted, 119-20, 132
Kozloff, Sarah Ruth, 33
Kramer, Mark, 21
Kroft, Steve, 4, 5-6
Kuhn, Thomas, 27

L.A. Law, 31
"Land Fraud and a Murder" (3/2/75), 50
Lando, Barry, xvii
"Las Vegas by the Sea" (9/1/74), 135
Laugh-In, 1
Leach, Edmund, 140
Lears, T. J. Jackson, 68-69
Lehrer, Jim, 120, 132
"Lena Horne" (12/27/81), 31, 77
letters, to *60 Minutes,* 6-7, 160-62, 176
libel, xviii
"Liberté, Egalité, Fraternité" (4/26/81), 39
Library of Congress, xix
"Libya's Qaddafi" (3/23/80), 139
"Life and Death in an Irish Town" (5/17/80), 31
Life magazine, 3, 73, 262*n26*
Lippmann, Walter, 70-73, 113-14
literary journalism, 8, 16, 20-22, 27, 29, 39, 42-43, 51, 169-70, 172-73
Loewenwarter, Paul, xvii, 81

Loman, Willy, 102-3
"Looking at *60 Minutes*" (9/27/81), 13, 66, 270*n37*
Los Angeles *Times,* 177
Luce, Henry, 72-73
Luckmann, Thomas, 14
Lule, Jack, 18

M*A*S*H*, 2
MacCannell, Dean, 94, 97
McClure, William, xvii, 81, 254-55*n4*
MacDougall, Curtis, 71-72
MacNeil, Robert, 120, 132
"Madame Minister" (9/19/82), 77
Madsen, Axel, xvi
Mailer, Norman, 22-23, 39
"The Making of a Murderer" (2/17/85), 50
"A Man Called L'Amour" (6/1/80), 139
"Man of Honor" (3/27/83), 89
Mander, Mary, 1, 28-29, 66, 75, 166
March of Time, 73
Marcus Welby, M.D., 2
"Martin Luther King's Family at Christmas" (12/24/68), 76, 89
"Marva" (11/11/79), 139, 160
"The McMartin Preschool" (2/4/90), 5
medium shot, 37-38, 54-56, 61, 82-84, 86-87, 164; defined, 185
Meet the Press, 2
metaphors, xxiii, 15, 18, 57, 106, 108, 115, 154, 164, 166-67, 171; cultural meaning of, 65, 140, 182-83
Middle America, 64, 78, 81-82, 89, 90, 96, 122, 134, 138, 174-75, 177-78, 265-66*n16;* virtues of, 10, 12, 28, 34-35, 40, 53-54, 61, 76, 88, 98-99, 105, 108, 110, 134-36, 145, 151, 153, 155-56; suspicious of authority, 19, 44; suburbs and, 94
Miller, Arthur, 102
"Mister Right" (12/14/75), 40, 77, 141
Mitchell, W. J. T., 179-80
modernity, 23, 69, 94-100, 101, 105-8, 141, 179, 183
"Momma" (10/14/84), 40
moral order, 63-67, 74-75, 88, 122, 124, 134, 157, 181
"More Than a Touch of Class" (4/7/74), 35, 78

Morse, Margaret, 18
Moses, Harry, xvii, 52, 57-59
Mott, Frank Luther, 72
Moyers, Bill, xxiii, 93, 138
"Mrs. Thatcher" (2/17/85), 31
muckraking, 8, 43-45, 155, 255*n5,* 259*n1*
Murder, She Wrote, 5, 33-34
Murrow, Edward R., xi, 26, 93, 256*n12*
mythology, xxiv, 89, 135, 137, 139, 141-42, 151, 157, 181, 183; male, xviii, 15; public, xix; "third term" mediation in, 34-35, 63, 266*n1;* defined, 137-40, 152, 266*n1;* individualism and, 137-57, 175

narration (news), 37, 39-40, 124-25, 130, 132; defined, 185-86 (*see also* voice-over)
narrative: definition of, 29, 33; opposition/conflict, 34, 49, 61, 63-64, 81, 83, 85, 89, 95-96, 101, 105-7, 110, 117, 136, 139, 140, 162-70, 173; closure, 130-31; time, 162-64; place, 164 (*see also* consensus narrative; news, narration; and news, as narrative)
NBC, 29, 181
"Neighbors" (3/13/88), 64
Nevin, Edward, 52-63
Newcomb, Horace, xix
news: as myth, xvii; as science, xvii, xxiii, 16-19, 24, 166, 180; hard vs. soft, 15-16; as entertainment, 15, 18; conventions, 17-18, 28, 29-42, 45, 47, 117, 163-65, 171, 180; as narrative, 18, 19-24, 26, 29, 42; corporations and, 18, 19, 22, 40, 49, 67, 161, 165, 168, 181; as commodity, 18, 41, 163, 167-68, 180-81; as mystery, 43-67, 74-75, 169; as therapy, 68-92; as adventure, 93-112; as arbitration, 113-36; reality and, 166-67 (*see also* formulas; common sense)
Newsweek, 41, 72, 118, 119
"New York City Is Falling Apart" (2/19/89), 99
New York *Times,* 16, 21, 113, 145, 155
"New York Yankee" (5/3/81), 76
nonsense, 114, 117-18, 122, 145-47, 149, 153 (*see also* knowledge, hierarchy of)
North, Oliver, 143, 155

objectivity, xxii, 8, 17-18, 19-20, 23, 27,

42, 44, 58, 73, 114, 117, 165, 178 (*see also* science)
O'Brien, Dean 95
Ochs, Adolph, 16
"The Oil Kingdom" (6/9/74), 110
"Oman" (8/24/80), 97
"Once upon a Time . . ." (8/25/85), 32
"One American Family" (2/4/90), 4-5
One Day at a Time, 2
"1000% Inflation" (3/12/89), 97, 111-12
opposition (*see* narrative, opposition/conflict)
"Over the Hill" (2/5/84), 77

"Paris Was Yesterday" (4/22/73), 97, 110
Park, Robert, 13
"Pavarotti" (11/4/79), 139
Pentagon, 39, 61-65, 154-55
Percy, Walker, 1, 68, 117, 158, 183
Person to Person, xi
personal journalism, 3, 21-22, 24, 29, 156, 180
Phillips, Drew, xvii
pilgrims (and modern tourists), 112
PM Magazine, 4
Poe, Edgar Allan, 47, 49
point of view, xxii, 17, 22, 36, 40, 81, 85, 153, 175, 181
political columns, 72
popularity (and news), 16-17, 25, 29, 42, 168, 179-81 (*see also* elitism)
postmodernity, xviii, 179, 183
precision journalism, 20
Prime Time Live (ABC), 4
production costs, of *60 Minutes,* 2-3
pseudo-event, 95
Pulitzer, Joseph, 16

"A Question of Mercy" (4/16/89), 122

radio news, 70-73, 261-62*n13*
Rather, Dan, xi, 4, 15, 25, 31, 39-40, 49, 51, 52-63, 68, 96, 99, 120, 122, 167; on television's global reach, 178
ratings, 2-3, 162
Reagan, Nancy, 141, 143
Reagan, Ronald, 5, 40, 77, 131, 141-45, 150, 151-52, 154-55, 156, 160
"The Reagans" (1/15/89), 143-45
realism, xxi, 11, 22-24, 41, 47-48, 52, 73, 152

Reasoner, Harry, 4, 31, 32, 49-50, 64, 76, 77, 100, 133-34, 149; on *60 Minutes* as anthropology, xvii; on origins of *60 Minutes,* 26; on ombudsman role of *60 Minutes,* 160
Reeves, Jimmie, 169
"Remember Pearl Harbor?" (12/3/78), 120
reporters: as characters, xxiv, 30-31, 42, 141, 166; as heroes, 9, 31, 40, 51, 61, 63-64, 85, 140, 157, 160; as well-informed, 13-15, 29, 54, 56, 57, 64, 86, 91-92, 95, 114-16, 122, 135, 141, 146; as detectives, 30, 43-67, 182; as analysts, 30, 68-92, 133-34, 142, 144, 182; as tourists, 30, 93-112, 134-35, 182; as referees, 30, 37, 113-36, 147, 182; as narrators, 37-39; as experts, 154
reporting: as science, xxiii, 16-19, 47, 113; as information, 9, 14, 19, 26; as story, 9, 19-24, 26, 27
reverse-questions, 36, 78, 256-57*n12*
Rieger, C. C., 44
"Rolls-Royce" (6/22/80), 101-10, 111-12; transcript of, 215-29
Rooney, Andy, xxi, 4, 6, 7, 118, 161-62, 250*n14,* 268*n3*
"Roy Cohn" (12/30/79), 139
"Roy Innis" (11/25/79), 139
Royko, Mike, 165, 167
"Rural Justice" (2/22/76), 100

"Saddam's Body Guard" (1/20/91), 32
Safer, Morley, 4, 15, 30, 31, 32, 39, 40, 50, 65, 76, 79, 80, 90, 96, 98, 100, 101-10, 120, 123-32, 145-51, 160-61; on origins of *60 Minutes,* 7
Sawyer, Diane, 4, 31, 32, 77, 78, 158
"The Scarlet 'A' " (8/25/85), 32
scene: defined, 185
Schafer, Roy, 69-70, 74, 251*n26*
Scheffler, Philip, xvii, 254-55*n4*
Schorr, Daniel, 46, 163
Schudson, Michael, 8-9, 17, 20, 44, 48, 73, 155, 165
Schutz, Alfred, 14, 115
science, xvii, xxi-iii, 18, 20, 25, 27, 47, 68, 72, 117, 139, 166 (*see also* news, as science; and objectivity)
See It Now, xi, 26-27, 40, 73, 256-57*n12*

segment: defined, 185
"The Selling of Retin A" (2/4/90), 5-6
seniority rights, 123-32
sequence: defined, 185
"Seward's Folly" (9/1/74), 100
"The Shah of Iran" (10/14/76), 76, 79-80
Sheehy, Gail, 22
"The Sheik" (12/23/79), 139
"Shirley" (4/8/84), 35
shot: defined, 186 (*see also* close-up; and medium)
Silverstone, Roger, 140
Simpson, Homer, 68
Sinclair, Upton, 44
"Sister Emmanuelle" (10/18/87), 158
The Smothers Brothers Comedy Hour, 1-2
Snyder, Mitch, 160
social change, xxiv, 159-62
"Social Security?" (3/2/75), 120
Solomon, Jean, xvii
sound bites, 12, 14, 17, 28, 36, 149
Stam, Robert, 40
Steffens, Lincoln, 44
Stein, Harry, 163
"The Sting Man" (4/12/81), 33
"The Stolen Cezannes" (10/14/79), 49
Stone, I. F., 9
St. Pierre, Suzanne, xvii, 5
Susman, Warren, 69

"Tales of the Texas Rangers" (12/29/85), 32
Talese, Gay, 21-22
"Tammy" (10/2/83), 77
That's Incredible, 2, 4
Thomas, Lowell, 72
Thompson, Hunter, 22
Thorburn, David, xxiv, 135-36
Three's Company, 2
Tiffin, John, xviii, 101
Time magazine, 3, 72-73, 262*n26*
"Titan" (11/8/81), 64
"To Live or to Let Die" (3/2/75), 120-22
transcripts, xix, 7, 39; 187-246
Tuchman, Gaye, xxii, 17
Turecamo, David, xviii
20/20 (ABC), 4, 41, 180

USA Today on TV, 4

values, xxi, 29, 47-48, 79, 85, 138, 143-44, 151, 161; premodern, 68, 105, 110, 112, 138, 183 (*see also* Middle America, virtues of)
Vieira, Meredith, 4
Vietnam War, 1, 8, 23, 90, 178
viewers, xix, 6-7, 30, 32, 39, 40, 42, 57, 61, 78, 94, 110-11, 116, 119, 137, 160-62, 168, 174-76
villains, 34, 37, 39-40, 48, 50-51, 57, 61-62, 64-65, 75, 79-80, 82, 96, 99-100, 108, 111, 119, 121-22, 130, 135 (*see also* institutions)
voice-over narration, 22, 28, 37, 39, 40, 56, 57, 61, 62, 83-84, 97, 116, 124, 125, 164; defined, 186

Wallace, Mike, xvi, xvii, 3, 4, 5, 31, 33, 35, 40, 43, 48, 49, 50, 52, 66, 76, 77, 78, 79, 80, 81-89, 91, 97, 98, 115-16, 120, 135, 141-44, 151, 163; on criticisms of *60 Minutes,* xviii; on origins of *60 Minutes,* 7; on interviewing, 12, 32-33, 154; on hard vs. soft news, 15-16; on popularity of *60 Minutes,* 25, 32-33; on medium shots, 36-37; on news conventions, 152-53, 154; on ombudsman role of *60 Minutes,* 159
Walters, Barbara, 36
"Warning: May Be Fatal" (12/14/75), 49
Washington *Post,* 45, 165
Wasserman, Al, xviii, 254-55*n4*
Watergate, 23, 25, 45-46, 154-55
Weinberger, Caspar, 154
Wershba, Joseph, xviii, 123, 254-55*n4*
West 57th (CBS), 4
"What Became of Eldridge Cleaver?" (5/18/75), 38, 81-89; transcript of, 203-14
"What Happened in Laos?" (3/30/71), 120-22
"What Killed Jimmie Anderson?" (3/2/86), 65
"Wheeler Dealer" (10/27/85), 32
White Paper (NBC), 3
White, Hayden, 74-75
"Who Shot Barbra?" (4/10/88), 50
"Why Me?" (5/18/75), 39, 123-32, 135, 159; transcript of, 230-46
Wicker, Tom, xx, 19-20, 80

"A Wild and Crazy Guy" (4/10/88), 77, 78
"Wildcat Trucker" (2/22/76), 96
Wilder, Thorton, 37
Will, George, 119
Williams, Bruce, 162
Williams, Palmer, xviii, 26, 254-55n4, 255n7

Wolfe, Tom, 20-21
Woodward, Bob, 45-46, 154-55

"Yanks in Iran" (1/2/77), 98
"Yasir Arafat" (2/19/89), 78
"Your Money or Your Life" (3/19/78), 51
"Yugoslavia" (2/17/80), 99

About the Author

RICHARD CAMPBELL is an assistant professor in the Department of Communication at the University of Michigan, where he teaches courses in broadcast journalism, popular culture, and television criticism. He holds a Ph.D. in Radio-Television-Film from Northwestern University, where he was a Danforth Fellow. He earned an M.A. in Communication from the University of Wisconsin–Milwaukee and a B.A. in English from Marquette University. Before returning to graduate studies, he taught English and journalism for five years at West Division High School in Milwaukee. He also worked briefly as a print reporter and a radio and television news intern and writer in Milwaukee.